Forging Diaspora

FORGING

Afro-Cubans and African Americans

ENVISIONING CUBA Louis A. Pérez Jr., *editor*

DIASPORA

IN A WORLD OF EMPIRE AND JIM CROW

Frank Andre Guridy

THE UNIVERSITY OF NORTH CAROLINA PRESS *Chapel Hill*

© 2010
THE UNIVERSITY OF
NORTH CAROLINA PRESS

All rights reserved

*Manufactured in the
United States of America*

*Designed and set in
Garamond Premier Pro
with Electra Display
by Rebecca Evans*

Parts of this book have been reprinted with permission in revised form from "'Enemies of the White Race': The Machadista State and the UNIA in Cuba," *Caribbean Studies*, Special Issue on Garveyism in the Hispanic Caribbean, 31, no. 1 (January–June 2003): 107–37; "From Solidarity to Cross-Fertilization: Afro-Cuban/African American Interaction during the 1930s and 1940s," *Radical History Review*, Special Issue on Black Transnational Studies, 87 (Fall 2003): 19–48; and "Feeling Diaspora in Harlem and Havana," *Social Text* 27, no. 1 (Spring 2009): 115–40.

The University of North Carolina Press has been a member of the Green Press Initiative since 2003.

Library of Congress Cataloging-in-Publication Data
Guridy, Frank Andre.
Forging diaspora : Afro-Cubans and African Americans in a world of empire and Jim Crow / Frank Andre Guridy.
p. cm.—(Envisioning Cuba)
Includes bibliographical references and index.
ISBN 978-0-8078-3361-2 (cloth : alk. paper)
ISBN 978-0-8078-7103-4 (pbk : alk. paper)
1. African Americans—Relations with Cubans—History—20th century. 2. African Americans—Race identity—History—20th century. 3. Blacks—Race identity—Cuba—History—20th century. 4. African Americans—Social conditions—20th century. 5. Blacks—Cuba—Social conditions—20th century. 6. African diaspora. 7. United States—Race relations. 8. Cuba—Race relations. I. Title.
E184.C97G875 2010   305.896′073—dc22
2009044821

cloth   14 13 12 11 10   5 4 3 2 1
paper   14 13 12 11 10   5 4 3 2 1

To *mi amor*, Deborah

Contents

Illustrations

Acknowledgments

This project would not have been possible without the generosity, support, and guidance of countless people who, in substantial and subtle ways, enabled me to survive the intellectual, physical, and emotional challenges that came with the writing of this book. This project initially grew out of my research on the dynamics of racialization in Cuban society and politics during the republican era. I realize in retrospect that my decision to shift my focus away from a history of racialization to a study of diaspora-making was shaped not only by my own intellectual evolution but also by the larger political nightmare that descended upon the United States and the world during the eight-year reign of George W. Bush. In a period that produced the worst forms of nationalist xenophobia in my lifetime, I felt compelled to write a history of the conditions that led people to find commonality across supposedly intractable differences rather than a history of the forces that divide people along racial lines. Given that much of this study was written during the era of post-9/11 U.S. empire-building, it is perhaps not by accident that its focus is on people who pursued narrow openings in an imperial structure during an earlier period when direct challenges to imperialism seemed ineffectual. Perhaps this study might modestly enhance our understanding of the workings of empire and the possibilities for its subversion.

The seeds of this project were planted during my time as a graduate student at the University of Michigan–Ann Arbor. I owe an immeasurable debt to my dissertation adviser, Rebecca J. Scott, for modeling what it means to be a relentless researcher. Her work continues to inspire me. Since our time together in Ann Arbor, my friend and colleague Adrian Burgos has continually offered smart advice, generous feedback, and constant support. This book would not have happened without the life-affirming relationships that I have had with Jane Carpenter, Millery Polyne, Judy Polyne, Daniel Alexander Jones, Susan

Walsh, Gina Pérez, Adam Berlew, Jamie Hart, Alex Vasquez, Jill Dolan, Stacy Wolf, Deborah Vargas, and Stacy Macías.

During a dream year as a scholar-in-residence at the Schomburg Center for Research in Black Culture, I had the privilege of benefiting from the feedback and support of Colin Palmer, Miriam Jiménez Román, Diana Lachatañere, Ken Bilby, Jeff Kerr-Ritchie, the late George Priestley, and Winston Kennedy. This book also benefited from the feedback and support of colleagues at the University of South Florida. Special thanks must go to the late Trevor Purcell, whose untimely passing I continue to grieve, and to my wonderful colleagues Deborah Plant, Cheryl Rodriguez, Edward Kissi, Kevin Yelvington, Barbara Cruz, Susan Greenbaum, Barbara Berglund, Fraser Otanelli, and Jacqueline Messing.

I am truly fortunate to be part of a number of dynamic intellectual communities at the University of Texas at Austin. I owe an immeasurable debt to the "Chapter Four collective": Deborah Paredez, Juliet Hooker, and Jemima Pierre, who read virtually the entire manuscript and gave me valuable feedback and steadfast support when I needed it the most. I am deeply grateful to my colleagues in the Department of History, especially Alan Tully, Jim Sidbury, Ann Twinam, Jonathan Brown, Susan Deans-Smith, Ginny Burnett, Seth Garfield, Tiffany Gill, Anne Martínez, Emilio Zamora, Tony Hopkins, Martha Newman, Laurie Green, Mark Metzler, Madeline Hsu, Karl Miller, Toyin Falola, Martin Summers, and Julie Hardwick, for the large and small ways they enriched my project and for making me feel like a valued citizen of our department. My colleagues at the Center for African and African American Studies, particularly Jossianna Arroyo, Ted Gordon, and Omi Osun Olomo, provide (and often reach beyond) exemplary models for senior colleagues of color. I also want to thank other colleagues and friends at UT for their intellectual generosity, including Elizabeth Engelhardt, Meta DuEwa Jones, Christen Smith, João Vargas, César Salgado, Robin Moore, Charlotte Canning, Jennifer Wilks, Cherise Smith, Jafari Allen, and John McKiernan-González.

Generous support from a number of institutions made the research for this project possible. The Institute for the Study of World Politics, the Consortium for a Stronger Minority Presence at Liberal Arts Colleges, and the Office of the Provost at Wheaton College provided critical support, as did the National Endowment for the Humanities, which provided the funds for a fellowship year at the Schomburg, and various units at the University of Texas at Austin, including the Department of History, the Institute for Historical Studies, the Center for African and African-American Studies, and the Teresa Lozano

Long Institute of Latin American Studies. My research in the United States was enhanced by the assistance I received from staffs at the Schomburg Center for Research in Black Culture, the Library of Congress, the Chicago Historical Society, the Beinecke Library at Yale University, the W. E. B. Du Bois Library at the University of Massachusetts at Amherst, the archives of Tuskegee and Hampton Universities, and the National Archives for Black Women's History at the Mary McLeod Bethune House. My research in Cuba was made possible by the support I received from many Cuban institutions. In particular, I want to thank Belkis Quesada y Guerra of the Instituto de Historia for her invaluable assistance in obtaining visas and access to the various archives and libraries on the island. My research also benefited from the assistance of the staffs in the Archivo Nacional de Cuba, the Archivo Histórico Provincial de Villa Clara, and the Archivo Histórico Provincial de Camagüey. *Mil gracias* to my friends and colleagues Mitzi Espinosa Luis, Violeta Luis, and Carlos Venegas for their invaluable assistance in locating important archival sources. I, like all scholars working on Afro-Cuban history, have benefited from the support and friendship of Tomás Fernández Robaina, whose commitment to racial equality and to the promises of the Cuban Revolution remain awe-inspiring. Words cannot describe the gratitude I feel toward Barbara Danzie León, Nelio and Mercedes Danzie, and Ramiro de la Cuesta. During our numerous remarkable encounters, they welcomed me into their homes, shared their documents and memories with me, and brought my project to life in ways that I never could have imagined. I cannot thank them enough. I yearn for the day when the U.S. travel ban and trade embargo will be demolished so that I can be in more regular contact with *mi familia cubana.*

Throughout the course of my research and writing, I had the privilege of being enriched by a wonderful group of colleagues in various colleges, universities, archives, and conferences who made valuable contributions to this project: Eric Arnesen, Gillian McGillivray, Marc McLeod, Matt Childs, Reinaldo Román, Pedro Pérez Sarduy, Jean Stubbs, Alejandro de la Fuente, Aline Helg, Fannie Rushing, Kelvin Santiago-Valles, Gladys Jiménez Muñoz, Agustín Laó-Montes, Marc Perry, Eileen Findlay, Michael Gomez, Robert Hill, Minkah Makalani, Mia Bay, Sam Roberts, Michelle Stephens, Carter Mathes, Joshua Guild, Gil Rodman, George Sánchez, Ben Vinson, Jim Sweet, David Kinkela, Ebru Turan, and Ruben Flores. I must make special mention of *mi hermano* Jorge Giovannetti, whose research skills and intellectual generosity never fail to amaze me. I have had the privilege of benefiting from the intellectual energy generated by the collective of the Tepoztlán Institute for Transnational History, especially Elliott Young, Pamela Voekel, Reiko Hillyer, David Kazanjian, Josie Saldaña, David Sartorius, and Micol Seigel. I am deeply grateful to Elaine Maisner of the University of North Carolina Press for her editorial insights, encouragement, and patience during the past six years, and I am also indebted to the two anonymous readers of the manuscript. This book benefited enormously from their advice and suggestions.

I am blessed to have a loving family who has encouraged me to be the person and scholar that I want to be. I am forever grateful to my parents, Amparo and Francisco, and my brother Daniel for their unwavering love and support and for being sources of comic relief. The Díaz, García, Toplitsky, and Guridy families have left their imprints on my life and on this book in innumerable ways. In recent years, I have been welcomed with open arms by my new family in San Antonio: Gilberto "Grouch" and Consuelo Villarreal, Tía Lucía Bustillo, and the rest of the Salinas, Bustillo, Lozano, Villarreal, and Rodriquez families, who have gone out of their way to make me feel part of their families.

This book is dedicated to *mi amor*, Deborah Paredez, who came into my life out of nowhere in 2003 and revolutionized it completely. I am forever grateful for all of the blessings she offers me every day. She read every sentence of this book and did the hard work of convincing me that I could, in fact, finish it. She is my life partner, soulmate, and now, co-parent to our baby girl, Zaya Alegría, whose joyous arrival marks the end of the long journey with this book and the beginning of so many more. May the revolutions continue.

Forging Diaspora

Introduction

Making Diaspora in the Shadow of Empire and Jim Crow

In May 1961, the *Crisis*, the organ of the National Association for the Advancement of Colored People (NAACP), published an article by the Afro-Cuban lawyer Juan René Betancourt titled "Castro and the Cuban Negro." Since the 1940s, Betancourt had been an activist against racial discrimination in Cuba, authoring three books and several journalistic pieces in defense of the rights of Cubans of African descent. In 1959, he had joined the hundreds of thousands of Cubans who celebrated the triumph of the revolution that overthrew Fulgencio Batista and put Fidel Castro and his band of revolutionaries in power. Betancourt, who had been a classmate of Castro at the University of Havana, participated in the new government's effort to abolish enduring practices of racial discrimination. He became "delegate-intervenor" of the National Federation of Negro Societies, a conglomeration of the long-standing mutual-aid and recreational associations that had been the centers of social, cultural, and political life for Afro-Cubans since the postemancipation period. Betancourt sought to "reactivate the normal activities of the Negro movement and to present the Castro government with a specific program designed to make the Cuban Negro a first-class rather than a fifth-class citizen." Despite the Afro-Cuban activist's initial enthusiasm for the revolution, his vision of the "Negro movement" soon clashed with that of the new regime, and he was unceremoniously dismissed by the government and forced into exile shortly thereafter. His *Crisis* essay was a passionate critique of the revolution's communist orientation to the question of racial discrimination, highlighting the government's dismantling of the Afro-Cuban societies. "One can truthfully say," Betancourt insisted to *Crisis* readers, "that the Negro movement in Cuba died at the hands of Sr. Fidel Castro." By pleading his case in the pages of the *Crisis*, the Afro-Cuban exile, like so many before him, appealed to African American readers to publicize his concerns.[1]

Betancourt's decision to seek out the NAACP was a routine act of cross-national exchange between Afro-Cubans and African Americans. Since the era of slavery, and particularly after the U.S. intervention into the Cuban War for Independence in 1898, Afro-Cubans and African Americans had reached across cultural and linguistic differences to develop cultural exchanges, forge economic relationships, and construct political solidarities. These interactions were based on the idea that they belonged to a larger African diaspora, or the "colored race," rooted in the perception of a shared history of enslavement and concretized by the motive to develop cross-national relations as a means of negotiating the intertwined processes of U.S. imperialism and of racism in Cuba and the United States during the opening decades of the century. These relationships were part of a plethora of Cuban-U.S. encounters constructed not by white elite businessmen and diplomats, but by black, upwardly mobile, and elite non-state actors in both countries who created small openings in the racialized imperial order for their own purposes. While African Americans have always had relationships with other Afro-diasporic populations, such as West Indians, Haitians, and Africans, among many others, Cuba's geographic proximity and its deep integration into the U.S. political economy created the conditions for a unique relationship between Afro-descended communities in these two countries. Thus, by sending his anti-Castro treatise to the NAACP, Betancourt was utilizing the institutional networks that had been built up over the previous six decades.

The changing landscape of world politics in the early 1960s intruded upon this older form of Afro-diasporic interaction. The Cold War affected all forms of transnational politics, forcing ideologically diverse political coalitions to choose between capitalism and communism. More importantly, decolonization and revolution in the "Third World" after World War II gave previously colonized populations a new investment in national modes of belonging. The 1950s and 1960s initiated the age of "national liberation struggles" when the "wretched of the earth" framed their demands within the dominant discourse of nationalism.[2] The drive for national sovereignty in the newly formed (or re-formed) states in Africa, Asia, and Latin America overshadowed forms of solidarity that were not driven by the precepts of nationalism. The Cuban Revolution played a pivotal role in this global transformation. The Castro government's explicit identification with African liberation struggles further cemented the legitimacy of the nation as a mode of political organization and transborder initiatives.

While Betancourt's protest did not fall on deaf ears, it was effectively counteracted by a new set of networks that were radically transforming the character of Afro-Cuban and African American interaction. These relationships were actively initiated by the new Cuban government, which courted African American support in a manner no Cuban state had attempted before. In 1959 and 1960, the Castro regime invited prominent African Americans to Cuba such as Joe Louis, Marian Anderson, and younger intellectuals and activists, including Amiri Baraka (then LeRoi Jones), Harold Cruse, and Robert Williams. In September 1960, Castro made a huge splash with African Americans by staying in Harlem's Hotel Theresa and meeting with Malcolm X after being snubbed by a midtown Manhattan hotel.[3] Moreover, the revolutionaries' antidiscrimination measures on the island seemed to strengthen their antiracist credentials. Many younger African American civil rights activists could not help but be fascinated by what was happening in Cuba. Taking up the cause of African Americans became part of the Castro government's propaganda war with the U.S. government in the early 1960s. At the same time, as Betancourt pointed out in his *Crisis* essay, the revolution rapidly dismantled the Afro-Cuban societies, thereby destroying the institutional basis of over sixty years of linkages between Afro-Cubans and African Americans. By 1961, the older networks created by the Afro-Cuban and African American associations were giving way to a new set of relationships heavily influenced by the Cuban state and its enemies in Washington. While African Americans' relations with Afro-Cubans continued after 1959, they would be subject to the policy imperatives of the Cuban and U.S. governments. Thus, the triumph of the Cuban Revolution and its symbolic self-fashioning as an antiracist regime dramatically altered the interactions of the two Afro-descended groups, a transformation that persists to this very day.[4]

While the Cuban Revolution was a powerful boost to African American and Afro-Cuban aspirations for freedom and equality in the 1960s, it overshadowed a rich history of social, political, and cultural relationships between these communities before the emergence of Fidel Castro. This book documents the institutional relationships and cultural interactions between Afro-Cubans and African Americans from the U.S. intervention of 1898 until the eve of the outbreak of the Cuban Revolution. By examining the hidden histories of cultural interaction between these communities in various contexts—from Booker T. Washington's Tuskegee Institute, to social and cultural movements such as Garveyism and the black transnational cultural "renaissance" of the 1920s and 1930s, to the black travel networks created during the Good Neighbor and early Cold War eras—this study illustrates the centrality of cross-national linkages to the ways Afro-descended populations in both countries negotiated the entangled processes of imperialism and racial discrimination. As a result of these relationships, Afro-descended peoples in Cuba and the United States came to identify themselves as being part of a transcultural African diaspora, an identification that did not contradict black aspirations for national citizenship.

Why Diaspora?

Why did Afro-Cubans and African Americans seek out each others' communities during the first half of the twentieth century? How does the concept of diaspora enhance our understanding of these initiatives? Answering these questions entails an examination of the ways in which perceived commonalities are enacted across cultural and national boundaries. If historians have documented the various ways the nation has been imagined by historical actors, we have yet to fully investigate how transnational modes of belonging are created and maintained. Such an inquiry need not discount the power of national allegiances. The struggles of Afro-Cubans and African Americans for citizenship rights within the political structures of the nation-states in which they lived have been well documented. However, the intertwined processes of imperialism and racial segregation compelled them to develop survival strategies that extended beyond the boundaries of the nation. These relationships were motivated by material incentives as much as they were by a desire for belonging. Afro-diasporic linkages presented concrete benefits, including opportunities for education, political support, artistic inspiration, and potential profits.

The notion of the African diaspora that informs this book goes beyond the traditional focus on the dispersal of the native people of Africa as a result of the slave trade. It highlights the importance of "routes" instead of "roots" to stress the importance of relationships between diasporic communities outside of the symbolic homeland of Africa in the reconstitution of the wider African diaspora. As anthropologist James Clifford has argued, "Transnational connections linking diasporas need not be articulated primarily through a real or symbolic homeland. . . . Decentered, lateral connections may be as important as those formed around a teleology of origin/return."[5] Thus, I view the African diaspora as both the dispersal of Africans through the slave trade and their ongoing social, political, and cultural interactions across various boundaries after emancipation. As a concept that illuminates the creation of cross-border communities, diaspora is a useful way to interpret cross-national, Afro-descended interaction that is not reducible to politicized forms of "black international-ism" or "racial solidarity." Although the historical actors in this study did not use the term "diaspora," preferring instead to use terms of the day such as the "colored race," "Negro," or the "Negro peoples of the world," the concept of diaspora gives definition to black supranational identifications while avoiding the pitfall of reifying the period's racialist language that represented African descendants as part of an essentialized "race."[6]

As a study of the rich and varied cross-national relationships created by Afro-descended populations in Cuba and the United States, this book aims to contribute to an understanding of the formation of diasporic communities in world history. While some scholars have sought to identify typologies of diasporas, starting with the Jewish model, this book instead takes up the task of documenting diaspora in action, or the ways Afro-diasporic linkages were made in practice.[7] The foundational work of historians and anthropologists on African cultural continuities and transculturation during the era of slavery has enriched our understanding of Afro-diasporic cultures in the Americas.[8] How-ever, the task of historicizing the actual making of diasporas after emancipa-tion and independence has yet to be accomplished. If the African diaspora has been continually remade through the "live dialogue" between Africa and the Americas, it is also reconstituted by the continuing interactions among African descendants outside the continent. The cross-national relationships analyzed in this book are small parts of a wider process of diasporization among African descendants after the end of slavery in the Americas.[9]

Foregrounding the exchanges between Afro-Cubans and African Ameri-cans complicates our understanding of the fields of "Cuban," "Afro-Cuban" and "African American" history. For historians of racialization in Cuba, this book underscores how Afro-Cubans viewed the issue of racial inequality not simply as a national question but also as one that pertained to themselves and African Americans as members of the larger transnational collective they often described as *la raza de color* (the colored race).[10] As Afro-Cubans struggled for citizenship rights within the Cuban republican system, they developed cultural, economic, and political ties with their black neighbors to the north as a complementary strategy to navigate the obstacles presented by imperial and racialized power in Cuba. As this book demonstrates, spearheading these initiatives were Afro-Cuban cultural and recreational societies, including the Club Atenas (Athens Club), the Unión Fraternal, and many others. For African American historiography, this book enacts Earl Lewis's call to situate

African Americans in a history of "overlapping diasporas."[11] Such an endeavor sheds new light on established topics in the field, such as the emergence of racial uplift ideology in the Jim Crow period, the Garvey movement, the Harlem Renaissance, and the early civil rights era. As we will see, whether it was Booker T. Washington's Tuskegee Institute, Marcus Garvey's Universal Negro Improvement Association (UNIA), Walter White's National Association for the Advancement of Colored People (NAACP), or Mary McLeod Bethune's National Council of Negro Women (NCNW), prominent African American leaders and their organizations sustained strong connections to Afro-Cuban associations during the first half of the twentieth century. Thus, historical actors whom African American historiography has tended to view as conservative accommodationists and integrationists also actively pursued relationships with people of African descent abroad. These interactions illustrate that African Americans across the political spectrum identified themselves as part of a larger diasporic collective as much as they did as U.S. citizens. Although African Americans' self-understandings were shaped by their interactions with people of African descent throughout the globe, Cuba's geographic proximity to the United States gave the "Negro in Cuba" particular significance and familiarity for African Americans.[12]

A diasporic perspective invigorates our reading of noteworthy Afro-Cubans who have long been known primarily for their activities as Cuban nationalists, including Juan Gualberto Gómez, Rafael Serra, and Nicolás Guillén. As chapter 1 demonstrates, Afro-Cuban patriots such as Gómez and Serra, among many others, venerated Booker T. Washington and his school in the heart of Jim Crow Alabama and argued that Afro-Cubans needed to follow his example. Furthermore, Afro-Cuban societies, including the elitist Club Atenas, had deep connections to African American institutions. The voluminous scholarship on "identity" has shown that one need not see diasporic activity as inconsistent with nationalist loyalties. As historians of racialization in Cuba have shown, people of African descent often did not see an incompatibility between their national and racial self-understandings, which often worked in tandem and could be mobilized in various ways at different moments.[13]

If diaspora-making is a process that extends beyond the cultural transformations engendered by slavery, what does it look like? How does one document the "decentered lateral connections" theorized by Clifford? The forging of diasporic linkages necessarily entails, as literary scholar Brent Edwards has shown, the messy process of translation and, inevitably, misunderstandings.[14] Projections, mistranslations, and disagreements over meaning are embedded in all forms of Afro-diasporic interaction. And yet, what is most striking is the ways in which Afro-Cubans and African Americans used whatever means at their disposal—broken versions of English and Spanish, bodily gestures, and communications of affect—to forge commonality across difference. As chapter 1 demonstrates, diaspora-making occurred when Afro-Cuban parents sent their sons and daughters to get an education at Tuskegee Institute in the heart of Jim Crow Alabama. Chapter 2 illustrates diaspora in action as Garveyites sang the Ethiopian national anthem in English and Spanish and marched in codified processions in a 1920s-era Liberty Hall in Cuba. Chapter 3 shows diasporization occurring when Langston Hughes felt transported to Africa as he experienced a *son* band in a Havana dance hall. Chapter 4 reveals diaspora-making as Afro-Cuban and African American associations and entrepreneurs developed their own tourist network and confronted the structures of the racial segregation of leisure in both countries. Taken together, these chapters historicize the formation of Afro-diasporic subjects out of these cross-national interactions that frequently transcended cultural and linguistic differences.

Empire, Race, and Diaspora in a U.S.-Caribbean World

The intimate ties forged by Afro-Cubans and African Americans were made possible by the emergence of a cross-border, transnational zone that I call the "U.S.-Caribbean world," a region that first emerged out of the trade networks of the eighteenth century and came to full fruition after the War of 1898. In the four decades before the outbreak of the Second World War, Caribbean and Central American economies and societies became more integrated into U.S.-controlled cross-border linkages. The boundaries of this supranational configuration stretched from the eastern seaboard of the United States southward along the Atlantic coast to the islands of the Caribbean basin, the shores of the Gulf of Mexico, the nations of Central America, and even the northern reaches of South America. This translocal zone linked the northeastern cities of Boston, New York, Philadelphia, and Baltimore to southern U.S. and Caribbean cities like New Orleans, Tampa, Key West, Havana, Kingston, Santo Domingo, San Juan, Limón, and Colón. Paving the way for these translocal linkages were emerging U.S. agricultural-export firms such as the United Fruit Company, the Cuban-American Sugar Company, and the South Porto Rican Sugar Company, among many others. These corporations became the primary channels of the U.S. economic presence in the region. With the growth of tourism in the 1910s and 1920s, United Fruit and other steamship companies transported not only bananas and sugar, but also tourists between U.S. and Caribbean ports. The expansion of steamship travel between the United States and Cuba highlights the increasing velocity of economic linkages in the opening decades of the century. At the turn of the twentieth century, most travel between the island and the U.S. mainland was dominated by the New York and Cuba Mail Steamship Company, also known as the "Ward Line." By 1931, the Ward Line was joined by the Vacarro Line, the United Fruit Company, the P. O. Steamship Company, and the Panama Pacific Line, among others. In the same period, United Fruit's "Great White Fleet" expanded from a fleet of 44 ships that could transport 350 passengers to one of 90 ships that carried 2,500 passengers throughout the region.[15]

Along with U.S. economic expansion into the region, armed intervention by the U.S. military and the spread of U.S. cultural forms also played critical roles in extending the borders of this transregional configuration. The U.S. military occupations of Haiti, Dominican Republic, Cuba, Puerto Rico, and Nicaragua, along with the creation of the Panama Canal, expanded the role of the United States in the politics of the region, bringing the Caribbean and Central America more tightly within the U.S. sphere of influence. Furthermore, U.S. cultural imperialism, whether in the form of Protestant missionaries or consumer culture, also played a decisive role in bringing Caribbean and Central American societies into the orbit of the United States.[16]

The extension of U.S. economic, cultural, and political influence into the Caribbean and Central America in the three decades after the War of 1898 effectively supplanted the older European-oriented Atlantic system in the region. This is not to argue the irrelevance of the European-Atlantic framework. Rather it is to suggest that a U.S.-Caribbean one provides more historical specificity than prevailing Atlantic models better suited to an earlier period of European domination, particularly the era of the Atlantic Slave Trade. In fact, what we see in the first half of the twentieth century is overlapping U.S. and European "imperial formations" under U.S. hegemony, not just in the region's independent republics, but also in the Caribbean colonies under British and French rule.[17]

Cuba's geographic proximity to the United States, its size as the largest of the Antilles, and its key role in U.S. imperial designs placed it at the center of this U.S. American empire in the Caribbean. Beginning with the U.S. occupation of the island in 1898 and the transition to civilian neocolonial rule in 1902, Cuba became entrenched in a rapidly expanding network of people and ideas traveling to and from the United States. The U.S. imperial encounter with Cuba was produced by a plethora of power-laden relationships created not only by white, elite, U.S. and Cuban politicians and businessmen, but also by a range of social actors from various class, racial, gender, and regional backgrounds, including philanthropists, adventurers, social reformers, educators, exiled political activists, soldiers, and so on, all with multiple self-understandings and all with their own particular interest in the U.S. presence in the islands. Thus, the U.S. imperial encounter with Cuba was not simply one "nation" occupying another. In fact, it is important to recall that Cuba was not yet a nation at this point. As historian Gilbert Joseph has argued, "U.S. power has been brought to bear unevenly in the region by diverse agents, in a variety of sites and conjunctures, and through diverse transnational engagements."[18]

Afro-descended populations were an integral part of many of these transnational encounters. People of African descent were the backbone of the labor force in the region during this era. This black transnational labor force included not only West Indians, but also people of African descent from the Spanish- and French-speaking societies of the region. Hundreds of thousands of Afro-Caribbean migrants left their homelands to work for U.S.-controlled industries in Panama, Costa Rica, Cuba, and New York City, among other places.[19] While black migrants moved throughout the Caribbean, other groups of black women and men moved on a more massive scale within the United States. During the era of the "Great Migration" hundreds of thousands of people of African descent relocated from the southern United States to various urban centers in the North, Northeast, and Midwest. From the outbreak of World War I through the 1920s, they numbered nearly 1.5 million, arriving in industrial centers such as Chicago, Cleveland, Detroit, and New York City, creating their own communities in the process.[20] The most famous of these destinations, of course, was Harlem, where 40,000 foreign-born people of African descent, mostly from the English-speaking Caribbean, settled in. Together with the already existing black population in these cities, the new immigrants provided a fertile base for movements such as Garveyism. Not surprisingly, the UNIA thrived in many of these newly developing communities, thereby forming a bridge between these U.S. cities and black settlements in Cuba and throughout the rest of the circum-Caribbean region. Thus, rather than classifying movements such as Garveyism as fundamentally either a "West Indian" or an "African American" phenomenon, this book's focus on Afro-Cuban participation in the movement shows how the UNIA was a transcultural movement that produced new Afro-diasporic cultures in the 1920s.[21]

To situate the Great Migration with the simultaneous Caribbean migration is to highlight the deepening connectedness of Afro-diasporic communities across national borders in this period. It is also to link the process of U.S. empire-building in the Caribbean and Central America with transformations occurring in the United States. Not unlike the upheavals produced by the Age of Revolution of the late eighteenth and early nineteenth centuries, the transformations created by U.S. empire-building and simultaneous black migration throughout the region created the conditions for unprecedented cross-cultural interaction.[22] What we see emerging during these decades was a U.S.-Caribbean, transcultural, Afro-descended population living in distinct nation-states while encountering forces that led them to pursue survival strategies beyond regional and national borders. By the late 1910s and early 1920s, this historic transformation was having a profound effect on the ways people of African descent in the U.S.-Caribbean world navigated the structures of racialized imperial power and imagined themselves and each other.

A close examination of the particular history of Afro-Cuban and African American interaction highlights this larger diasporic transformation in a historically specific transnational setting. This historic specificity is rooted in not only Cuba's unique history of racial formation during the colonial period, but also its position as a neocolonial republic under immense U.S. cultural, political, and economic influence, which brought the island into greater contact with U.S. racial understandings. The U.S. presence in Cuba not only shaped the construction of Cuban national identity, as historian Louis Pérez convincingly demonstrated, but also reshaped racial ideas and practices. To be sure, the impact of U.S. imperialism on racial dynamics in Cuba involved, as Pérez writes, a process by which "North American prejudices were easily transposed into a Cuban ambience" in a way that "could serve as a rationale for discrimination in Cuba."[23] However, the relationship between U.S. and Cuban racial ideas was much more intricate. The impact of the U.S. presence on racialization in Cuba can be best represented as a complex process of cross-fertilization between Cuban and U.S. conceptions of race. The cross-border movement of racial understandings encompassed a wide range of encounters between Cuban and American people of European descent, as well as African Americans and Afro-Cubans. The emergence of branches of the Ku Klux Klan in Cuba during the 1920s illustrates the intermeshing of racial systems. In 1928, Cuban and U.S. Klan members portrayed themselves as "an institution founded in the year 1866 in the United States of America," while insisting that their "fundamental goals and principles are exclusively Cuban." Rather than constructing a comparative model that posits a clash between two distinct racial systems, this study shows how the Cuban-U.S. imperial encounter produced an assemblage of racial understandings that enveloped the two countries in a larger transnational system of racial formation.[24]

The benefits of viewing Cuba and the United States within a continuum of hemispheric racial systems illuminate the ways racial segregation in both countries stimulated the forging of Afro-diasporic linkages. Whereas the racial segregation of African Americans in daily life in the United States is well known, the history of racial exclusion in Cuban society, particularly in the realm of leisure practices, is more obscure. To be sure, the spheres of the workplace and politics were clearly cross-racial before 1959. But the arenas of leisure and recreation generally were not, as shown by the emergence of separate cultural and recreational societies throughout the republican era. With the exception of Afro-Cuban musicians, Cubans of African descent were routinely excluded from the clubs of the white Cuban elite, such as the infamous Havana Yacht Club. But much like African Americans, Afro-Cubans turned segregation into congregation by forming a vast array of organizations that became the lifeblood of their cultural life across the class spectrum.[25] These associations, known as the *sociedades de color* (colored societies), which first emerged out of the *cabildos de nación* (African-based fraternal societies) of the colonial period, were the primary initiators of Afro-Cuban contacts with African American institutions. The most famous of these societies was the Club Atenas, an association formed by a small group of Havana-based Afro-Cuban intellectuals in 1917. While the elitist tendencies of these associations are well known, their functions as cultural institutions and as spaces of diasporic interaction have tended to be overlooked. Throughout the prerevolutionary period, groups like Club Atenas and the Unión Fraternal actively pursued connections with African Americans by sending their literature to black institutions in the United States, hosting African American travelers, and publicizing the achievements of the *negro americano* in their publications and at their activities. As chapter 1 demonstrates, the very existence of the Club Atenas's headquarters can be traced to an African American source. The building's architect, Luís Delfín Valdés, was an Afro-Cuban graduate of Tuskegee in 1908. Thus, the Afro-Cuban societies played central roles in the forging of Afro-diasporic linkages throughout the prerevolutionary era.

As the conditions created by empire accelerated contact between Afro-Cubans and African Americans, the ideologies of empire in turn shaped their understanding of these encounters. The imperial assumptions in diasporic encounters were embedded in the postemancipation ideology of racial uplift, which resonated deeply with upwardly mobile blacks throughout the diaspora.[26] As the historiography of the Pan-African movement showed long ago, diaspora projects emanating from blacks in the West were frequently based on the assumption that they were more "civilized" than Africans on the continent of Africa. In short, the task of uplifting the "race" from the vestiges of slavery fell on the shoulders of African descendants in the diaspora, particularly African Americans, who often saw themselves as the leading lights of the global "colored race." This hierarchical understanding of the diaspora's relationship to the continent was replicated in African Americans' perceptions of their relationship with Afro-Cubans. Their status as citizens (however partial) of the most powerful nation in the hemisphere combined with their well-known struggles against Jim Crow segregation accorded them a special place of importance within the African diaspora. Moreover, their ambivalent position vis-à-vis U.S. imperial expansionism further complicated their understanding of their relationship to other diasporic populations. At times they opposed U.S. empire-building, while in other moments they supported it as a means to secure their own citizenship rights within the United States.

Afro-Cubans' understanding of their relationship to Africa and African Americans was equally complex. While African cultural practices permeated the daily lives of most Afro-Cubans, the elites and aspiring classes tended to avoid public identification with Africa.[27] Yet to shy away from an "African" identification was not to reject a black self-understanding. At the same time, Afro-Cubans shared the assumption that their African American counterparts were the leaders of the global "colored race." Juan René Betancourt's declaration in the 1950s, "Negro American, the discriminated men of the world entrust themselves to you," in many ways underscores Afro-Cuban attitudes toward members of their "race" in the United States throughout this period. However, Afro-Cubans often used this hierarchical notion of diaspora strategically. Through their apparent subservience they sometimes manipulated African Americans' self-perceptions in order to gain concrete benefits from their more privileged neighbors to the north while never forfeiting their rightful place as Cuban citizens and members of the "colored race."

To acknowledge the class-based and imperialist assumptions embedded in notions of diaspora is not to make the argument that diasporization was little more than imperialism in blackface.[28] Such claims misread the options for action available to African descendants in both countries in the opening decades of the century and the ways in which they made empire work for them. As this book shows, regardless of their views on U.S. imperialism, African Americans and Afro-Cubans often chose to use the imperial structure toward their own ends rather than forge direct challenges to it. Aspirations for freedom and equality could not be achieved simply by fighting for citizenship rights within the context of the nation alone. As a historical phenomenon that created the circumstances for all types of cross-border linkages, empire building opened up potential avenues for Afro-Cubans and African Americans to achieve freedom, equality, and upward mobility. Therefore, traversing the routes of empire became a means to an end that often fell short of the particular goals of U.S. officials and businessmen in Cuba. Seeing how that story unfolds should enrich our understanding of the complex relationship between diasporization and empire building.

Diaspora in Action: Historical Actors on the Move

This book's emphasis on black cultural and educational institutions biases the study toward relatively privileged persons of African descent in both countries. Political leaders, students, activists, artists, intellectuals, and entrepreneurs fill the vast majority of the pages of this book, even though the points of contact between Afro-Cubans and African Americans extend across different social classes.[29] Despite the limitations of this approach, it is important to focus on black elites as a significant part of Afro-Cuban and African American historiography. As a contribution to African American studies, this book examines diasporic initiatives among the African American elites and the experiences of upwardly mobile Afro-Cubans engaged in diaspora-making in Cuba beyond the realm of Afro-Cuban religion and folklore. With the exception of the recent scholarship on race and politics in republican Cuba, the historical experiences of Afro-Cubans who do not fit into the categories of slaves, patriots, musicians, workers, communists, or *santeros* (santería practitioners) have generally been overlooked. Elizabeth McHenry's assessment of recent African Americanist scholarship rings true for studies of Afro-Cubans. "Against the backdrop of the 'authentic' actions of their less-privileged counterparts," McHenry writes, "the perspectives of the black middle and upper classes, their activities and their actions have been considered as indicative of one of two things: the desire to assimilate into the white middle class, or the passive acceptance of white domination and accommodation to racial segregation." This narrative, she argues, "oversimplifies the complexity of their actions; in doing so it also grossly underestimates the complexity of the experience of black Americans in the United States."[30]

While the attention to black elites in this study aims to complement existing trends in Afro-Cuban and African American historiography, the predominance of men in this study underscores the masculinist nature of many Afro-diasporic encounters and illustrates the ways men of African descent in Cuba and the United States bonded on common gender assumptions about who should dictate the future of the "colored race."[31] Chapter 3, for example, examines the relationships of Langston Hughes, Nicolás Guillén, Gustavo Urrutia, and José Antonio Fernández de Castro and highlights the homosocial worlds of Afro-Cuban and African American intellectuals and their white peers in these movements. In addition, this study foregrounds the moments when black women in both countries intervened in these largely male-dominated circles. By the 1930s and 1940s, newly formed black women's organizations such as the National Council of Negro Women and the Asociación Cultural Femenina became active agents in the forging of these connections. Thus while this book is not a gender analysis, it is one that is attentive to gender dynamics in the process of diasporization.

The book is organized as a series of encounters between Afro-diasporic peoples in the United States and Cuba. Drawing upon archival sources in both countries, this study foregrounds specific spaces of diasporic interaction to convey the essence of diaspora-making by following historical actors as they move across borders. Each chapter examines a fundamental aspect of diasporization in the twentieth century: material incentives, performance and embodiment, cultural production and its reception, and tourism. It begins in chapter 1 with an examination of the connections forged by Booker T. Washington's Tuskegee Institute in Alabama with Cubans of African descent during the onset of U.S. imperialism in Cuba in 1898. The chapter shows how the interactions between the school and prospective students were driven largely by the agency of black people themselves in both countries even in the midst of U.S. imperial designs in Cuba. Upwardly mobile Afro-Cubans were eager to study at Tuskegee because Booker T. Washington's message of "up from slavery" resonated with their own experiences. The chapter highlights the importance of material incentives in the making of Afro-diasporic linkages by showing how aspirations for an education animated Afro-Cuban desires to attend Tuskegee.

Chapter 2 examines the forging of diasporic relationships in the 1920s within the context of Marcus Garvey's Universal Negro Improvement Association (UNIA). Rather than analyze the UNIA as simply an English-speaking, U.S.-based political movement, I view the organization as a transcultural phenomenon that enabled Cuban and Anglophone African descendants to enact a diasporic commonality. Key to this process was the association's vibrant performance culture, which enhanced the ability of Garveyites to communicate across linguistic and cultural differences. While the U.S. intervention in Cuba in 1898 set the stage for greater interaction between Afro-Cubans and African Americans, the expansion of the U.S. presence in the Caribbean during the 1910s and 1920s, along with concomitant African American and Afro-Caribbean migration throughout the region, further accelerated this process. The role of Garveyism in this broader transformation is clear in Cuba, the country that had the largest number of UNIA divisions outside the United States. Cuba's geographic position at the center of this imperial formation made it an important cultural crossroads between Afro-Cubans and English-speaking African descendants from the United States, Central America, and the Caribbean. The result of these changes was a mass movement that created a new transcultural understanding of the African diaspora, one that explicitly foregrounded the diverse histories of the "Negro peoples of the world."

Chapter 3 continues the theme of cross-cultural interaction by underscoring the role of promoters and audiences in the forging of the connections between the Harlem Renaissance and the *afrocubanismo* movement. In both Cuba and the United States, previously denigrated cultural forms, such as the blues, spirituals, rumba, and the *son*, were taken up by writers, musicians, and artists to create a new diasporic cultural aesthetic. The chapter interprets the immense traffic between these cultural movements as evidence of diasporization, rather than as mere background information for two distinct national movements. Key figures in these exchanges were poets Langston Hughes and Nicolás Guillén, as well as their promoters, including José Antonio Fernández de Castro, Gustavo Urrutia, and Arturo Schomburg, and Hughes himself. Even when the writers and artists themselves denied or downplayed these cultural exchanges, the audiences and promoters of their work actively linked the two movements together. The interactions between promoters, audiences, and artists inaugurated new understandings of Afro-diasporic cultures that celebrated, rather than rejected, the expressive cultures of the black working classes in both countries.

Chapter 4 underscores the importance of black tourism in the process of diasporization from the early 1930s until the dawn of the Cuban Revolution and the civil rights movement in the 1950s. Spurred on by African American and Afro-Cuban entrepreneurs and organizations, black travelers with some means began to view themselves as "tourists" eager to visit other parts of the world where people of African descent lived. Cuba's pleasant climate, geographic proximity, and large population of African descent made it a particularly attractive place to visit for African American travelers, especially since a passport was not needed for entry to the country. The expansion and transformation of passenger travel service from steamships and railways to buses and airplanes in this period expanded opportunities for interaction between Afro-Cubans and African Americans. However, black tourism had to contend with persistent transnational structures of racialization that pervaded every corner of the transit industry from Havana to the Jim Crow South and the northern United States. Therefore, the chapter not only shows how instances of racial discrimination against black travelers helped propel activism in both countries, but also documents the strategies black entrepreneurs and organizations used to assemble a tourist network that relied upon segregated African American and Afro-Cuban institutions and businesses. In this way, the chapter is a continuation of the book's central theme of diaspora-making as a form of adaptation, of Afro-descended populations developing their own transnational strategies to counter persistent forms of racial exclusion within the imperial structures that governed travel and leisure between Cuba and the United States in this period.

Finally, the book concludes with an epilogue that traces the histories of Afro-Cuban encounters with African Americans after the triumph of the Cuban Revolution in 1959. Drawing upon fieldwork and interviews conducted in Havana, it narrates the story of Ramiro de la Cuesta, an alumnus of Bethune-Cookman College and a product of Afro-Cuban and African American linkages during the prerevolutionary era. I use these reflections on my interviews to meditate on the meaning of Afro-diasporic encounters in the past, present, and future. De la Cuesta's experience highlights a bygone era that might have increasing relevance to a new epoch of Cuban-U.S. relations that could be on the horizon.

CHAPTER ONE

Forging Diaspora in the Midst of Empire

The Tuskegee-Cuba Connection

In November 1901, a group of students arrived at Tuskegee Institute from Cuba with a letter of introduction from Juan Gualberto Gómez, the famous Afro-Cuban patriot. Gómez had exhibited his nationalist credentials during his fierce battle for Cuban sovereignty against the U.S.-imposed Platt Amendment in the Cuban Constituent Assembly. Now, only a few months later, he sent four students to Tuskegee, the famous school for African Americans in the nation that had successfully thwarted Cuban independence. Among these pupils was his son, Juan Eusebio. "I hereby take the liberty of recommending to you Lorenzo del Rey Jr. the bearer of this letter," the elder Gómez wrote in English to the school's principal, Booker T. Washington, "who wishes to be admitted in the Institute whose Directorship you fill with so much tact and credit. . . . I ask of you, as you are so kind always, to admit him." While Gómez revealed that del Rey was unable to pay for his education, he insisted that the student was "sufficiently advanced in machinery, and [would] work while there so as to be less onerous to the Institute." Gómez hoped that the school would "make a man of him," as well as the other students who arrived with his son, including Ramón Abreu, Nicolás Edreira, and Romualdo Cárdenas. The longtime advocate for Afro-Cuban education thanked Washington in advance for accepting the students and promised to "create an Association here whose purpose will be to send every year a number of students to Tuskegee, where tuition will be paid by said Association." Gómez concluded his letter by expressing his admiration for Washington's "love for the advancement of your brothers."[1]

Gomez's letter to Washington highlights the Tuskegee Institute's role in the formation of Afro-diasporic linkages at the turn of the twentieth century. It also provides revealing evidence of two men who have usually not been viewed by historians as diasporic subjects beyond their national contexts. Interpreting this letter requires one to go beyond existing portrayals of both of these well-known figures: Gómez—the Afro-Cuban nationalist loyal to *Cuba Libre*—Free Cuba; Washington—the African American accommodationist acquiescent to Jim Crow segregation. In the midst of imperial transitions in Cuba and the United States at the turn of the twentieth century, both became key players in the formation of cross-national relationships between Afro-Cubans and African Americans. The fact that Gómez, an iconic Cuban nationalist figure, sent his son to a black American school in the U.S. South illustrates the material benefits that relationships with African Americans could provide for Afro-Cubans even at the precise moment of Cuban national formation. Hundreds of other Afro-Cuban parents and guardians did the same, not as an act of diasporic political solidarity, but in the hope of obtaining some sort of advanced schooling for their sons and daughters due to the absence of viable options in their homeland. Thus, Tuskegee became a site of diasporization not only through Washington's efforts, but more importantly through the agency of people of African descent who were inspired by his message of "up from slavery." In this way, Afro-diasporic subjects in Cuba and other parts of the diaspora gave the Tuskegee phenomenon a meaning that transcended the racial politics of the United States in the Jim Crow era.[2]

Aspiring Afro-Cubans like those who were advised or assisted by Gómez found Tuskegee to be an attractive school for their teenage sons, and occasionally their daughters, because of its growing international reputation. In an era when racial segregation was becoming the governing principle of education in the southern United States, Tuskegee, and its predecessor Hampton Institute, championed what became known as the "Hampton-Tuskegee Idea" of industrial education for people of African descent. Tuskegee became the preeminent model of industrial training. Founded by ex-slave and Hampton graduate Booker T. Washington in rural Alabama in 1881, the institute grew rapidly and superseded Hampton as the most prominent and best-endowed school for African Americans. Tuskegee quickly developed a national and international stature, attracting thousands of students from across the United States and other countries, including hundreds of Afro-diasporic students from the African continent, the Caribbean islands, and Central and South America. As this chapter shows, Afro-descended students from Cuba and Puerto Rico were among the first students from abroad to enroll at Washington's school, due to the islands' geographic proximity to the United States and their centrality to the plans of U.S. imperial expansion.[3]

In many ways, Afro-Cuban encounters with Tuskegee mirrored the larger power relations embedded in the U.S.-Cuban imperial encounter at the turn of

Representatives of the different nationalities in the 1908 class of Tuskegee Normal and Industrial Institute. *Clockwise from top left*: Saturnino Sierra Feijoo, Puerto Rico; Edward Andrens Anthony, Togo; Bethel Aldrick Posey, San Andrés Island, Colombia; Iwane Kawahara, Japan; Alexandre Lavard, Haiti; Luís Delfín Valdés, Cuba; and Alvin Joristophones Nealy, United States.

the twentieth century. Washington, like many African Americans at the time, tried to harmonize his loyalty to the United States with an identification with the worldwide colored race. His attempt to apply his model of racial uplift to Afro-descended populations abroad, including Cuba, was a manifestation of these conflicting allegiances. Despite the imperial dimensions of the Tuskegee connection to Cuba, it was not the product of U.S. imperialist designs. Instead, the relationship was created largely by the school and Afro-Cubans themselves. Rather than wage a counteroffensive to imperialism, the Tuskegee-Cuban connection shows how many Afro-diasporic subjects in Cuba and the United States attempted to take advantage of the opportunities created by the emerging imperial structure. Afro-Cubans and African Americans reached across national borders as a strategy to negotiate the changing configuration of power in a moment of imperial formation. To be sure, diasporization in the midst of empire was marked by unequal power relations; however, this does not negate the lasting effects of the Tuskegee-Cuba connection. Tuskegee remained an educational option for upwardly mobile Afro-Cubans into the 1920s. More importantly, it laid the foundation for Afro-diasporic interaction between Afro-Cubans and African Americans in subsequent decades.

Despite the apparent applicability of Washington's model of industrial education to Cuba, by and large his grand vision of Cuban Negroes studying at his school and returning to their homeland employing industrial methods did not come to pass in the ways he might have anticipated. Many Afro-Cuban students, like other pupils at the school, resisted Washington's rigorous curriculum and were expelled by the institution. Those who remained at the school and became loyal supporters of Tuskegee took apart their principal's message and clung to what they could use to their own purposes. Afro-Cuban alumni of the institution were empowered by Washingtonian racial uplift, not to become good farmers or domestic workers, but to become black professionals and entrepreneurs. Moreover, the emergence of Afro-Cuban institutions inspired by Washington, such as the Instituto Booker T. Washington in Havana, shows the influence of the Tuskegee principal's ideas even among those who never came to Tuskegee.

Analyzing the Tuskegee-Cuba relationship complicates our understanding of the transnational dimensions of African American history during the Jim Crow era. The basic assumptions that tended to guide interpretations of black American politics during the Jim Crow era characterized Washington and his followers as "accommodationists" while his rival W. E. B. Du Bois and his "Talented Tenth" adherents were positioned as more progressive (and internationalist) historical actors.[4] These assumptions informed the most in-fluential source on Washington and Tuskegee: the fourteen-volume published version of the Booker T. Washington Papers, compiled by Washington biog-rapher Louis R. Harlan during the 1970s and 1980s.[5] The few documents on Washington's effort to educate Afro-Cubans (and Afro–Puerto Ricans) that appear in the published volumes, as well as most subsequent scholarship, give the impression that Washington was little more than an agent of U.S. imperial-ism.[6] Yet the published volumes, which contain approximately 5 percent of the entire collection housed at the Library of Congress, do not include a wealth of contrary evidence, especially the letters from students and others from Cuba and Puerto Rico who attended or expressed interest in attending the school. Therefore, giving attention to the archive beyond the published volumes opens up interpretations of the Tuskegee phenomenon that transcend the nation-based narrative of African American history.

A close examination of Tuskegee's connection to Cuba also enhances our knowledge of the ways Afro-Cubans experienced the imperial transition. As historians have shown, Cubans of African descent fought for their citizenship rights within the Cuban separatist movement and the newly formed Cuban re-public.[7] Yet, they also sought opportunities for themselves outside the confines of the Cuban state in formation. They had to. Even when they felt an intense investment in the Cuban nation, their uncertain material circumstances and the absence of local educational options compelled them to look elsewhere, particularly since the Cuban state was controlled by the U.S. occupation forces. The U.S. intervention and occupation of Cuba exacerbated racism on the island. Yet, it did not stop Afro-Cubans from pursuing openings in the emerging imperial structure for their own benefit. In this regard, Afro-Cubans were no different than other aspiring Cubans of this era.[8]

While the U.S. intervention in Cuba helped prompt Afro-Cubans to seek out Tuskegee for an education, it also provided openings for African Ameri-cans. While many African Americans were opposed to U.S. expansionism, others embraced it enthusiastically, especially when the "Spanish-American War" and the subsequent occupation of the island seemed to present new op-portunities for material advancement and secure citizenship rights. Forging linkages with Afro-descended people abroad not only was the agenda of pro-gressive (from a twenty-first-century perspective) Pan-Africanist intellectuals such as Du Bois, but was, in fact, part of the political and quotidian strategies of entrepreneurially minded African Americans such as those who considered themselves adherents of Booker T. Washington's ideas. Cuba's proximity to the

United States and its centrality to the war effort made it particularly attractive for aspiring black men. If empire opened up new opportunities for many white Americans, it also opened up potential outlets, albeit more limited ones, to African Americans.

Tuskegee and the African Diaspora in the Age of Empire

In 1898, Booker T. Washington was on his way to becoming the most powerful black leader in the United States. His notoriety rapidly increased after his 1895 Atlanta Exposition address, also known as the Atlanta "Compromise" speech, in which he told a predominantly white Southern audience, "In all things purely social we can be as separate as the fingers, yet one as the hand in all things essential to mutual progress." Washington's stature was enhanced by the support of prominent figures among the white U.S. political and economic elite. After Washington's speech, many, if not all, roads led to the little town in the middle of the state of Alabama. Visitors and their money flowed into the school to see Washington's "miracle" of black education. Moreover, the annual Tuskegee Negro Conference, which attracted visitors to discuss the "Negro problem," made it the de facto political center of black America in the opening decade of the century, whether his northern black elite opponents liked it or not. His ability to extract resources from philanthropists, including some leading industrialists, enabled him to make his educational institution, Tuskegee Institute, the most noteworthy school for people of African descent in the country at the time.

Tuskegee's emergence as a model of African American education enhanced Washington's stature, not just in the United States, but throughout the world. The Tuskegee principal was viewed by his admirers, black and white alike, as a leader of the "Negro race" worldwide. It was a role that he strategically embraced, even if he was a "provincial" man at heart.[9] As European imperialism became more entrenched in Africa, white philanthropists and colonial officials saw the "Hampton-Tuskegee Idea" applicable to the African continent. European colonial officials were eager to apply Washington's model of "industrial education" to various educational and agricultural schemes in different parts of Africa.[10] The institution's prestige was also enhanced by its hosting of the International Conference on the Negro in 1912, which included a wide range of participants who sought to apply Washington's model of industrial education to Africa and other parts of the diaspora. In the two decades before the emergence of Harlem as a black political and cultural capital, one could argue, Tuskegee was the prime epicenter of Afro-diasporic activity in the world.[11]

But Washington's international influence was first felt, not in Africa, but in the United States' "new possessions" in the Caribbean and the Pacific acquired in the War of 1898. As tensions between the United States and Spain escalated after the USS *Maine* exploded in February 1898, Washington and other African American leaders throughout the country saw the prospect of war presenting an opportunity to stake claims to equal citizenship. The eventual triumph of Jim Crow in the U.S. South has perhaps prompted us to overlook the fact that the impending war with Spain in 1898 seemed to offer a real possibility for African American men to stave off the onrushing tide of disfranchisement. Many saw the war as a moment when they could prove their worthiness for genuine political and social equality through their military service. Although black men had previously distinguished themselves in the Civil War and in the various wars against Native Americans, their participation in a military conflict with a foreign power could finally affirm African Americans' loyalty to the nation. Throughout the country, black activists called for the recruitment of African American volunteers into the armed forces. Such arguments were palpably gendered. Military service, as historian Michele Mitchell has shown, could not only further claims to full U.S. citizenship, but also enable black men to demonstrate their manhood. If white men in the United States and Europe could take up the "white man's burden," African American men could make their own claim to imperial citizenship by articulating their own "black man's burden." In this way, African American men sought to bring their aspirations for equal citizenship in the United States in line with their desires to play a leading role in the regeneration of the "race" as a whole.[12]

Booker T. Washington joined this chorus of African American voices agitating for participation in the conflict after the explosion of the *Maine*. In March 1898, he proposed to John Davis Long, the secretary of the navy, the idea of "placing at the service of the government at least ten thousand loyal, brave, strong black men in the South" for military service. Washington volunteered to take responsibility of this awesome task. He based his proposal on the racialist idea that black people could handle the tropical climate of Cuba better than whites. "The climate of Cuba is peculiar and dangerous to the unacclimated white man," the Tuskegee principal warned. Conversely, black soldiers would be ideal for the Cuban campaign because "the Negro race in the South is accustomed to this climate."[13] While federal and state leaders seem to have ignored Washington's proposal, President William McKinley eventually allowed African American men in select states to enlist as volunteers in the U.S. military later that year. The invading army included not only the Ninth and Tenth Cavalries, two regular black regiments, but also a number of newly formed volunteer infantries, including the Eighth Illinois, the Ninth "Immunes," and the Twenty-third Kansas Infantry.[14]

As black men were volunteering for military service, the Tuskegee principal found himself in the position of a broker for U.S. interests in Cuba who needed "Negroes" for their projects on the island. As Washington's notoriety increased, many U.S. citizens sought him out to recommend black folks for work in the "new possessions." As is generally known, powerful whites, including President Theodore Roosevelt, were asking Washington to recommend African Americans for government positions. Roosevelt was just one of hundreds who sought out Washington for guidance on how to incorporate "Negroes" into their plans. As the U.S. occupation of Cuba took shape, Washington received numerous requests from white missionary, charitable, and business organizations to recommend African Americans for their interests in Cuba. In November 1899, Osgood Welsh of the Constancia Sugar Company asked Washington to send to Cuba "a few proven men" to become "the advance guard of workers in the cane fields of the island." However, Welsh made sure the Tuskegee principal understood that his interest in black workers was simply "a practical question of bringing together a supply and a demand." Thus, Welsh informed Washington that while he "would have nothing to do with a sudden irruption in large numbers of American negroes into Cuba," he would "under intelligent guidance bear a hand in making the experiment of enlarging the field of American negro work."[15]

U.S. military officials stationed in Cuba also sought out the Negro race leader to inform him of opportunities for skilled African American workers in Cuba. Presley Holliday, the white sergeant major of the black Tenth Cavalry, informed Washington of the job prospects for tailors at his post in Manzanillo, Cuba. "Tailors are always in demand at posts garrisoned by the regular army," Holliday wrote, "and for that reason, in most military posts they are nearly always given the advantage of free rooms where they can live and run a shop, and also the advantage of boarding with a troop or company at very reasonable rates." Holliday insisted that if "a tailor, backed by a good recommendation, present[ed] himself at this post he would in all probability be given these same privileges; and I know from experience that should his work prove satisfactory he would always have all the work he could do."[16]

But white Americans were not the only ones interested in bringing "Negroes" to Cuba. African Americans sought to create their own opportunities on the island. In some quarters, the occupation revived emigrationist sentiment among African Americans. Aspiring black entrepreneurs, clergymen, and soldiers spearheaded the call to consider relocation to Cuba. Since the late eighteenth century, people of African descent in the United States had launched numerous emigration and colonization movements. At the turn of the twentieth century, such a movement was largely inspired by the heroism of Afro-Cuban *mambises* (insurgents), especially Antonio Maceo, and tales of the absence of color lines on the island. The black press in the United States reported numerous stories from African American soldiers stationed in Cuba that touted the supposed opportunities available to aspiring colored men. Elite African Americans such as John L. Waller were a major force in reviving emigrationist sentiments in Kansas. Waller, a longtime emigrationist who captained the Twenty-third Kansas Infantry, claimed African Americans could prosper in Cuba. Another black midwesterner, James Nathaniel Hughes, the father of the famous poet Langston Hughes, seems to have felt the same way. In late 1901, he left his pregnant wife, Carrie, behind to try to make a life for himself in Cuba. While Hughes's activities on the island are unknown, whatever venture he sought for himself seems to have failed because he returned to the United States the following year. These tales of Cuba as a racial paradise notwithstanding, relatively few African Americans emigrated to the island. Moreover, some of the ones who did found themselves disappointed with conditions in Cuba.[17]

But to be satisfied with highlighting the futility of black emigrationist dreams, as some historians have tended to do, leads one to ignore the experiences of those who did emigrate abroad. One of these was R. M. R. Nelson, a black American entrepreneur from New York who engaged in a variety of business activities in Cuba for more than two decades. Like the elder Hughes, the enterprising Nelson viewed Cuba as a place of economic opportunity for people of African descent. "I came to Cuba July '98 as a 'camp follower,'" Nelson informed Booker T. Washington in a 1904 letter, "and ever since I have been preaching riches in Cuba." Nelson, who was keenly attuned to investing trends on the island, asked Washington and "other representative Afro-Americans" to invest in a land project in eastern Cuba, a region that was being flooded with U.S. capital. He claimed to have access to a significant portion of 1.5 million acres of "nearly all virgin land, containing all classes of superior woods and (24) twenty four 'denounced' gold, copper, iron and manganese claims."[18] While Nelson was unable to secure Washington's support for this project, he continued undeterred to do business on the island into the 1920s, courting "representative Afro-Americans" along the way. In a 1924 letter Nelson wrote to Charles Henry Douglass, the owner of the Douglass Theatre in Macon, Georgia, he emphatically affirmed his reasons for remaining in Cuba by insisting that on the island, "I CAN BE what I am, More than HALF A MAN."[19]

John Stephens Durham's activities also illustrate the ways some African Americans navigated the imperial racial order in Cuba. Durham was a long-time friend of Booker T. Washington who kept a regular correspondence with the Tuskegee principal for almost two decades. Durham was in many ways the prototypical "Talented Tenth" figure, even though he had a close relationship with Washington, the supposed enemy of the northern black American elite. Born to a "colored" Philadelphia family, he was educated at elite schools, including the Institute for Colored Youth and eventually the University of Pennsylvania. Durham was apparently fair-skinned enough to pass for white, which likely enhanced his ability to obtain positions that were usually the domain of whites. Still, he "pride[d] himself on being Negro, while he would pass anywhere for a white man," one press profile reported. After practicing as a lawyer in Philadelphia, he managed to get himself into the U.S. diplomatic corps, replacing Frederick Douglass as the ambassador to Haiti in 1893. Ten years later, with Washington's help, he became part of the U.S. government's legal team in the Spanish Treaty Claims Commission. His work for the commission seems to have impressed Edwin Atkins, the New England sugar baron who was one of the most influential sugar planters on the island. In a 1907 letter, Washington happily informed Durham that Atkins had showered him with unsolicited praise, that he felt Durham was "by long odds the most efficient man connected with the Spanish Claims Commission," and that the African American mill manager "had the very highest reputation as a business man." Washington concluded that Atkins's faith in Durham "seem[ed] to be unlimited."[20]

Durham's reputation must have helped him land a position as manager of the Central Francisco in Camagüey, a sugar mill constructed by Manuel Rionda and largely financed by the Philadelphia-based McCahan Sugar Refinery. "I have recently closed with an American company to take charge of a sugar property on the south coast of Cuba," Durham enthusiastically reported to Washington in April 1905. "They pay me $9,000 a year and a commission on annual profits in stock." Francisco had floundered since its construction, and the company hired him to expand and to make changes. "They want to double the plant," he reported to the Tuskegee principal, "so you see, I have not laid a bed of roses for myself."[21] Durham's time on the Spanish Treaty Claims Commission and his Philadelphia connections, not to mention his light-skin privilege, undoubtedly helped him obtain a position that few people of African descent could fathom.

The presence of some number of African Americans, however small, among those from the United States who flowed into Cuba during the occupation and beyond, reveals that U.S. expansionism was a complex phenomenon that included a wide variety of participants and produced multiple outcomes. Even the presence of white southerners among the U.S. occupiers could not entirely prevent African Americans from creating spaces for themselves in Cuba. African Americans participated in furthering the objectives of U.S. government officials and businessmen, but they could also enact their own understanding of their presence in Cuba, as was the case when many of them joined the U.S. military as an expression of solidarity with Antonio Maceo.[22] African Americans used whatever connections they could—military service, political connections, or light-skin privilege—to find a place for themselves within the new imperial structure. It is within this larger context of African American engagements with U.S. interventionism in Cuba that one must situate the linkages Booker T. Washington's school forged with Afro-Cubans.

Forging the Tuskegee-Cuba Connection

In July 1898, Washington began developing a plan to extend his model of industrial education to Cuba. His advisors readily approved of his idea and encouraged him to publicize the initiative in the press. William Baldwin Jr., the railway magnate who was also head of Tuskegee's Board of Trustees, told Washington that he thought the "idea of getting the papers to take up the Cuban Tuskegee question [was] a good one." However, Baldwin advised the Tuskegee principal to hold off on informing the U.S. government of his plans. "We can get the endorsement from Washington [D.C.] later, just as well as beforehand," Baldwin wrote, "and it is important that you should not lose any of the credit."[23] The two men's correspondence reveals that Washington and his advisors had conceived of the Cuba project well before the U.S. occupation of the island took shape.

Soon after the end of the war, Washington skillfully worked his way into the community of social reformers who sought to carry out their work in Cuba and announced his desire to recruit Cubans to study at Tuskegee. In "Industrial Education for Cuban Negroes," published in the *Christian Register* in August 1898, he argued that Tuskegee and Hampton could play important roles in helping Cuba recover from the destruction engendered by the War of Independence.

> One-half of the population of Cuba is composed of mulattoes or Negroes. All who have visited Cuba agree that they need to put them on their feet the strength that they get by thorough intellectual, religious, and industrial training, such as is given at Hampton and Tuskegee. In the present depleted condition of the island, industrial education for the young men and women is a matter of the first importance. It will do for them what it is doing for our people in the South.[24]

Washington left no evidence of his precise motivations for bringing Afro-Cubans to Tuskegee. This is unsurprising, given his dissembling personality that has bedeviled his observers for more than a century. However, it seems reasonable to conclude that his program fit nicely with his own political agenda at the time. Educating some of the "mulattoes or Negroes" in the islands of the Caribbean would certainly enhance Tuskegee's legitimacy, not only among white Americans, but also within African American leadership circles, where an increasing number of critics were becoming unsettled by Washington's growing influence. Taking up the education of Cubans and Puerto Ricans of African descent would allow Washington to enhance the power of his influential patronage network, known as the "Tuskegee Machine."

Whatever his reasons might have been, Washington quickly began his recruitment effort in the summer of 1898. To get his project going, he utilized his well-honed "navigation" skills that were making him the most prominent black educator in the United States. The Tuskegee principal's objective was to find black people and sympathetic whites who would support his project. As he had been doing since he founded Tuskegee, the "Wizard," as he was eventually called by some of his admirers and critics, worked his magic. He turned to his closest confidants in the school's executive council, including Emmett Scott, his trusted private secretary, and Warren Logan, the school's treasurer, to take charge of the initiative. The first challenge, of course, was funding. In the weeks that followed the publication of his article in the *Christian Register*, donors began to send money to Tuskegee for the Cuba project. In late August, Scott informed his boss that Massachusetts donor W. W. Blackman gave "$150.00 for Cuban education in response to your appeal."[25] Others soon followed. After reading about Washington's effort in the press, Olivia Phelps-Stokes offered funds for Washington's Cuba program. Within a few years, the school's budget had a "Cuban Fund" for students from the island. Washington even drew from the pockets of Edwin Atkins, the American sugar baron and one of the more powerful players in the Cuban sugar industry, who made modest contributions to Tuskegee.[26] In subsequent years, Washington continued to secure money from Olivia and her sister Caroline Phelps-Stokes. In effect, the extension of the "industrial education" paradigm to Afro-Cubans foreshadowed the well-known Phelps-Stokes program for the education of Africans that was established a decade later.[27]

While Washington's call for funds was quickly answered, he was still faced with the actual task of recruitment. Who would find the students? How would he get them to Tuskegee? Once again, the Tuskegee principal skillfully maneuvered his way among powerful whites. Henry B. Plant, the founder of the massive railway and steamship empire in the South and the Caribbean known as the Plant System, operated railways throughout Florida, Georgia, and Alabama, steamship service from Tampa to Key West and Havana, as well as several hotels along the coasts of Florida. In early October 1898, Tuskegee contacted Plant to see if he would provide a free pass for a recruiter to travel from Alabama to Cuba. Remarkably, Plant granted the pass a few weeks later. However, he impressed upon Washington that the Tuskegee agent traveling with the pass would "say nothing whatever of the receipt of the enclosed transportation . . . as the issuance of this transportation I would not like to be considered as a precedent for similar action in other cases." Plant's granting of the pass to Tuskegee is striking, since it took place in the moment when conditions facing African American travelers were becoming more difficult in light of encroaching Jim Crow segregation. Thus, it is not surprising that Plant did not want word to get out that his company was granting free transit to a person of African descent.[28]

Washington's Cuban recruitment effort illustrates the complex relationship between Afro-diasporic peoples and U.S. capital in this period. He used the same skills that he had employed to convince whites to do right by the Negro in the United States to launch his Cuban program. Washington's recruitment strategies show that like the formation of the African diaspora in the era of the Atlantic Slave Trade, diasporization at the turn of the century was made possible by the transnational structures of empire. If black sailors and slave rebels took advantage of transport systems that were designed for their exploitation during the slave trade, black mobile subjects in the postemancipation period also used the "tools of empire," as historian Daniel Headrick called them, for their own purposes. The creation of nation-states in the Americas did not curtail this long-standing practice of travel and communication.[29]

To locate prospective pupils, Washington turned to Thomas Austin, a student at Tuskegee who was a native of Key West. To Washington, Austin was the ideal person for the job because he was "one of our most reliable students and has had considerable contact with the Cubans and speaks the Spanish language."[30] Washington's characterization of Austin's language skills was probably accurate, since the student probably was exposed to Cuban émigrés who had been settling in Key West since the 1840s. Armed with the Plant System's transportation pass, Austin traveled to Tampa and Key West to find Cuban students in November 1898. Soon after his arrival, his principal gave him further instructions. "If you can secure enough promising students in Tampa and Key West," Washington instructed Austin, "I do not want you to go to Cuba, but if you cannot secure enough in Tampa and Key West to make up the number to eight go to Cuba for them. . . . If you can find students that you can depend upon in Tampa and Key West you could leave them there until you return from Cuba and pick them up on your return, or you could send them direct here without waiting as your judgment dictates. I hope I have made myself clear with you."[31]

Washington's decision to send Austin to locate Cuban students in Key West and Tampa before going to the island made sense because a significant number of Cuban émigrés were people of African descent. Key West and Tampa, like New York, were sites of Afro-Cuban participation in the Cuban separatist cause. Afro-Cubans forcefully linked the independence movement to their own desires for true social and political equality. While the importance of these cities as centers of support for *Cuba Libre* is well known, their roles as parallel, interconnected zones of diasporic activity by Afro-Cubans is virtually unknown. As the plethora of publications from the period shows, Afro-Cuban activism was connected to, yet autonomous from, the goals of Cuban independence. Not surprisingly, a number of these figures corresponded with, and were admirers of, Booker T. Washington and other African American leaders. Figures like Rafael Serra moved between Florida, Cuba, and New York to found *sociedades de instrucción y recreo* (instructional and recreational societies), which were designed to educate illiterate Afro-descended people. Many were associates of Juan Gualberto Gómez, including Teofilo Domínguez, and Miguel Gualba, among many others, who coordinated organizations and their publications in Havana, Key West, and Tampa designed to link together the interests of the Cuban "colored race" in these towns. Thus, when Austin arrived in Florida in December 1898, he encountered the remnants of the Florida branch of the transnational Afro-Cuban émigré community that was struggling for social and political equality and who were well aware of the parallel African American struggle.[32]

Austin's language skills and familiarity with Cuban communities did little to help him find students in Tampa and Key West. "I am sorry to report that my progress is poor," Austin informed Washington soon after he arrived in Florida, "due to the fact that they are more anxious to return to Cuba." "On to Cuba" was the sentiment among Cubans in these towns, Austin wrote in a letter with stationery that had precisely that slogan across the top. The Tuskegee student's claim highlights the return movement of Cuban émigrés who were part of the "tide flowing into Cuba" after the war was over.[33]

While Austin was trying to recruit students in Tampa and Key West, his principal was pursuing pupils through his connections with black soldiers serving in the U.S. occupation forces in Cuba. Washington contacted Allen Alexander Wesley and William Barnett, two members of the Eighth Illinois Infantry stationed for garrison duty in San Luis de Cuba, a small town on the eastern end of the island. A native of Indiana, Wesley was a graduate of Fisk University, where he met Margaret Murray Washington, the black social reformer who was also the Tuskegee principal's wife. Wesley had followed the Cuban War for Independence closely, particularly the exploits of Antonio Maceo. In 1898, he enlisted as a surgeon in the Eighth Illinois Infantry and was eventually commissioned as a major. Wesley and other black American soldiers conveyed their admiration for the "Bronze Titan" when they visited the Maceo family home in Santiago de Cuba.[34]

Wesley and his fellow regiment mates enthusiastically looked for students in Oriente. He informed Tuskegee that he had "gotten all the officers stirred up over the matter." While they were confident that they could easily locate students, they were less certain of the precise terms of the school's offer. "There seems to be some confusion as to [the] details in sending the persons you request," Wesley wrote to Washington in October 1898. "It is no easy matter to get parents to consent to send their children 2 or 3 thousand miles away from home into a strange land without some kind of assurance that they will be well taken care of and the more especially girls." Wesley's comment on the reluctance of Cuban parents to send young female students in particular reveals the underlying gendered dynamic among Afro-Cuban students at Tuskegee.[35]

By December, Wesley had successfully located families who were interested in sending their children to Tuskegee. "We have decided to send a boy and a girl from Santiago," Wesley informed Washington. "The parents are very eager for these two to go," Wesley insisted. "It is a brother and sister, of 14 and 12 respectively." Despite this assistance from Wesley and Barnett, it appears that these students were never able to go to Tuskegee because there was no afford-able means of transport from Santiago to Tuskegee in 1898–99.[36] By the summer of 1899, however, Austin and Thomas Jackson, another Tuskegee recruiter, brought eight students to the school from Cuba—all of them from Havana.[37]

While Washington was working with his own recruiters, he was also finessing the support of U.S. companies in Cuba. In October 1899, the school contacted Robert Lyman of the Spanish-American Iron Company, a mining interest with properties in Daiquirí, east of Santiago de Cuba. Washington contacted Lyman to find a way to bring the students that Wesley had found earlier that year, who apparently had not yet left for Tuskegee. With the departure of the Eighth Illinois from the island earlier that year, the school had lost contact with the Afro-Cuban parents in Santiago who wanted to send their children to the school. The two had met at one of Washington's speaking engagements that year. Lyman, like many white businessmen who heard the Wizard speak, was moved by the Tuskegee principal's lecture. He thanked Washington for the "pleasure your lecture gave me" and pledged to help him send the students to Tuskegee. A few months later, Lyman informed Washington that he had contacted Joaquín Castillo, a veteran in the Cuban Liberation Army and "one of the leading Cubans in Santiago," to assist them in finding students.[38]

It was through Lyman that Tuskegee was able to gain access to the U.S. military government in Cuba. The previous year, the school seems to have been able to obtain free passage on a warship from the War Department for a recruiter and Cuban students to bring them to the United States.[39] But now, Washington sought the support of the U.S. occupation authority in Cuba directly. Lyman wrote General Leonard Wood soon after he became military governor of Cuba in January 1900, informing him of Washington's desire to bring Cuban students to Tuskegee. "It has occurred to me that perhaps you might like to utilize this opportunity to do a good turn for some of your Cuban constituents," the Spanish-American Iron executive wrote the general.[40] Lyman's letter was followed up by one from Tuskegee, in which the school asked Wood if he could send them "two or three young men or women of the Negro race." The military governor agreed soon thereafter, and he arranged for the occupation government's Department of Charities to send Manuel Gutierrez, Segundo Carbó, and Alberto Rojas, three students from Remedios, to Tuskegee later that year.[41]

Although the military government's Department of Charities sent some students to Tuskegee, its role in the school's relationship to the island was ultimately quite limited. The surviving evidence in the Booker T. Washington Papers at the Library of Congress indicates that the government played a direct role in sending only a few students to the school. Most pupils went to Tuskegee through their own efforts and the efforts of their parents or guardians, along with key help from Washington's African American network. The path Gutierrez, Carbó, and Rojas took to Tuskegee makes this clear. Even though the Department of Charities sent the students to New Orleans, the school still had to find a way to get them from Louisiana to Tuskegee. For this task, the Wizard called upon Colonel James Lewis, a prominent African American veteran of the Union army who was the surveyor general in New Orleans. Lewis was a black Republican activist and a member of the Afro-American Council, the proto–civil rights organization that was originally founded by T. Thomas Fortune, a well-known African American journalist and Washington confidant. In the spring and summer of 1900, Lewis was part of the cadre of black activists Washington was secretly working with to combat Jim Crow segregation in New Orleans. While Lewis was quietly corresponding with Washington about the attempts of the "white trash," as he called them, to pass the Separate Street Car Law in Louisiana, the colonel agreed to meet the students at the port and provide them with transportation to Washington's school. After Lewis managed to get a half-priced train ticket for the "well-behaved" boys, he sent them on their way "furnished with meals, a lunch on train and 50 cents in cash."[42] Thus, Washington's network of friends and associates played a key role in his transnational initiative even as they were collaborating on the domestic struggle against encroaching Jim Crow segregation.

The U.S. military government played a more important role in disseminating the Spanish translation of *Up from Slavery*. Soon after it was first published, Grace Minns, a Boston-based social reformer, proposed to Washington the idea of translating the book into Spanish "for the purpose of introducing it into Cuba." Minns, a member of the Department of Charities, felt that the underdeveloped state of the island's education system made it ripe for Washington's program of industrial education. She pointed out that the island had "practically no industries except the manufacture of cigars and sugar.... All of the arts which made good homes and in which such emphasis is laid at Hampton and Tuskegee, are practically unknown to the rank and file of the people." Despite the fact that Minns misread the productive capacities of the island's population, particularly its Afro-descended urban artisanry, she remained convinced that "the soil in Cuba is ready for the seeds from Tuskegee and Hampton to be planted." By the spring of 1902, with Washington's permission, Minns had arranged for the book to be translated and published by D. Appleton and Company.[43] The Spanish title, which Minns herself crafted, was *De Esclavo á Catedrático* (From Slave to Professor). "The term catedrático in Spanish signifies a professor in a university," Minns explained to the Tuskegee principal, "a professor with a chair, a place from which he speaks. It seems to me to tell the story of 'Up from Slavery' very well." Minns thought that the original title "would not translate well, and might moreover be thought to have some political significance." Minns's concern about the "political significance" of a literal translation of "Up from Slavery" reveals her own position as a white social reformer who wanted to present a carefully crafted message to Afro-Cubans that would not stir up too much "political" trouble. The concern with the political implications of the book was likely heightened by the fact that it would be disseminated precisely in the moment when Cubans were fighting U.S. interests for universal manhood suffrage in the new Cuban Constitution.

Despite these anxieties, the military government's Department of Charities distributed copies of the book throughout the island. The book included several illustrations of Tuskegee and its students, dutifully performing their industrial curriculum. One year later, Minns happily informed the Wizard that "one thousand copies of your book are now spread all through Cuba." Minns felt confident that the book would "be read by the children in the public schools, in the orphan asylums, by patients in the hospitals, by old men and women in the almshouses, by employees in the cigar factories, and by a large number of persons who are interested in the administration of the schools, the charitable institutions, and in public affairs."[44]

Minns's bold prediction turned out to be somewhat accurate. An examination of the incoming correspondence in the Tuskegee files of the Booker T. Washington Papers shows that the widespread circulation of *De Esclavo a Catedrático* had a great effect. Persons of African descent throughout the island were inspired by the Wizard's autobiography and by his work at Tuskegee. It is not surprising that they would be awed by his autobiography. After all, the island's political and economic turmoil made such a story virtually unthinkable for the vast majority of Afro-Cubans. From the time of the book's publication until Washington's death, hundreds of letters of admiration from Cuba poured into Tuskegee. One reader, Marcelino Callaba Pérez, a soldier in the Cuban army, who identified himself as a "twenty-four year old young man of the colored race" inquired about attending the school after reading *De Esclavo a Catedrático*. Writing from his post at Camp Columbia, he informed Washington that the "great adventures" he read in the Tuskegee principal's autobiography reminded him of his own, which he saw as "similar." Callaba desired to leave the army to pursue his studies to obtain the title of "Doctor of Veterinary Medicine." Callaba's letter illustrates how the "from slave to professor" story inspired many Afro-Cubans to achieve greater upward mobility.[45]

Washington also received praise from Cuban readers who defined themselves as white. One of the more fascinating letters came from Gavino Barnet of Matanzas, who found the book significant in light of the memory of the La Escalera Conspiracy of 1844, when slaves and free people of color were executed by the Spanish colonial government. He wanted the Tuskegee principal to know that he was writing "from the place, city, and nei[gh]borhood, where many years ago, (1844), and when I was even a white infant" a "good many colored men, slaves and free, were shot by order of the General Governor of the Island (the hard hearted General Leopoldo O'Donnell), after having been submitted to most insufferable martyrdoms for a supposed conspiracy against the white people." To Barnet, the publication of Washington's book and the creation of Tuskegee was a significant sign of progress in light of the history of repression of slaves and free people of color in Cuba. "For those reasons," Barnet sent "through the sea, the most hearty and deep congratulation for so a high work you have realized."[46]

Such responses to Washington's book would have pleased Minns. And yet it is clear that Washington and Tuskegee's reputation was rapidly spreading among Afro-Cubans themselves apart from the Department of Charities' efforts to circulate his book. Many more heard about Tuskegee from Cuban students who were already at the school. Throughout the opening decades of the twentieth century, Washington received thousands of letters from students and their parents throughout the African diaspora expressing their interest in attending Tuskegee. Letters of interest poured in from across the United States, as well as from areas as far away as Cape Coast, in the Gold Coast of West Africa; Demerara, British Guiana; Limón, Costa Rica; Bahia, Brazil; Puerto Plata, Dominican Republic; and Port-au-Prince, Haiti. Washington and the Tuskegee story tapped into the deep desires of people of African descent to obtain an education in the Age of Empire. Washington's own recollections of these desires in his autobiography, "it was a whole race trying to go to school," could have applied to Afro-Cubans at the turn of the twentieth century.[47] While the ex-slave's story influenced many throughout the world, it was most influential in Cuba, and to a lesser extent Puerto Rico, because of the islands' relatively recent history of abolition, their geographic proximity to the

United States, and their more direct contact with U.S. empire-building in ways that Afro-descended populations in other places had not experienced up to that point. The convergence of the U.S. intervention with Afro-Cubans' desire for an education made them particularly receptive to the "Hampton-Tuskegee Idea."

Who were the members of the "whole race trying to go to school" from Cuba? And why did they want to go to this faraway place in the middle of rural Alabama? The multitude of letters from Afro-Cubans in the Booker T. Washington Papers at the Library of Congress helps answer these questions. The letters, some written in Spanish and others in English with varying degrees of fluency, communicate the stories of folks who have been largely overlooked in modern Cuban historiography. While African Americans' efforts at getting an education in the postemancipation period have been well documented by historians, Afro-Cuban mobilization for schooling in this period is not as well known. Instead of examining these movements as comparably discrete phenomena, the analysis presented here highlights the convergence of Afro-Cuban and African American efforts on behalf of education since they did, in fact, come together at Tuskegee in this period.

The "why" question is in many ways easier to answer. For Afro-Cubans at the turn of the twentieth century, there were few alternatives for advanced schooling. Nearly all of their letters highlighted the lack of educational opportunities on the island. Education on all levels had always been limited in Cuba during the Spanish colonial era. The meager opportunities that did exist were curtailed even more by the War for Independence. The destruction wreaked by the war and the collapse of Spanish colonial rule only intensified Afro-Cuban aspirations for an education. Juana María Cárdenas and Carmen Navarro bluntly informed the Tuskegee principal in 1900 that they had "strive[d] in our country to fulfill this desire but we cannot do it here and now all our hopes are in your hands."[48]

Since the postemancipation period, descendants of slaves and free persons of color in Cuba had made educational access a top priority in Afro-diasporic conceptions of racial uplift. It was the decisive factor that would propel the "race" to break free from the last vestiges of slavery. The lack of educational opportunities was frequently foregrounded by Afro-Cuban societies in the immediate postemancipation period. In 1893–94, Juan Gualberto Gómez's Directorio Central de las Sociedades de la Raza de Color (Central Directorate of the Societies of the Colored Race) spearheaded a campaign to demand that the colonial government provide greater educational access to Afro-Cubans.

Although Spanish authorities instituted legislation to expand schooling on more than one occasion, its laws and decrees were largely worthless. Public education remained inadequate under Spanish colonial rule and Afro-Cubans continued to be largely excluded from the most desirable private schools. Thus, Afro-Cuban desires to attend Tuskegee should not be surprising since Washington's inspiring story resonated with their own understanding of racial uplift, born out of their own experiences in a postemancipation society.[49]

A good number of the Afro-Cubans who sought admission to Tuskegee were black tradesmen struggling to navigate their way through the challenges of Cuban society in the moment of imperial transition. Not surprisingly, they found Tuskegee's curriculum of "industrial education" especially appealing. One such letter came from Eleno Lino of Havana in 1902:

> Having heard by a friend of mine, the opportunities afforded by your night school to poor colored men who are ansious [*sic*] to have a better education I write you these few lines to see if there is any room for me. I am a Cuban by birth, 18 years of age strong, able bodied and willing to work. I am a taylor [*sic*] by trade and could pass examination in reading, writing, add[ition], subtract[ion], multiply and divide, but I do not know English. This letter is [written] by a dear friend. Hoping to have an early answer from you encouraging my desires. I am your humble servant.
> —*Eleno Lino*[50]

Lino was part of a wave of Afro-Cuban skilled workers who viewed Tuskegee as a chance to refine their skills and advance themselves socially and economically. Bernardo Calderón, a mechanic from Havana, informed Washington in 1912 that his motivation for attending the school was to make himself "independent from the 'patronos' [bosses]." Calderón claimed that while being a mechanic insured that he would not "die of hunger in Cuba," he felt that further vocational training would ensure that he could establish a family and have, as he put it "the peaceful old age that I desire."[51] What we see in a number of these letters are the hopes and aspirations of segments of what historian Michele Mitchell has called in an African American context the "black aspiring class," skilled workers who belonged neither to the rural laboring majority, nor to the educated black elite, who sought opportunities to advance themselves in the face of racism and colonialism.[52]

Some of them were quite mobile, as was the case of Brijida Cabrera, a domestic worker living in New York City in 1900 who wanted to send her son to Tuskegee. "I am a widow in poor circumstances residing in N.Y. at present working for a private family and as I am of Cuban nationality," she wrote in English on the letterhead of the Hotel Muro in Manhattan to Washington. Cabrera's son, Miguel Marín, was "colored, speaks and writes the English language and inclined to be bright and of excellent behavior."[53] A few months after Marín was admitted, Cabrera wrote the school from Havana inquiring about her son. The letter was written on the letterhead of The Inn, one of the Plant System Hotels that was based in Tampa. Apparently she had not been in touch with Miguel, as her letter indicated that she was offended by the fact that the school accused her of being indifferent toward her son. "Believe me, I love him well as my only child and would like to do all that can help to make him happy," Cabrera snapped at the school. As proof of her concern, she asked school administrators if Miguel had received the box of candy that she sent while she was in Baltimore.[54] Cabrera's class status is hard to define. She, like many other Cubans at the time, seems to have traversed the migratory lines of labor that extended from Cuba, New York, and Florida. Her correspondence gives a glimpse of the life of a mobile domestic worker who was able to find employment in multiple cities in the emerging U.S.-Caribbean world.

While domestic workers like Cabrera were among those who sent their children to the school, it was the elite segments of the Afro-Cuban population who were more prominent among the students sent to Tuskegee. Many of the students who sought admission to Tuskegee were connected to influential leaders such as the Afro-Cuban patriots Juan Gualberto Gómez and Martín Morúa Delgado, both of whom were among the tiny number of black elected officials in the early years of the Cuban Republic. For example, Leonardo Ibañez came to Tuskegee as a result of the efforts of Gómez, who was his godfather. He arrived at Tuskegee in September 1903 after Gómez asked the school to admit him. In his request, the Afro-Cuban leader assured the school that the student's guardian, Fermín Zuñiga, would "pay his scholarship annually without fale [sic]" and insisted that Ibañez was a student who would "observe good conduct in every respect."[55] Hence it is clear that some—perhaps most—of these students were members of the tiny Afro-Cuban elite who were scrambling for educational opportunities in a period of uncertainty.

Like Ibañez, many of these pupils were friends and family of the first group of Afro-Cubans who came to the school. This becomes clear upon an examination of the recruitment of students in the early years. Luis del Risco, a student from Havana who studied at Tuskegee for three years, convinced the school to admit his brother Armando in the fall of 1901. When del Risco discovered that his brother's expenses would have to be paid by his family, he cunningly reminded his principal of his supposed promise to cover Armando's expenses. Celestina Ramírez, who was one of the few Afro-Cuban young women who studied at Tuskegee, managed to get her sister Sixta admitted. She too pleaded with the school to cover her sister's expenses. "I know that the rest of the Cubans have found that they will not have to pay their school," Ramírez wrote Washington that same fall. "And I think if my sister is Cuban to[o], she ought not to [pay] any thing," she noted, "or if she has to [pay], I am very willing to give her my place and then I will go home." Both students were granted their requests for admission with funding for their siblings.[56]

A key figure in the school's student recruitment efforts was Alfredo Pérez Encinosa. Pérez was among the first students who arrived in Tuskegee during the 1898–99 year. In his first year, the audacious student skillfully maneuvered his way into the school's administrative hierarchy. In the spring of 1899, he offered his services as a recruiter on the island, informing Washington that he was willing to help the principal find more students in Cuba. "I would like you to give me the opportunity to gather some Cuban boys and girls for you," the student wrote. "I could do so in three weeks and can guarantee you some very nice boys and girls. After my stay of three weeks I shall return. I pledge myself to do so." If Washington doubted his student's sincerity, Pérez told him that he could have the military governor, John Brooke, send "a soldier [to] meet me at the ship and escort me to my home and tell him to not let me stay over four weeks and therefore I will be under his charge and be compelled to return."[57]

Washington apparently did not grant Pérez his request. However, one year later, the persistent student again asked the Tuskegee principal if he could go back to Cuba for the summer. "You must remember that you told me to go to Cuba as soon as I had here two years," the insistent Pérez wrote to his principal, "and I told you that it was too long and then you told me that you will let me go this summer if you could find that the government transport will care [for] me and I must say that you're trying to fool me." "Now Mr. Washington I mean business," he warned. He pleaded to the Tuskegee principal to "think of a son who is absent from his only dear mother since [18]98 and is very anxious to see his mother and his free country."[58]

Pérez's persistent pestering was ultimately successful. The school let him and Antonio Soto, a fellow Cuban student, return to the island in the summer of 1901.[59] As promised, he, as did Soto, recruited a number of students in Havana for the school. By the beginning of the fall term, eleven more pupils arrived from Cuba. That same summer, Tuskegee made arrangements with the Department of Education of the Insular Government of Puerto Rico to receive twenty students per year beginning that year. Thus, in the fall of 1901, the school suddenly found itself with a sizeable number of pupils from the Spanish-speaking Caribbean.[60]

Pérez and Soto had no trouble finding people who were interested in Tuskegee in the summer of 1901. Washington had already been alerted to Afro-Cuban interest in his school the previous summer. Thomas Austin, the Tuskegee recruiter who seems to have relocated to Havana from his native Key West soon after his graduation, informed Washington in the summer of 1900 that there were "several Cubans who, after learning that I was from Tuskegee, have asked me to find out for them if there are any chances of them getting there [sic] children in your school. I am in position to get boys or as many girls as you wish."[61] Austin was not exaggerating. Some of the families he met when he first went to Cuba wrote the school inquiring about admission. Ramón Edreira, who met Austin the previous year and had wanted to send his brother and cousin to Tuskegee, wrote Washington that summer asking if they could be admitted. Manuel Valdés, a friend of Soto's, begged to have himself and two others admitted because they all were left "ruined by the war." Carlos Pierra Edwards communicated similar sentiments to the school while also emphasizing the particularly dire situation for students of color on the island. Pierra wrote with the hope of sending his fifteen-year-old daughter to the school. "We have no facilities for educating our children here, especially if they are colored," Pierra wrote, "this being the true cause of the great percentage of illiteracy among the inhabitants." Despite his interest, it appears that his daughter did not attend the school.[62]

Afro-Cuban young women, Pierra's daughter for one, had a much more difficult time than young men getting into Tuskegee. If craftsmen from Cuba found Tuskegee's "industrial" program to be suitable for their sons, young black Cuban women found the "normal" aspect of the school's curriculum appealing. However, many of them were unable to pursue the promise of Tuskegee. In some cases, they were overlooked and ignored by the school and the U.S. occupation government. Juana Cárdenas persistently pestered the school for admission. After unsuccessfully applying for admission in 1900, she wrote the school again one year later. "With great pains I have saved the money to pay my way to your Normal College," Cárdenas wrote on 28 June 1901. "On the 8th of June of last year I received a letter from you where it was stated that you were unable to pay the transportation of new students from Cuba, but that you might provide otherwise. Are you able and willing to help me? If it is [so], and I pray the Lord it will be so, He and my family will thank you for it."[63] Despite

Cárdenas's persistent efforts, there is no record of her attending the school. Of the eleven new students who went to Tuskegee in the fall of 1901, only two of them were female: María Casanova, who came with her brother Patrocino, and Sixta Ramírez, the sister of Celestina Ramírez, who was already a student at the school. The relative absence of Cuban female students was a pattern that held true. Throughout the two decades of Cuban attendance at Tuskegee, only four of the students were females.

The relative absence of Afro-Cuban young women at Tuskegee is striking. The school was plain about its commitment to coeducation—a fact that is clear in all Tuskegee publications at the time. Tuskegee, like other black American schools, saw itself as preparing special roles for women in its project of racial uplift. Moreover, there is ample evidence of the school's attempt to recruit Afro-Cuban female students. Among the students that the school initially sought to recruit in 1898 was Manuela Gómez, the sister of Juan Eusebio and daughter of Juan Gualberto Gómez. "It is most kind of you to wish me to send Manuela," Manuela Gómez, their mother, wrote Washington in December 1898. "I will speak to Mr. Gomez about it and if he consents I shall write to you immediately." Apparently, the elder Manuela was unable to convince Juan Gualberto to send their daughter to go to Tuskegee. No record exists of her attendance at the school.[64]

Since parents were eager to send their sons to the school to learn a trade, one would think that they would also be willing to send their daughters to become teachers. As in African American communities, the black woman teacher was highly esteemed by Afro-Cubans—the apex of female achievement and respectability. And yet, it seems clear that patriarchal norms guided the thinking of Afro-Cuban parents, who sought to keep their teenage daughters in the home. Moreover, the idea of sending them to a faraway place in another country must have been anathema to many parents. Allen Alexander Wesley, the surgeon in the Eighth Illinois Regiment, made this exact point as he was trying to recruit students for the school in the fall of 1898. So too did Robert Lyman, the employee of the Spanish-American Iron Company, who also tried to recruit students for Tuskegee. In 1900, he informed Washington that he solicited the help of Joaquín Castillo Duany, the Cuban Liberation Army general in order to get boys and girls for the school. Castillo seems to have informed Lyman that while he was able to locate male pupils, he was unable to recruit females. According to Lyman, Castillo was "unable to secure a girl as old as fourteen as the mothers object to letting them go away at that age and wishes to know if one of nine or ten years will do." While the limitations of this source—coming from an American who was likely unaware of gender dynamics in Cuba—are clear, Lyman's communication of Castillo's point is still revealing. It suggests that perhaps Cuban parents were unwilling to send their daughters during the age when the potential for sexual activity was greater. It also highlights the patriarchal structure of domestic labor. Parents might have been unwilling to let their teenage girls leave because they were old enough to contribute to the reproduction of the household. Lyman's admission resonates with Susan Greenbaum's discussion of the patriarchal dynamics that prevailed in Afro-Cuban households in Tampa during this period. Boys were encouraged to get an education while girls were not.[65]

While Afro-Cubans were the primary initiators of the Tuskegee-Cuba connection, occasionally a few prominent white Cubans sent students to the school. Their letters to Washington indicate that they viewed Tuskegee as a place to send Afro-Cuban charity cases, particularly orphans. For example, Gonzalo de Quesada, a Cuban patriot, diplomat, and associate of José Martí, contacted Washington about the possibility of sending a student to Tuskegee in August 1909. Quesada inquired about the possibility of sending the thirteen-year-old son of Julio Hernandez, a "colored journalist" from Santiago de Cuba who had been "recently deceased leaving several children in the greatest misery."[66] Francisco P. Machado, a Cuban politician from Sagua la Grande who held several governmental positions, paid for two students, Pedro Nuñez and Alfonso González Ruíz, to go to Tuskegee. While Machado's connection to the school is unclear, it is likely that he became aware of it through his previous association with the Cuban Educational Association, a program formed in 1898 and designed to educate mostly elite white Cubans in the United States. In a 1910 letter, Machado, who had previously been a member of the Cuban Department of Education, thanked the Tuskegee principal for the "kind attention to my wards in your school."[67] Quesada's and Machado's correspondence with Tuskegee again illustrates the ways Cubans across the color line viewed the school as an appealing institution for Afro-Cuban youth.

In the three decades after 1898, dozens of Cuban students studied at Tuskegee. Afro-Cubans continued to arrive at the school well into the 1920s. The highest number of Cuban students at Tuskegee in a given year was twenty-three, during the 1905–6 academic year.[68] Indeed, Afro-Cuban attendance at the school was at its high point during the first decade of the century. Between 1898 and 1910, an average of fifteen students from Cuba attended the school. During the 1910s, the number of Cubans dropped gradually to around ten students each year. While most pupils came from Havana, some arrived from other parts of the island, such as Sagua la Grande, Guantánamo, Santiago de Cuba, and Santa Clara. Sagua la Grande, on the northern coast of the island, seems to have supplied a disproportionate number of students during these years. This is likely due to the town's particular history of economic and social linkages with the United States.[69]

After a decrease in the number of students during the First World War, the Cuban population at Tuskegee underwent a modest increase during the 1920s. Many of the students who studied at the institution during this period had English surnames, suggesting that perhaps they were children of West Indian migrant workers who resided in Cuba, or perhaps some were descendants of the small number of African Americans who settled on the island after 1898.[70] As mentioned above, the vast majority of Cuban students at Tuskegee were male, a stark contrast to the Puerto Rican student population, which had a large presence of females during these years.[71]

The Tools of the Trade: Craftsmanship and Craftiness at Tuskegee

The girl, coming a stranger from her home in the city or country, is lost in a crowd of girls new to dormitory life. New surroundings and new conditions are everywhere. New emotions, new purposes, new resolutions chase one another in her thoughts, and she becomes a stranger to herself only to find her bearings first in her own room. Here Maine and California, far-away Washington and Central America, meet on common ground. Alabama and Georgia alone feel kinship from geographical propinquity.
—*Margaret Murray Washington*[72]

Margaret Murray Washington's portrait of the new female student could be applied to all new pupils when they first arrived at the school, including those from abroad. As the passage above points out, Tuskegee's students came from areas throughout the Americas. The multitude of images of nameless black students working on the school grounds churned out by the Tuskegee propaganda machine might lead one to assume that they were all black southerners. Yet while students from Alabama and Georgia comprised a large percentage of the school's population, others arrived from all over the United States and other parts of the African diaspora. Thus, when Afro-Cubans arrived at the school, they did not just encounter English-speaking students but heard English spoken with different accents. As the opening decade of the century unfolded, the school's student body became even more varied as students from Cuba, Puerto Rico, Haiti, Jamaica, and other parts of the Caribbean, Central and South America, and Africa arrived in greater numbers. The contemporary category "African American" thus obscures the presence of international students at the school as well as the great diversity within the group of African American students themselves. Accounting for the transcultural quality of the student population should enable us to avoid imposing a preexisting notion of national or cultural "difference" informed by contemporary standards of racial identification on the past and help to illuminate conflict and distinctiveness as historical actors viewed them. An examination of the Tuskegee files of the Booker T. Washington Papers reveals that tensions between the school administrators and Afro-Cuban students were usually rooted in the power dynamics between them rather than an inherent incompatibility between southern U.S. and Cuban cultures.

When Afro-Cuban students first walked onto the grounds of Tuskegee Institute, they must have been awed by what they saw. In the opening decade of the century, the philanthropic money pumped into the school funded its rapid expansion. By the time Cubans began attending Tuskegee, the school's property had grown to nearly 2,500 acres. New buildings were being constructed, and more land was incorporated into the campus. The new arrivals were also probably anxious at the sight of a student population of approximately 1,500 working all over the school grounds: uniformed students working in the farm and the foundry, marching in military drills, laying bricks for a new building, making mattresses, and washing dishes.

The core activities of Tuskegee's students centered on the school's physically demanding program of industrial education. To Washington, industrial education had four objectives:

To teach the dignity of labor.
To teach trades, thoroughly and effectively.
To supply the demand for trained industrial leaders.
To assist the students in paying all, or a part, of their expenses.[73]

Washington's vision of education was heavily influenced by the ideas of Samuel Chapman Armstrong, founder of Hampton Institute, whom his biographer describes as Washington's "great white father." Throughout his career as educator and race leader, Washington never failed to espouse the virtues of Armstrong's vision. Armstrong's curriculum of manual training was based on his belief in the inherent inferiority of black people. People of African descent did not have the intellectual capacities for a liberal arts education, according to Armstrong. The Hampton principal believed that manual labor would instill the necessary moral values to regenerate the supposedly downtrodden race. Like Hampton's curriculum, Tuskegee's program of study was also based on the centrality of manual labor. Industrial training would not only equip blacks with the ability to be economically competitive, but it would also be a way of building "character." Thus, like Armstrong, Washington believed manual labor had a moral value. To be sure, Tuskegee benefited from this curriculum in that it provided access to cheap student labor. Ultimately, Tuskegee aimed to mold its students into morally upright people.[74]

While Washington was heavily influenced by Armstrong's vision of industrial education, he repackaged his mentor's ideas in significant ways, arguing that black educators played a decisive role in the uplifting of the race. Like most African American leaders of the time, Washington believed in the notion of racial uplift—the idea that blacks needed to pull themselves up from the degradation of slavery. Some scholars have viewed Washington and Tuskegee as "Armstrong and Hampton in blackface." However, such claims underestimate the significant differences between the actual implementation of the curriculums of their respective schools.[75] A key difference between them was that Tuskegee was largely run by people of African descent. The school's faculty believed that having black teachers and administrators would provide powerful role models for students—a shining example of self-help and "Negro achievement." In the words of Robert Russa Moton, Washington's eventual successor, Tuskegee was the "most convincing evidence of the Negroes' ability to work together for mutual regard and mutual helpfulness."[76]

Tuskegee's curriculum was based on the idea that intellectual and manual labor went hand in hand, what Washington called "dovetailing." While the school became known for its industrial curriculum, Washington routinely argued that it did not ignore academic preparation. At Tuskegee, he insisted, students could productively combine academic and industrial training. Washington pointed to the school's practice of requiring students to work at the school. Tuskegee's plethora of publications proudly highlighted the centrality of student labor in the construction and furnishing of school buildings. Thanks to the school's practice of dovetailing, Washington argued, "students [were] able to build and equip a large building from top to bottom, inside and out, and the object lessons of their own handiwork stand clustered over many acres, a city in itself built by young colored men."[77]

Like other African American schools at the time, Tuskegee insisted that its students dress in a manner that conveyed respectability. Students wore uniforms and were not allowed to wear bright colors. Along with its strict dress code, the school implemented Washington's obsession with cleanliness: "One thing that I have always insisted upon at Tuskegee," he wrote in *Up from Slavery*, "is that everywhere there should be absolute cleanliness. Over and over again, the students were reminded . . . and are reminded now—that people would excuse us for our poverty, for our lack of comforts and conveniences, but that they would not excuse us for dirt."[78] Cleanliness would be enacted through Armstrong's "gospel of the toothbrush." Washington explained to his readers that "no student is permitted to remain who does not keep and use a tooth-brush." The school principal personally saw to it that his fanatical obsession with cleanliness and order was followed at the school by conducting his own investigation of the students and their work. Washington made this clear in *Up from Slavery*, when he described the school's insistence that students dress neatly, that "all the buttons were to be kept on their clothes, and that there must be no torn places and no grease-spots." Washington proudly proclaimed that these lessons in comportment had been "so thoroughly learned and so faithfully handed down from year to year by one set of students to another that often at the present time, when students march out of chapel in the evening and their dress is inspected, as it is every night, not one button is to be found missing."[79] As historian Stephanie Shaw has argued, Tuskegee's emphasis on comportment was typical of many African American schools in this period. Educational institutions such as Tuskegee saw themselves preparing a cadre of "race men" and "race women" who would be the vanguard of the project of racial uplift.[80]

The school's fierce preoccupation with comportment also highlights the school's emphasis on embodied activity. Tuskegee propaganda frequently touted the mantra of "learning by doing," which revealed not only the school's industrial education curriculum, but also the more basic point that students needed to prove their education less through "academic" activity (such as reading and writing) and more through embodied practices: making mattresses, constructing buildings, milking cows, cooking food, and so on. Tuskegee students were expected to be physically productive, a philosophy that echoes historian Martin Summers's discussion of the influence of gendered understandings of "producer values" among African American men in the early twentieth century.[81]

Washington believed his rigorous industrial education program to be particularly pertinent to the supposedly backward Cubans who enrolled in his school. As always, the Tuskegee principal presented a carefully constructed public image of the school as an agent of civilization vis-à-vis the students from Cuba and Puerto Rico. In December 1899, he told a reporter from the *Memphis Commercial Appeal*, when asked if he had experience with students from Cuba, "Yes we have a number of them in our school. They do fairly well and I can not see why they should not be educated into being good American citizens, though such a training must necessarily be a matter of time."[82] Washington communicated a similar message to Samuel McCune Lindsay, the commissioner of education in Puerto Rico, a few years later. "Our experience with some *Cuban* students is that they have to remain here about two years or longer before they really acquire the American spirit," he informed Lindsay.[83] Washington's self-presentation as an agent of "Americanization" demonstrates his well-known ability to appeal to white sensibilities. However, his foregrounding of his Americanness also likely reveals how national identifications infused his hierarchical understanding of his role vis-à-vis the larger "colored race." Those members of the race who needed to be lifted up were not just poor black southerners, but also those from the more backward branches of the race in Africa and other parts of the diaspora. To Washington, the project of racial uplift was a global one. Tuskegee's leadership, like many African American leaders at the time, saw the school playing a key role in the larger "regeneration" of the diaspora.

As Washington preached the gospel of cultural imperialism to white Americans, he found his students to be less than cooperative disciples. Far from being sponges who uncritically soaked up Tuskegee ideology, Afro-Cuban students took apart the school's message and used what they saw fit, often on their own terms. If Washington was the "master of the Tuskegee plantation," he gave the impression to his students that he was a benevolent one.[84] Over the years, they flooded the principal's office and the school's executive council with letters expressing their various concerns. Moreover, they craftily tried to appeal to Washington's public image as a noble servant to get what they wanted, even at times pitting the benevolent leader against his own staff.

If the Tuskegee principal ruled the school in an authoritarian fashion, he could not completely impose his will on his pupils. In fact, students continually pushed for things that they wanted by regularly appealing to Washington's paternalism. Tuskegee's critics, then and now, have tended to overlook the ways students engaged the program of industrial education. Despite the voluminous literature on Washington and Tuskegee, it is striking that so little attention has been paid to the actual experiences of the students who attended the school. While some scholars have criticized Washington's acquiescence to white philanthropy, such critiques do not take into account the ways students refined the school's objectives. If the institute promised to teach students the "dignity of labor," it could not prevent pupils from trying to avoid manual labor as much as possible. The school's promotion of the image of students dutifully performing agricultural labor such as cutting sugarcane, for example, obscured the fact that the last thing most Afro-Cuban students wanted was to work in sugarcane fields as many of their ancestors did under slavery. If the school promoted the idea that graduates would become carpenters and domestic laborers for white potential donors, some Cuban graduates left the school as architects.[85]

Many of the students from Cuba were unwilling to submit themselves to Tuskegee's strict and demanding curriculum. The Tuskegee files of the Booker T. Washington Papers contain many references to the disciplining of Cuban students. Some were suspended, some were expelled, and others ran away. Juan Gualberto Gómez himself apologized to Washington for the behavioral problems some Cuban students were causing the school. In a 1903 letter, Gómez admitted that he knew "some of the Latin students do not observe good conduct." In his view, this was because some Afro-Cuban parents sent their sons to Tuskegee "thinking that your institution was an asylum, to correct those boys who in their own home gave much trouble."[86] Gómez's claim might reveal the divergent motivations of Afro-Cuban guardians for sending their children to Tuskegee. Indeed, the school's reputation for strictness, a core tenet in the project of racial uplift, might have appealed to parents eager to instill strict moral codes in their children.

While Afro-Cuban resistance to Tuskegee's strict code of conduct might have been based on the particular temperament of students sent to the school, it was less likely to be rooted in any innate incompatibility of the Cuban students' "Latin culture" with African American culture.[87] Such claims do not stand up to a full investigation of the school's records. Indeed, Afro-Cuban students were not disciplined by the school at a higher rate than the African American students. Moreover, it is important to recall the youthful ages of the student body. Many teenage youths, regardless of their national or cultural background, would resist having to straightjacket themselves into a uniform while performing undesirable, backbreaking labor. Furthermore, disciplining students was a central part of the Tuskegee curriculum. In this regard, Tuskegee resembled other boarding schools of the era.

Students' ability to deflect Tuskegee's "lessons" occasionally emerges in the inadvertent admissions that show up in the correspondence of school officials. Washington himself admitted to Samuel McCune Lindsay that Puerto Rican students "like to dress gaudily and extravagantly, to spend much time in powdering their faces," activities that the school actively sought to discourage.[88] Similarly, Washington admitted to Warren Logan, the school treasurer, that the school had to address the "large amount of money spent by the Cuban students for clothing."[89] Even more revealing was Logan's admission to Washington in January 1899 that the students "seem to regard that they are conferring a great favor upon the institution by being here."[90] Logan's telling complaint hints at the ways Afro-Cuban students sought to assert their agency against the school's civilizing mission. Part of this attitude could have been based on the relatively elite backgrounds of many of the students from Cuba. While they rarely failed to show their gratitude to Tuskegee, they refused to passively submit to the school's strict codes. Their frequent demands for adequate clothing and food could have been motivated by their perception of the kinds of treatment they expected as elite students.

Almost from the outset of their arrival, the students from Cuba voiced their concerns about their treatment at the school. Two areas of conflict that routinely emerged between Cuban students and the school's staff were clothing and food. While the school preached the importance of a neat appearance, students from the island routinely complained of inadequate clothing. In the fall of 1899, a group of students wrote an angry letter of protest to Washington after an incident in which they clashed with another student and with Alonzo Kenniebrew, the school surgeon. Among the issues the students raised was their lack of adequate apparel. "Why is it Mr. Washington," the students asked, "when we ask for clothes or anything we need, we are asked so many questions and sometime [don't] get it?" The letter, which was signed by a number of Afro-Cuban students, including the bold Alfredo Pérez Encinosa, also expressed the needs of Celestina Ramírez, the lone young woman among the Cuban student population at the time. "The following is a list of the articles she asked for that she needed," the students informed Washington: "two dresses, three pair stockings, one trunk, half a dozen handkerchiefs, 1 corset, 3 shirt waist, 1 comb, 1 hair brush, 3 Under shirts, 3 pair pantalettes, 1 pair shoes."[91]

Ramírez herself was not afraid to express her concerns to the Tuskegee principal directly. In a 1901 letter, she complained about the school's onerous financial demands on her family. "My mother is poor and she is not able to get 8 dollars every month and she is as poor as any of the famil[ies]," the young Cuban woman complained. Moreover, she compared her unsatisfactory condition with the more favorable treatment she felt that other students received from the school. "It is very funny that these other girls just come and already they [have] every thing they need and winter clothes etc.," Ramírez informed the Tuskegee principal, "and I have been here two years and a half [and I] haven't got anything to wear." As a student specializing in millinery, she objected to the fact that she was expected to pay "for the system I have to use on my trade[.] I did not paid [*sic*] it but because [I] thought to ask you about it." Finally, as one of the few Afro-Cuban female students at the school, she alerted Washington to what she saw as the unequal treatment she received during the previous summer in comparison to the male students from Cuba. "I work as much as any body does," Ramírez complained, while the "Cuban boys did not do anything."[92]

Manuel Gutierrez similarly challenged the school to live up to its professed values. Gutierrez was one of the Cubans sent by Leonard Wood, the U.S. military governor, in 1900. Gutierrez managed to stick it out at Tuskegee, eventually graduating in 1909. However, in a 1906 letter, he expressed his complaints about his "miserable condition" at the school. According to Gutierrez, Wood gave him the impression that "the school had accepted to pay every student who came with me everything they needed, including doctor bill[s]." However, he found himself with "nothing to wear" and with a toothache that he could not address due to lack of funds. He also claimed that the school promised him a suit once he reached a satisfactory academic standing. "How am I going to have my record good in Rhetoric," the student asked, "when I cannot get up there because I have not anything to wear[?]" Here again, the school's emphasis on embodied forms of learning is clear, as well as the pressures students must have felt to perform these tasks in proper attire. Moreover, Gutierrez claimed that Major James Ramsey, the school's commandant of cadets who was in charge of disciplining male students, withheld suits from Afro-Cuban students, suggesting again that perhaps the school felt the need to control their adornment practices. "I want to go home next summer, and carry good tidings to the people of my community, and those of the whole island," Gutierrez insisted, "and also bring more to be educated, but if the treatment that the Cubans as a whole are getting here goes on this way, I will have to write to him who recommended me here, and to my people."[93]

Gutierrez's veiled threat to report his mistreatment to his people back home was a rhetorical strategy employed by a number of dissatisfied Cuban students. In their 1899 letter of protest to Washington, the students informed Washington that they "started to write the *N.Y. Herald* about how the Cubans were treated at Tuskegee, but when we reflected and thought of the harm it would do the school, we refrained from doing so, especially on your account, because you are responsible for us and we do not want to put you to any trouble."[94] If Afro-Cuban students were to adhere to Washington's "gospel of the toothbrush," they insisted on having the necessary equipment from the school to embody the school's curriculum. Their subtle attempts to use Washington's ideas for their own advantage shows that they learned Tuskegee's lessons better than the administration realized. Their behavior mimicked Washington's own tried-and-true strategy of making requests of more powerful figures while feigning humility and making subtle threats at the same time. In short, while the school taught students craft-making, it also inadvertently taught them how to be crafty.[95]

While the ability of Afro-Cuban pupils to use craftiness to express their concerns to Washington is clear, their capacity to wage collective efforts with other students is less certain. This is because the relationship between Afro-Cuban pupils and the wider student body is difficult to ascertain, largely due to the nature of the documentation in the Tuskegee files of the Booker T. Washington Papers, which presents a view of student life from the perspective of the principal's office and the Executive Council. Although little evidence of tensions articulated along national and linguistic differences exists, neither is there documentation on the making of cross-national Afro-diasporic identifications among the students at the school. The diasporic awareness of Afro-Cuban students and their parents that comes through in their correspondence with Washington does not appear in the scant evidence on the cultural life of students at the school. The lack of evidence of cross-cultural interaction among the students cannot be attributed to the policies of Washington and his staff. Aside from creating English classes for the Spanish-speaking students, they did not seem to segregate the Spanish-speaking students from the larger student body. It appears that Tuskegee's administration approached foreign students with the same objectives as they did with other pupils: to instill the virtues of industrial education.

The tendency for the students from Cuba and Puerto Rico to bond at Tuskegee makes sense not only because of their common language and colonial heritage, but also because they comprised the vast majority of the foreign student population during the first decade of the century.[96] Furthermore, many Spanish-speaking students tended to be admitted at the lower "preparatory" grade levels, mostly, it seems, to address their limited facility with English, although many Afro-Cuban pupils had at least a basic command of the language before or during their time at the school. Cuban–Puerto Rican solidarity is apparent in a number of the petitions they sent to the school's administration. In 1910, Antonio Escabí, a Puerto Rican member of the "Cuban and Porto Rican Club," asked if the group could have permission to take a day off to "celebrate our national holiday." Interestingly, the "national holiday" they requested was March 22, which was actually the anniversary date of the abolition of slavery in Puerto Rico. Since Puerto Rico did not have an independence day, it is striking that these students chose to celebrate abolition instead, highlighting their own identification with emancipated slaves. While it appears that the school agreed to the club's request, on other occasions it denied petitions for days off to celebrate other Cuban and Puerto Rican "national holidays." While these petitions were likely motivated by a desire to escape the school's onerous labor demands, they also illustrate the persistence of national and cultural identifications among the Cuban and Puerto Rican students who attended Tuskegee.[97]

Although cultural differences with the larger English-speaking student population likely facilitated Afro-Cuban bonding with students from Puerto Rico, such distinctions did not prevent a number of Afro-Cuban pupils from establishing close relations with the upper reaches of Tuskegee's administration. Exhibiting a keen awareness of Washington's public persona, Afro-Cuban students knew how to appeal to his status as a leader of the wider "Negro race." They appealed to their principal's public identity not only for strategic purposes, but also because they themselves adopted his model of the entrepreneurial "race man." One of these students was Alfredo Pérez Encinosa, who used his close relationship to the principal's office to convince the school to let him help recruit students from Cuba. From the time of his arrival in 1899 until his departure in 1905, Pérez imposed his enterprising spirit on the school's faculty and staff. During his time at Tuskegee, he was engaged in a variety of entrepreneurial activities that would have made any member of the National Negro Business League proud. Probably picking up on the premium the school placed on "proper" adornment, he created his own little laundry business at the school. During the summers, Pérez went to Cuba, working as a translator and a printer. His work with Cuban newspapers must have put him in touch with Rafael Serra, the famous Afro-Cuban journalist and admirer of Booker T. Washington. Serra's book, *Para blancos y negros*, featured a few articles on Washington and Tuskegee. Pérez translated Tuskegee's catalog for Cuban readers. In a 1904 letter written from Havana, he proudly reported his activities to Washington's secretary, Emmett Scott. At the end of the letter, he tellingly described himself with a reference to another diasporic population: "I am the Cuban 'Jew,'" the ambitious student wrote.[98]

Although the "Cuban Jew" was regularly disciplined by the school for misconduct, he nevertheless made a favorable impression on the Tuskegee principal himself. In a letter written to his friend John Durham, the African American sugar mill manager in Cuba, Washington offered a rare and detailed commendation of his student. Washington marveled at Pérez's entrepreneurial skills, describing him as a "remarkable boy and one that you can thoroughly trust." Washington initially saw Pérez as a "seemingly green, unpromising fellow," but eventually he became "one of our best students" who exhibited a "remarkable talent for business." "I shall not be surprised if he turns out to be a rich man soon after he gets out in life," Washington surmised. He continued:

> He always has something to sell, and has the knack of making a teacher or student feel that they should have what he has to sell. On a good many occasions I have heard of his borrowing money from various teachers out of which to operate his business, but in each case he has been careful to return the loan. I remember that two years ago when he returned to the school from his summer vacation that I told him we were going to cut him out of the laundry business by reason of the fact that we were going to do such good laundry work on the school grounds that students would have no occasion to send their collars and cuffs away for laundering; he smiled, and within two hours he returned to me and showed me a large laundry list which he had gotten from students and teachers.[99]

Pérez's enterprising personality and savvy invariably allowed him to excel at Tuskegee. In 1905, he became the first student from Cuba to graduate from the school.[100]

After Pérez departed Tuskegee, he maintained contact with Washington and the school and continued to fashion himself as a black entrepreneur. He considered himself Washington's "Cuban disciple." After working as a representative of the Parker Pen Company in Cuba, he obtained a scholarship from the Cuban government to study at the Royal Veterinary College of London in 1907. In a letter he wrote to the school in April of that year, Pérez exhibited his own racial awareness and the recognition that he was one of the few Afro-Cubans able to study in Europe. "I am the only 'dark horse' in the race," Pérez proudly informed Washington from England, "and it is my intention to finish the course before the other white Cubans that have come to this country to study." Thus, Pérez left Tuskegee, not as a poster child for the industrial worker, but as someone who instead latched onto Washington's model of black entrepreneurship.[101]

Like Alfredo Pérez Encinosa, Julio Despaigne developed a close relationship with the Tuskegee principal. Despaigne arrived from Guantánamo sometime during the 1904–5 school year and studied at Tuskegee for three years before departing in 1908. A few years later, however, he retuned to the school to study for three more years before graduating in 1914.[102] Throughout Despaigne's tenure at Tuskegee, he fashioned himself as Washington's advisor, informing the principal of the ways the school could better accomplish its mission. "During the last term I have been observing the progress of the Institute," Despaigne wrote in a September 1905 letter, "and I have seen that there are yet many things to do." In his correspondence with Washington, the young Cuban student boldly offered suggestions to improve the school, such as serving more appetizing food to students, installing a barbershop at the institute, and improving the lighting in Rockefeller Hall, one of the dormitories on campus.

Despaigne also seems to have acted as a spy for Washington, informing the principal when students disobeyed the school's rules. While Tuskegee proudly proclaimed to the outside world that the school taught its students the "gospel of the toothbrush," Despaigne informed Washington that "a very large number of students use the tooth brush only to adorn the wash-stand." He also notified the principal of the ways students averted the consequences of the school's regular room inspections. While students made their beds for inspectors, they "disorder[ed] them and put clean and dirty clothes on them" once the inspection was over. While school officials supposedly did not tolerate the use of tobacco on school grounds, Despaigne provided the alarming news that "almost every student of Tuskegee smokes." If school catalogs promised donors that it taught students the "dignity of labor," the officials learned from Despaigne that his fellow students from Cuba "beat work every day and worked only two or three hours in the day." In fact, Despaigne reported that a fellow Cuban student bragged to him that Tuskegee "was good for the lazy." Moreover, Despaigne was not afraid to tell on his teachers, highlighting the ways in which they failed to teach Cuban students how to write correct English. "The teacher that was correcting my mistakes told me that she have [sic] no time for that, so you will excuse the mistakes you will find in my letter." Like the other students from Cuba, Despaigne warned Washington of the negative consequences that might ensue if news of student disorder got back to Cuba. "It will be very lamentable that at the end of three or four years when they go home their fathers do not see their improvement." The principal's office took

Despaigne's letter seriously. Emmett Scott forwarded the letter to the appropriate faculty members and told them to "make note of all he says."[103]

While Despaigne's correspondence kept the principal's office abreast of the disobedient behavior of students, a letter he wrote on 7 April 1906 exhibits his awareness of Tuskegee's relationship to the wider African diaspora. On this occasion, the audacious Despaigne shared with the principal his thoughts on the "the present state of those members of our own race who are still in Africa," who, he felt, were being exploited by European colonial rule. Despaigne argued that the best way for Africans to secure their independence from European colonialism was by "training themselves like Hampton, Tuskegee, and the other schools like these two are doing with the negros in this country." Thus, the young student saw Tuskegee and Hampton playing a vital role in the goal of racial uplift, not just for persons of African descent in his native Cuba, but also on the African continent itself.[104]

Juan Eusebio Gómez was another student who became a Washington protégé. Gómez was one the first students who came to Tuskegee in the fall of 1898. He left soon after his arrival because of health reasons, but he returned in 1901 and went on to graduate in 1906. Gómez eventually roomed with Booker T. Washington Jr. at Tuskegee and later accompanied him to Phillips Exeter Academy in Exeter, New Hampshire. "Gómez," as he was affectionately called by the school principal, maintained intimate ties to the Washington family until the Wizard died in 1915. In a letter of introduction that Washington wrote on Gómez's behalf, he praised the young Afro-Cuban in terms that were unusually effusive by his own standards. "I have not only known him as a student for a number of years," the Tuskegee principal wrote, "but during the greater part of the present year, he has been a member of my own family and I, in this way, have had opportunity to get a clear and definite insight into his fine character. He has stayed at my home as I have stated, for a period of nearly a year and during all this time I have not found anything to criticize him for, but on the other hand, have found much to commend and praise him for."[105] Washington's glowing recommendation illustrates the intimate ties between the families of two of the most prominent Afro-descended leaders, one in Cuba and the other in the United States. The relationship was born less out of a common ideology between Washington and Juan Gualberto Gómez than out of the precarious material circumstances that prompted the Afro-Cuban leader to send his son to Tuskegee.[106]

Despite the close ties between the Gómez and Washington families, by the late 1910s Afro-Cuban enrollment at Tuskegee significantly diminished. The decline of the Cuban presence at the school was rooted in a variety of factors. First, the opportunities for an advanced education in Cuba increased during the 1920s. Scattered evidence indicates that Afro-Cubans took advantage of the expanded educational opportunities on the island. The sons and daughters of the old Afro-Cuban artisan class joined the tiny, but growing Afro-Cuban professional class and began earning degrees in Cuban schools.[107] Second, Washington's death in 1915 not only hastened the decline of Tuskegee's prestige among Afro-Cubans but also severed the interpersonal relationships between Washington and Afro-Cuban families that had been the engine of the school's relationship to Cuba. After the Wizard's death, those who desired to attend black schools in the United States probably looked to other institutions, such as Howard University, which supplanted Tuskegee as the most popular destination for aspiring black students during the 1920s.

Tuskegee and the Emergence of the Afro-Cuban Elite

The impact of the Tuskegee-Cuba connection went beyond the experiences of the students who attended the school. Throughout the first two decades of the century, Washington and his institution were a source of inspiration for many Afro-Cubans. This is clear in the formation of the Instituto Booker T. Washington, an organization initiated autonomously by Afro-Cubans in Havana and designed to bring the "Hampton-Tuskegee Idea" of industrial training to Cuba. In 1905, Emilio Céspedes Casado informed the Tuskegee principal that he and his brother had founded the school and named it after him. "We have established a[n] educational institution in Havana for youth of the colored race," Céspedes wrote Washington. "We feel genuine admiration for your personage and we wish you a long life so that you can leave your truly advanced labor." Céspedes asked for a portrait of the Tuskegee principal to put in the school's main room so as to "inspire Cuban youth" to follow his example. The Afro-Cuban educator closed his letter by declaring to Washington that he and his brother "belong to the Negro Race."[108]

The founding of the Instituto Booker T. Washington illustrates one of the ways in which Tuskegee's principles assumed organizational form among Afro-Cubans. Although little documentation exists on the institute, it seems that the organization plugged itself into the already existing network of *sociedades de color* ("colored societies") that emerged in postemancipation Cuba. The involvement of the Céspedes brothers in the creation of the school highlights the ways in which Afro-Cuban male leaders saw the compatibility of Washington's ideas with their own understanding of racial uplift. Emilio's brother was none other than Miguel Angel Céspedes, who later would become the longtime president of the Club Atenas and one of the more powerful black leaders in Cuba.[109]

But Tuskegee's impact on Afro-Cubans extended beyond the founding of the Instituto Booker T. Washington by the Céspedes brothers. Indeed, perhaps the most important outcome of the Tuskegee-Cuban connection was the school's role in the physical construction of the headquarters of the Club Atenas, the most prominent Afro-Cuban society during the republican era. As historians have shown, the association was largely created by the emerging Afro-Cuban professional class. Its headquarters, which opened with much fanfare in 1929, was designed by Tuskegee alumnus Luís Delfín Valdés, one of the prized members of the new Afro-Cuban elite. Valdés was trained in Tuskegee's pathbreaking architectural program headed by Robert R. Taylor, the foremost African American architect of his time. While Washington rarely failed to highlight the ways his school taught students brick-making and relied on student labor to construct school buildings, his school also pioneered the training of black architects. It is no wonder that Washington claimed, in *Working with the Hands*, that "students are able to build and equip a large building from top to bottom, inside and out, and the object lessons of their own handiwork stand clustered over many acres, a city in itself built by young colored men."[110]

Tuskegee's emerging architectural program attracted many aspiring "young colored men" such as Luís Delfín Valdés. In fact, nearly all of the male pupils from Cuba who successfully survived Tuskegee's curriculum were students in the architecture program. Valdés arrived at Tuskegee with one of the first groups of Afro-Cuban students in 1899. By 1906, he was informing Washington of his "great love for drawing" and his ambition to become an architect.[111] After graduating from the school two years later, he returned to Cuba and established a successful career as an architect. In many ways Valdés exemplified Washington's objectives when he initiated the Tuskegee-Cuba program: to educate students from Cuba and send them back to the island with the skills to advance the development of their own people. In another sense, Valdés did not fit the image of the yeoman black farmer or craftsman that the school used to pull at the heartstrings (and purse strings) of white donors. Instead, he epitomized the emerging black professional who used Tuskegee as a mechanism of upward mobility. As one of the founding members of the Club Atenas, he designed its new headquarters (which still stands at the corner of Zulueta and

The Club Atenas in Havana, shortly after it opened in 1930. Courtesy of Yale Collection of American Literature, Beinecke Rare Book and Manuscript Library.

Apodaca streets in Havana today). Unlike most of Tuskegee's straightforward brick buildings, the Atenas structure was much more lavish, made of "masonry and reinforced concrete, floors of marble and white granite from Carrara . . . with all of its doors and windows made of wood, crystal, and cedar." The Atenas building symbolized the club's elitist self-fashioning as an organization that reflected the "degree of culture, spiritual elevation, and intelligence of the elements that we represent."[112]

But the building was more than a symbol of Afro-Cuban elitism. While Atenas's membership remained confined to elite Afro-Cuban men, the association was a consistent advocate for Afro-Cubans' citizenship rights throughout its history. Moreover, as we shall see in subsequent chapters, it became a key space of Afro-Cuban and African American interaction in succeeding decades. Indeed, the members of the association affiliated themselves with those African Americans whom they saw as their equals—noteworthy members of the "colored race" in the United States whom the association hosted when they traveled to Cuba and whom it promoted in its cultural activities, including Langston Hughes, Mary McLeod Bethune, W. E. B. Du Bois, and countless others. The edifice made a deep impression on Hughes during his 1930 visit to Cuba, who described it as a "large building with a staircase of marble, beautiful reception rooms, a ballroom, a comfortable library, a fencing room and a buffet." Hughes, like many other African American visitors to the Atenas building, came away impressed by the club's headquarters, claiming that "colored people in the United States had no such club." The club's headquarters was literally and figuratively a concrete manifestation of the diasporic linkages engendered by the Tuskegee connection to Cuba. Like the relationship between the Gómez and Washington families, the Atenas building epitomized the relationships between the Afro-Cuban and African American elites that emerged during the opening decades of the twentieth century.[113]

Conclusion

The Tuskegee connection to Cuba illustrates how diaspora-making was a complex process embedded in, but not reducible to, the dynamics of imperial power relations. Washington, like a number of African Americans, saw the U.S. occupation of Cuba as a chance to prove his worthiness as a U.S. citizen and to enact his vision of racial uplift among African descendants abroad. While Washington's plan did not produce a population of black farmers, craftsmen, and domestic workers in Cuba, Afro-Cubans nevertheless were eager to use Tuskegee as a ladder toward upward mobility in the absence of other options for an advanced education. Thus, the story of the Tuskegee-Cuba connection forces us to rethink our understanding of the phenomenon of Washingtonian racial uplift. Rather than characterizing the Tuskegee program in Cuba as simply a mechanism of white supremacy, examining the ways Afro-Cubans interpreted the message of "up from slavery" reveals their ability to reshape Washington's brand of racial uplift. In this sense, we will see that Marcus Garvey was but one of thousands of Afro-descendants outside the United States who repackaged the ideas of the "Great Accommodator" into their own vision of racial self-improvement. At the same time, Afro-Cubans' resistance to Tuskegee's civilizing mission, and their tendency to ally themselves with students from Puerto Rico, illustrates the ways in which diasporic experiences did not dissolve national and cultural identifications among the students.

But for Afro-Cubans, national and diasporic identifications were never mutually exclusive. Julio Despaigne's April 1906 letter to Booker T. Washington reveals how Tuskegee was a place where some Afro-Cubans learned their position vis-à-vis the larger African diaspora in the early twentieth century. Despaigne must have felt particularly reflective one day when he wrote to his principal. Witnessing the growth of the institution, due in part to the recruitment of international students such as himself, Despaigne suggested to Washington that it would be a good idea to bring "members of our race who are still in Africa" to study at the school. "I believe with [a] good train[ing]," he wrote, "those people will rise nicely. Therefore, I wish you [would] look for a way to bring one hundred African[s] here. Fifty males and fifty females." After warning Washington of the opposition such a program would encounter from "enemies of the Negro," Despaigne suddenly posed the following question to his principal: "Are the Phillipino[s] negros?"[114]

Despaigne's letter highlights the ways that his experience at Tuskegee enabled him to wrestle with his own self-understanding as a person of African descent in Cuba and a member of a larger collective who were objects of imperial power. His written reflections provide a glimpse of diaspora in action by revealing the complicated ways persons of African descent struggled to understand the forces that formed them in the Age of Empire. Moreover, Despaigne's preoccupation with the African continent shows the importance it had for some of the Cubans of African descent who found themselves in this mini-African diaspora in the deep South. Despaigne's experience and the experience of his fellow classmates illustrate the complicated ways they came to identify themselves as racialized diasporic subjects.

If Booker T. Washington's death signaled the decline of Tuskegee's role in the remaking of Afro-diasporic linkages in this period, it did not curtail the velocity of Afro-Cuban interaction with their black neighbors to the north. In the ever-changing map of the diaspora, a powerful social movement emerged after the Wizard's death, launched by another Tuskegee disciple. This movement would galvanize not only the Afro-diasporic populations in the United States, the English-speaking Caribbean, and Africa, but also the transcultural communities that lived and worked in the urban centers and sugar mills of the island of Cuba.

CHAPTER TWO

Un Dios, Un Fin, Un Destino
Enacting Diaspora in the Garvey Movement

In the summer of 1929, local authorities in Sagua la Grande, Cuba—the same city that sent a disproportionate number of students to Tuskegee Institute—became alarmed upon becoming aware of a troubling "*velada*" (evening gathering) held on 28 July by Division 55 of the Universal Negro Improvement Association (UNIA). Among those who spoke at the event were members of the Sagua branch, including Simón A. Taylor, J. Crawford, D. Brooks, R. P. Moncrief, Sra. I. Walker, G. O. Moses, and Tertius Wignall, who were described by investigating officers as being of "American or English nationality."[1] While Garveyites spoke, the police report made note of "an individual known as Cuellar" attentively taking notes in the manner of a journalist. Even more disturbing to police officers, however, were the speeches given by Afro-Cubans who attended the event, including Lázaro García, who raised the issue of "El Negro ante de la liga de naciones" (the Negro before the League of Nations); Rogelio Galindo, the Cuban president of the UNIA's Havana Division, who reminded listeners about the "fines y objetivos de la asociación" (aims and objectives of the association); and Antonio Sierra Acosta, the Sagua division's vice president, who told everyone in attendance that "El Negro sin miedo" (the Negro has no fear). The festivities ended with attendees singing the Cuban national anthem and the Garveyite Ethiopian national anthem.

While the meeting was structured to follow the order of proceedings stipulated by UNIA organizers in the association's parent body in New York, investigating officers noted that certain Afro-Cuban speakers deviated from the program. As Afro-Cuban members spoke that evening, the attention shifted from the UNIA's vision of a worldwide movement of the people of African descent to the more specific grievances of people of African descent on the island. Arturo Moreno, head stoker of the United Railways Company, initiated the shift from the program. He was followed by Sierra Acosta, the Sagua Division's most prominent Cuban member, who informed everyone of the racially discriminatory practices of the United Railways Company, pointing out that "not one Negro could be found holding a job among the best paid of the railroad's private guards."[2]

With the chorus "*Avancen hacia la victoria, que Africa sea libre*" (Advance to victory so that Africa can be free) from the "*Himno Etiópico Nacional*" (Ethiopian national anthem) still ringing in their ears, the police canvassed the neighborhood for opinions about the proceedings they witnessed. They found that some local whites could not help but notice that speakers at the *velada* "expressed themselves in harsh terms for those of this class," while blacks in the neighborhood praised the "splendor of [UNIA] speeches, music, and songs, even though they were in English." As the report made its way through the local, provincial, and national branches of the Cuban state in subsequent weeks, governmental officials decided that the time had come for the "total suppression" of the Garvey movement in Sagua and other parts of the island.[3]

This account of the UNIA "fiesta" in Sagua la Grande not only provides a rare glimpse at Garveyite activities in Cuba, but it also highlights the ways in which the association became a space where culturally diverse African descendants on the island could enact a notion of diasporic commonality even as they grappled with their linguistic and cultural differences. It illustrates that while Garveyism in Cuba was largely comprised of English-speaking immigrants from the Caribbean and the United States, Afro-Cubans could use the movement as a platform to voice their own concerns. Sierra Acosta used the Garveyite stage to express the long-standing Afro-Cuban complaint about their exclusion from the more lucrative jobs in the Cuban republic. Moreover, the police report provides glimpses of the association's performance culture, which showcased the oratorical and performative skills of its members, evidenced by the government's claim that local Afro-Cubans praised the group's speeches, music, and songs. Giving speeches and recitations and singing songs were central activities in the Garveyite experience. Within the performative space of Garveyite *veladas*, Afro-Cuban men such as García, Galindo, Moreno, and Sierra Acosta could articulate their own understanding of their place within the larger collective that Garveyites called "the Negro peoples of the world."

This chapter highlights the role of the Garvey movement in the making of Afro-diasporic linkages between Cubans and Anglophone African descendants during the 1920s. If the U.S. intervention in Cuba in 1898 set the stage for greater interaction between Afro-Cubans and African Americans, the expansion of the U.S. presence in the Caribbean during the 1910s and 1920s along with concomitant African American and Afro-Caribbean migration throughout the region further accelerated this process. The UNIA was both a product and catalyst of these transformations. Following the movements of Garveyites throughout the eastern seaboard, the Caribbean, and Central America enables us to see the emergence of a U.S.-Caribbean world, linked together by translocal networks of capital, labor, and ideas. Cuba's geographic position at the center of this imperial formation made it an important cultural crossroads between Afro-Cubans and English-speaking African descendants from the United States, Central America, and the Caribbean. Thus, it is a particularly apt location to examine the process of diasporization among diverse Afro-descended peoples. The result of these changes was a mass movement that created a new transcultural understanding of the African diaspora. If the history of nations in the Americas is a history of "intermeshed transculturations," so too is the history of the distinct yet interconnected populations that comprise the African diaspora.[4]

Like the Cuban students with English last names who attended Tuskegee in the 1920s, the women and men of the Garvey movement were products of the cultural transformations enveloping Afro-diasporic communities during this period. The association founded by Marcus Garvey and Amy Ashwood in Kingston, Jamaica, in 1914 had by the 1920s ballooned into a mass movement that was made up of Afro-diasporic people from a vast array of cultural, linguistic, and national backgrounds. In the nine years after its inception in Cuba in 1920, the Garvey movement steadily grew in various towns throughout the island. By the middle part of the decade, Cuba had the largest number of UNIA branches outside of the United States.[5] While Garvey was busy fighting his own legal and political battles in the United States in the mid to late 1920s, his followers in Cuba used the association to meet their own social, political, and cultural needs. In the process, the UNIA employed the dominant discourse of nationalism to construct a principle of affiliation that transcended the nation. The Cuban government's surveillance of divisions of the UNIA in 1929 underscores the efficacy of the association's transcultural diaspora project.

The power of the UNIA's message stemmed in part from its "race first" ideology. In a period when the dominant images of Afro-descended peoples were steeped in racist caricature, the Garveyite program of self-reliance and race pride galvanized people of African descent throughout the diaspora. However, Garveyism was also based on patriarchal models of nationhood, in which the message of "race first" was a coded language for "men first." Like other Pan-African movements, Garveyism projected the image of Africa as a land with a glorious past of kings and queens that needed to be brought into the modern present by blacks in the diaspora. Moreover, the militaristic thrust of the UNIA, influenced by both World War I and the movement's appropriation of the combative Zionism of the Old Testament, ensured that the project of African redemption would be based on discipline and hierarchy. These two principles were important because Garvey self-consciously patterned the movement after Euro-American empires, with its own elaborate titles, military, and steamship line—in short, an "imperial model of diaspora," as Michelle Stephens has argued. Therefore, the ideological underpinnings of the movement illustrate the contradictions embedded in the Garveyite effort to unite the "Negro peoples of the world."[6]

An analysis of Garveyite ideology, whether one characterizes it as black nationalism or black fascism, only partially explains the significance of the movement. As the police report in Sagua suggests, the UNIA's appeal across linguistic and cultural differences was due to its relentless effort to use performance to enact an African diaspora. The notion of performance posited here uses it in its broadest sense, not simply as formal theatrical events, but as any embodied practice that involves the witnessing and/or participation of an audience. This includes activities such as parade processions, speeches, bodily gestures, and the printed word itself. As Elin Diamond has argued, performance is both a process—"a doing"—and a product—a "thing done."[7] In the Garveyite world, embodied activities such as elocution, marching, singing, and uniform-wearing were designed to enact their vision of an African diaspora. The UNIA's embodied activities could reinforce already existing Garveyite ideologies, but the unstable character of performance always presented the possibility for their alteration.[8] As the Sierra Acosta example above reveals, a performance-attentive analysis allows us to account for the ways Garveyites could deviate from their scripts and assert their agency even within the most codified structures of performance. Such an approach also enhances our understanding of the complex gendered dimensions of the UNIA experience by illuminating moments when men and women could reaffirm or alter Garveyite gender codes. Rather than overlook these performances in a quest for documenting more "tangible" evidence, the analysis of Garveyism put forth here makes the supposed "ephemeral" a central part of the UNIA's history in Cuba. Like Tuskegee's project of "learning by doing," the UNIA insisted on the importance of embodiment. As Garvey himself insisted in 1924, "To organize negroes we have to demonstrate; you cannot tell them anything; you have got to show them."[9] But unlike the "Hampton-Tuskegee Idea" of industrial education, the UNIA's project expanded upon Tuskegee's emphasis on embodied activity in ways Washington could not have fathomed two decades before. In this sense, Garveyism redefined "movement" in more ways than one by showing how bodily movement could function as a crucial element in self-making.

Garveyism in the U.S.-Caribbean World

Garveyism has been primarily an Anglophone story, one that is usually centered on the UNIA's home base in Harlem and the English-speaking Caribbean. More recent studies of Garveyism have documented its influence in the Spanish-speaking Caribbean and Central America. Yet these areas were not simply "outposts" of the UNIA but rather were intricately connected to the activities of the association's parent body in Harlem.[10] English-speaking African Americans and West Indians were not the only constituents of the Garvey movement. There were also Spanish- and French-speaking Afro-Caribbeans, some of whom also spoke English. Garveyites were also immersed in other "languages," the discourse of black Christianity and of patriarchy, the language of the British empire, and the rhetoric of Cuban nationalism. Garveyites were familiar with all of these languages, and they sought to articulate their understanding of diaspora amid these linguistic collisions.

Garveyism became a transcultural phenomenon in Cuba because West Indian migrants did not stay confined to the company towns controlled by foreign sugar companies in the eastern provinces of the island. West Indian migrants maintained their language and their allegiance to the British empire; but they did not live an isolated existence in Cuba, settling in various locales throughout the island, including urban areas such as Havana, Santiago de Cuba, and Sagua la Grande.[11] What is more, the racial segregation of leisure practices in Cuba compelled them to develop relationships with Afro-Cuban communities on the island. As this chapter shows, the UNIA often worked with Afro-Cuban associations, the dominant cultural force in the lives of people of African descent on the island, even in moments when their aims and objects diverged ideologically. In fact, UNIA Liberty Hall meetings were often held within the headquarters of Afro-Cuban organizations.

Examining Garveyism as a transcultural phenomenon entails interrogating both the mythology of the movement and prevailing understandings of Afro-diasporic social movement historiography. Historian Judith Stein made this point over twenty years ago when she argued that most scholarship on Garveyism at the time had failed to relinquish "contemporary politics long enough to comprehend the historical Garvey." In a more recent assessment of scholarship on the UNIA in the Spanish-speaking Caribbean and Central America, Robert Hill, the preeminent historian of the movement, highlighted the "delicate screen of myth" that still pervades studies of Garveyism. His concern was the frequently used label "radical" as it has been applied to the UNIA, which is based on a 1960s–70s postdecolonization, post–civil rights, Black Power understanding of "radical" as an antiracist, anticolonial, and at times, anticapitalist movement.[12] Guided by these assumptions, our understanding of the radical Afro-diasporic subject has often been framed in comparative terms, juxtaposing the supposedly more advanced "race conscious" Anglophone black people with the presumably less conscious black people in Latin America. Such narratives not only misread Afro-diasporic self-understandings in the Spanish-speaking Americas, but they also obscure the common assumptions that guided Afro-diasporic activism across national, cultural, and linguistic borders. The examination of Garveyite encounters with Cubans of African descent put forth in this chapter aims to complicate comparative narratives by providing a more nuanced portrayal of the commonalities and differences that Garveyites from different cultural backgrounds perceived in each other.[13]

Comparative approaches do not adequately account for the UNIA experience in Cuba and elsewhere because Garveyites constantly transgressed the borders that underpin comparative racialization studies. Garveyites, like many Afro-Caribbean people at this time, were on the move in more ways than one. Many of the women and men of the Garvey movement called multiple places home. They might have been born in Cuba, raised in Panama, and moved to Costa Rica, before returning to Cuba. The life of the UNIA organizer was also one of constant mobility. Selling stocks for Garveyite enterprises entailed traveling to places like Philadelphia, Boston, Baltimore, New Orleans, and Havana. This mobile Afro-diasporic population was the catalyst for Garveyism's multilingual, transcultural movement.[14]

Following the movements of Garveyites across borders illustrates that the movement was a product of the U.S.-Caribbean world, a particular cross-border zone with boundaries that were discernible by the end of the 1910s. The circulation of capital and labor that was unleashed by the emergence of U.S. expansionism spread throughout the Caribbean, leading to the reconstitution of Afro-diasporic communities, not only in the Caribbean and Central America, but also along the Atlantic and Gulf Coasts of the United States. By the time Garveyism emerged on the scene, corporations that were based in the northeastern and Gulf Coast states, including railway and steamship compa-

nies, had become more potent forces in the lives of the region's laboring majority. Corporations such as the United Fruit Company created webs of transnational linkages with the intent to generate huge profits from bananas and
sugar. However, these linkages also produced the conditions for a wide range
of transnational relationships between cities and towns in the United States
and the Caribbean that transcended the particular objectives of the company.
U.S. economic expansion was coupled with the creation of the Panama Canal
and the military occupations of Haiti, the Dominican Republic, Cuba, and
Nicaragua, which expanded the role of the United States in the politics of the
region. Although European colonial powers maintained a presence, the societies of this region continued to gradually redirect their attention away from
the European-Atlantic relationship that originated during the era of the transatlantic slave trade.[15]

If U.S. economic and political expansionism created a complex imperial
formation that included the Caribbean and U.S. coastal communities in the
South and Northeast, the massive migration of Afro-descended peoples, particularly those from the British Caribbean colonies, dramatically changed
the demographic complexion of the region. Hundreds of thousands of Afro-
Caribbean migrants left their homelands to work for U.S.-controlled industries in Panama, Costa Rica, Guatemala, Cuba, and New York City, among
other places. Since the beginning of the building of the Panama Railway in the
mid-nineteenth century, hundreds of thousands of Afro-Caribbean peoples
had migrated to Central America for work opportunities. During the U.S.-
controlled Canal Project in 1904–14, British West Indian migrant workers became the core labor force in the Canal Zone. An estimated 150,000 to 200,000
West Indians migrated to work in Panama in this period, transforming cities
like Colón into black enclaves. Following the completion of the canal and the
temporary decline of the banana industry during the years of World War I,
many British West Indian migrants left Central America for Cuba to take advantage of labor opportunities in the island's sugar industry. Some 130,000 to
140,000 migrated to Cuba during the first three decades of the century, many
of them coming from Panama and Costa Rica. They were joined by approximately 183,000 migrants from Haiti.[16]

While black migrants moved throughout the Caribbean, other black bodies were moving on a massive scale within the United States. During the era of
the "Great Migration" in the United States, hundreds of thousands of people
of African descent relocated from the South to various urban centers in the
North. From the outbreak of World War I through the 1920s, nearly 1.5 mil-

lion people of African descent migrated from southern states to industrial centers such as Chicago, Cleveland, Detroit, and especially New York City, the destination of 40,000 foreign-born, Afro-descended people, mostly from the English-speaking Caribbean. Garveyism thrived in these newly developing communities. Together with the existing black population in these urban areas, the new migrants provided a fertile base for the UNIA.[17]

Linking Caribbean and African American migration together highlights the conditions for accelerated contact between Afro-diasporic communities throughout the Americas in this period and underscores the ways U.S. empire-building in the Caribbean and Central America intersected with the transformations occurring in the United States. Black migrants from the southern United States encountered Afro-Caribbean peoples in northern cities, creating the conditions for unprecedented cross-cultural interaction, even as it also set the stage for intergroup tensions within the context of racism and labor exploitation. What we see emerging during these decades was a U.S.-Caribbean transcultural, Afro-descended population that was a product of their engagement with U.S. expansionism throughout the region. By the late 1910s and early 1920s, this historic transformation was having a profound effect on the ways people of African descent in the U.S.-Caribbean world navigated the structures of racialized imperial power and imagined themselves and each other. The Garvey movement was a manifestation of these new Afro-diasporic imaginings of community.

While Garveyism often touted itself as a "Back to Africa" movement, namely that it worked for the establishment of a black nation on the African continent, it also strived for the general uplifting of the "Negro race" within local contexts. Despite the UNIA's diasporic scope, it took a stronger hold in the United States, the Caribbean, and Central America. Garveyites took their Black Star Line (BSL) ships along the routes of the major steamship companies: from New York City to Havana, Cuba, to Limón, Costa Rica, to Kingston, Jamaica, and Colón, Panama. When the BSL failed, they boarded the ships of the United Fruit Company's "Great White Fleet" to organize black people around the U.S.-Caribbean world. Even though the association's core constituents were more likely to be from the Anglophone branches of the African diaspora, Spanish- and French-speaking people of African descent were also key members in the organization.

The UNIA's transcultural membership is clear in the biographies of many of its members, many of whom were shaped by their experiences of movement across borders. Garvey's well-known radicalization process engendered by his travels throughout the Caribbean and Central America is strikingly similar to that of more obscure UNIA members. Characterizing Garveyites as "African American," "West Indian," and "Cuban" misses the ways mobility created transcultural subjects with multiple self-identifications. For example, Louis La Mothe and Elie García were two key members of the UNIA's leadership circle who were born in Haiti. La Mothe left Haiti and worked as an elevator operator in New York City before he joined the UNIA in 1919. His apparent experience as a seamen led Garvey to hire him to work for the BSL, eventually serving the corporation as traffic manager in Havana. Likewise, García migrated from Haiti to New York, arriving in 1916. After working for a U.S. government laboratory in West Virginia during World War I, he relocated to Philadelphia, where he began to be involved in business activities associated with the BSL. Eventually, García became a part of the corporation's board of directors. He also was a key member of the UNIA's 1920 delegation to Liberia. While La Mothe's and García's trajectories were likely shaped by their class position, they nevertheless personified the transcultural composition of some UNIA members.[18]

The UNIA's African American leaders were also shaped by their experiences of cross-border movement. Perhaps the most important African American member throughout the association's history was Henrietta Vinton Davis. Born in Washington, D.C., in 1860, Davis first made a name for herself as an actress and elocutionist in the transnational black theater circuit. While her career aspirations as an actress were circumscribed by racism and sexism, Davis earned the reputation as one of the most prominent black elocutionists in the late nineteenth century, garnering praise from figures such as Frederick Douglass and Booker T. Washington.[19] She performed throughout the United States and the Caribbean, where she toured as a member of the Jamaican Garden Convent Theater. A few years later, Davis joined the UNIA and quickly became part of Garvey's inner circle, occupying various positions within the UNIA's parent body, including "international organizer." Of all of the members in the UNIA's parent body, Davis was perhaps the most frequent participant in the association's fund-raising tours to Cuba and Central America, suffering through a number of the association's disastrous voyages on BSL ships, not to mention Garvey's own persecution during his mail fraud trial. Moreover, her theater background undoubtedly enhanced her importance to the UNIA, given the association's performance culture.[20]

An even more revealing example of the Garvey movement's transcultural and transnational constituency was Eduardo Morales. Morales was born in

Cuba but raised in Panama, where he developed his racial awareness and his political activism. Like so many other African descendants in the Americas, Morales was inspired by Booker T. Washington's example. In 1910, he wrote Tuskegee inquiring about translations of the school's literature in Spanish. "Owing to the great demand for negro literature among the Spanish speaking," Morales wrote, "I am obliged to appeal to you as one who I reco[g]nize as leader of our race." Illustrating his own entrepreneurial proclivities, as well as a diasporic awareness even before he joined the UNIA, Morales informed the school that he had "already sold among them 'The Story of my Work and Life.' They ask me to inquire if they can get 'Tuskegee and its people' in Spanish, or something like it."[21]

Nine years later, Morales was one of the more vocal leaders of the UNIA in the Canal Zone. Along with William Preston Stoute, the Barbadian leader of the United Brotherhood labor union, Morales led the famous canal workers strike of 1920. For Morales, the strike was an opportunity for the divided black population to overcome the cultural differences that had stifled racial organizing. Morales's rousing speeches never failed to extol the virtues of Garvey's masculinist "race first" philosophy, themes that would he would continue to preach a short while later as a UNIA leader in Cuba. In a meeting in Panama, Morales asked his fellow male canal workers, "Do you want to prevent, when you get up in the morning and go one way in search of work, [that] your wife is compelled to go to those white people and beg them for permission to scrub their floors? You will prevent that if you join the union." For Morales, unionism was merely the first step on the road to Pan-African nationhood. Rejecting national identities, Morales declared, "I am a Panamanian but I do not call myself one." Morales insisted, "We should all be one and call ourselves negroes." In another speech, the UNIA leader attacked skin-colorism among the local Afro-diasporic population: "Our direct object is Racial Success; physically, morally, intellectually and financially. In order to achieve Racial Success, we must first realize that however fair our complexion may be, however straight our hair may be, as long as we possess the minimum amount of Negro blood in our veins, we are considered Negroes." Morales's explicit racial/diasporic consciousness, which was informed by his travels throughout the U.S.-Caribbean world, contradicts the prevailing comparative race relations model that differentiates the Anglophone race-conscious black person from the unconscious or naive, Afro-descended Latin American.[22]

After the repression of the 1920 strike in Panama, Morales became a prominent UNIA official, attending the association's annual convention in Harlem and relocating to Cuba with a new position as "high commissioner." His UNIA activities continued in subsequent years. He testified on behalf of Garvey during the UNIA leader's mail fraud trial in 1923. According to trial transcripts, Morales claimed he was living at a Harlem address, once again illustrating the centrality of cross-border movement in the UNIA experience.[23] It was in Cuba where the diverse backgrounds of La Mothe, Davis, and Morales converged, giving the UNIA a distinctive transcultural quality. But the UNIA's uniqueness in Cuba, which distinguished it from the Garveyite experience in Panama and Costa Rica, rested with the fact that Cuba already possessed a large native-born Spanish-speaking population of African descent with its own race-based organizing traditions. Afro-Cubans were among the largest Spanish-speaking Afro-descended populations in the circum-Caribbean region. Although they suffered from racial discrimination like all other black peoples in the region, their undeniable participation in the founding of the Cuban nation gave them a prominent status in the national imagination. If the UNIA was to be successful in Cuba, it needed to develop strategies to appeal to Afro-Cubans. What it found was a population with its own understanding of its position vis-à-vis the Cuban nation and the larger "colored race."

The Common Ground of Racial Uplift

The grounds for commonality between the UNIA and Cubans of African descent were found in their similar understandings of the ideology of racial improvement. Racial improvement, or racial uplift, posited the notion that the "colored race" could pull itself out of the depths to which slavery had supposedly plunged it by pursuing education, thrift, and the other dominant Western values of the day. Since the postemancipation period, the project of racial uplift had been central to Afro-diasporic social, cultural, and political organization. Like other black benevolent and fraternal organizations founded by upwardly mobile classes in the African diaspora, the UNIA was specifically dedicated to racial "improvement." While historians have shown the similarities between African American and West Indian conceptions of racial improvement, they have not yet documented their striking parallels with Afro-Cuban understandings of racial elevation. As we have seen in Afro-Cuban gravitation toward Booker T. Washington's ideas, Afro-Cubans also had their own conceptions of racial improvement that were born out of their own experiences in a postemancipation society, as well as their encounters with uplift discourses abroad.

The UNIA's vision of racial elevation and all of its class and gender contradictions has been well-documented by historians. Garveyism's project for Pan-African nationhood was rooted in, yet departed from, preexisting versions of racial uplift. Like many Afro-diasporic organizations of the time, the UNIA was preoccupied by the politics of respectability. The UNIA's brand of respectability was an eclectic blend of Victorian notions of morality with the traditions of African American prophetic Christianity. Article 5, section 39, of the association's constitution and Book of Laws required all UNIA officers to "maintain a high order of respectability."[24] Garveyite organizers translated their culture of respectability into a Cuban ambiance. The Sagua division of the UNIA, for example, prohibited the drinking of rum "or any other beverage that contains alcohol in the halls of the association."[25] The UNIA put a major emphasis on possessing "culture" and demonstrating it through elocution, Victorian dress and decorum, and "refined" cultural practices.

Key to the UNIA's project of respectability was its gendered understanding of education and "self-culture." That Garvey's initial efforts were inspired by the Tuskegee model of uplift is made clear in his effort to solicit Booker T. Washington's help in establishing an industrial school in Jamaica. Washington's program of industrial education appealed to Garvey due to his own membership in the Jamaican and Afro-diasporic artisan class. While Garvey ultimately abandoned his efforts to form a school to fulfill his larger ambitions for the "Negro peoples of the world," his association continued its emphasis on education. Among the main objectives of the association listed in article 1, section 3, of the UNIA's initial constitution was its goal to "establish Universities, Colleges, Academies, and Schools for the racial education and the culture of the people."[26] Garvey continually argued that if the race were going to achieve "success," then it needed to be led by men who mastered the tools of Western modernity. The result of these educational efforts would be the creation of the "self-made man": the idea that men could achieve their aspirations through "character," self-control, and intelligence. The idea of the self-made man was buoyed by the entrepreneurial enthusiasm that gripped African American communities after World War I, which convinced many men of African descent that they could become rich and powerful like the Rockefellers and the Carnegies.[27]

The Garveyite vision of racial improvement shared similarities with Afro-Cuban notions of racial uplift, which were articulated in terms such as *superación* (overcoming), *regeneración* (regeneration), and more frequently, *mejoramiento* (improvement).[28] At the core of the project of racial improvement during this period were three basic tenets. First, the Cuban of African descent was in a state of backwardness due to the experience of slavery. This notion of racial backwardness, or as one Afro-Cuban journalist put it, "our racial decadence," was based on the dominant positivist racial thinking of the day, which posited a social Darwinist notion that certain "races" were naturally stronger than others.[29] Second, the primary responsibility for bringing the colored race out of this state of backwardness belonged to the "youth," those young men (and some women) who were more removed from slavery and would lead the colored race to a glorious future. In the words of a member of the Afro-Cuban aspiring class, the youth would rid the colored race of "the sufferings of our ancestry." Third, as we have already seen in Afro-Cuban engagements with Tuskegee, the guiding light of racial improvement was education. Afro-Cubans viewed education, in the words of historian Alejandro de la Fuente, as "virtually sacred."[30] Epifanio Calá, a leading member of the Afro-Cuban aspiring class, argued that "the press and the school" were the means for making a man of the colored race into an "entirely regenerated, respected citizen, who is respected for his virtues and his talent, a factor in civilization, and an exponent of national dignity!"[31]

If the UNIA was an organizational manifestation of a larger racial improvement phenomenon, the *sociedades de instrucción y recreo* (educational and recreational societies) commonly known as the *sociedades de color* (colored societies) were concrete expressions of the Afro-Cuban brand of racial elevation. As noted in the previous chapter, the colored societies were a network of associations that served mutual-aid, educational, and recreational purposes for persons of African descent in Cuba. Led by Juan Gualberto Gómez, the colored societies played an important role in securing educational access for Afro-Cubans during the 1880s and 1890s.[32] While these Afro-Cuban societies had their roots in the colonial period, many new organizations emerged after the U.S. intervention in the Cuban War for Independence in 1898.[33] After the inauguration of the Cuban republic in 1902, these organizations continued to proliferate throughout the island. Afro-Cubans formed many sport clubs, literary societies, recreational societies, and feminist organizations. These associations were important social centers not only because they provided needed functions for their members and the community at large but also because they instilled a sense of accomplishment among people of African descent. Thus, like African Americans in the United States, Afro-Cubans transformed the meaning of racial segregation by creating organizations that served as important centers of social interaction and collective empowerment.[34]

Like the UNIA, Afro-Cuban societies posited a gendered understanding of racial uplift that foregrounded the aspirations of black and mulatto men. For most upwardly mobile Afro-Cubans, the responsibility of regenerating the "Cuban colored race" was primarily placed on the shoulders of its "enlightened" and "cultured" men. Following the model of civilian black manliness established by Juan Gualberto Gómez, the ideal enlightened man of African descent was, in the words of the Afro-Cuban magazine *Alma Joven*, "el tipo del *self-made*" (the self-made type), one who emerged from his artisan roots to embark on a career that demonstrated his culture.[35] A 1921 seminar hosted by the Club Atenas, the leading Afro-Cuban society of the era, exemplifies this model of black manhood. The event, hosted by Belisario Heureaux, the son of Ulises Heureaux, the ex-president of the Dominican Republic, celebrated "Our Enlightened Men in Cuba and Puerto Rico." Not surprisingly, the conference praised the achievements of Afro-descended men of both countries, including Juan Gualberto Gómez, Martín Morúa Delgado, José Celso Barbosa, and Rafael Cordero y Molina. Cultured men such as Barbosa, who was educated in the United States, were, in the words of Canales, "the prototype *antillano* [Antillean] of our ethnic class." Here we see a racialized notion of manhood that was transnational in character and that emphasized the contributions the educated man of the "colored race" made to Cuba and the Caribbean more broadly.[36]

Though always fraught with tensions along the lines of class, gender, and color, these Afro-Cuban institutions were centers of social life during a period in which most leisure activity on the island remained racially segregated. Until the Cuban revolutionary government shut down most of the colored societies in the early 1960s, they existed in every Cuban city and in smaller towns in the countryside. Some performed strictly recreational functions, while others focused more on education. Most did both. The existence of multiple societies in a given city was frequently a manifestation of the class and color divisions within urban Afro-Cuban communities. In cities such as Santiago de Cuba, elite and lighter-skinned Afro-Cubans tended to separate themselves from their darker-skinned counterparts. The sheer number of these Afro-Cuban organizations is an indication of their importance to Afro-Cubans and the urban community at large. The names of these associations reflect the forward-looking attitude of the Afro-Cuban aspiring class. Names such as "El Progreso" (progress) "La Luz" (the light), "La Bella Unión" (the beautiful union), and "El Fénix" (the phoenix) reveal the stamp of racial improvement ideology, which was central to the mission of these societies. Moreover, a number of the associations were named after prominent Afro-Cuban patriots, including Antonio

Maceo, Juan Gualberto Gómez, and José Antonio Aponte, representing the effort to project an Afro-Cuban identification that was central, yet distinguishable from the larger Cuban national identity. In short, these Afro-Cuban societies were part of a larger diasporic pattern of benevolent, fraternal, and mutual aid associations that included the UNIA.

The most noteworthy Afro-Cuban society of this period was the Club Atenas. The association was founded in September 1917 by the emerging Afro-Cuban elite in Havana. The club's identification with Greek history illustrates the occidentalist orientation of its membership. Among the organization's founders were politicians, lawyers, doctors, dentists, professors, students, merchants, and journalists, along with aspiring class folks such as "*empleados*" (employees) and tailors. Some were counted as members due to their prestige and their credentials as Cuban patriots, including Lino D'ou and José Gálvez.[37] A number of the club's founding members had connections to Tuskegee Institute, including lawyer and cofounder of the Instituto Booker T. Washington, Miguel Angel Céspedes, and Luís Delfín Valdés, the Tuskegee-trained architect who eventually designed the club's headquarters in the late 1920s.[38] While the club always promoted its "patriotic labor" for the Cuban nation, its roots in the Tuskegee-Cuba connection and its self-image as the guiding light of the Cuban "colored race" gave it an Afro-diasporic orientation. The association's elite status was revealingly described by the African American journalist Margaret Ross Martin, herself a member of the club in the late 1920s and early 1930s, who characterized it as "Cuba's most exclusive cultural, social and recreational organization among the colored people."[39]

The Club Atenas's elitist racial uplift ideology is clear in the association's mission. The club claimed that it was "an institution that represents the degree of culture, spiritual elevation, and intelligence of the elements that we represent, as well as their aspirations for constant progress."[40] While the Club Atenas celebrated the accomplishments of the "colored race," its "fruitful labor" was geared toward continuing the work of racial improvement. This was the logic behind the formation of various "sections" by the organization, including those of letters, science, fine arts, moral interests, and recreation. These branches of the group were to model respectable forms of social activity for Afro-Cubans. By coordinating activities through its various sections, the club sought the "improvement of the moral, intellectual, and material condition of our inferior social classes."[41] Like Afro-descended elites elsewhere, Atenas celebrated its "cultured" membership while projecting an image of responsibility for the supposed "inferior social classes" of the colored race in Cuba.

While resonances clearly existed between Afro-Cuban and Garveyite understandings of racial improvement, there were also some clear differences. The
most obvious dissimilarity was Garveyism's explicit "race first" transnationalist
vision of diaspora that foregrounded an identification with the larger colored
race rather than with a particular nation-state. The UNIA's particular extra-
national vision of Afro-descended people is demonstrated in its newspaper,
Negro World. On the publication's division reports page, readers could learn
about UNIA activities throughout the African diaspora. What is especially
striking was the translocal method of reporting. Rather than simply document
happenings from different nation-states, or different provinces, the division
reports classified Garveyite branches by city or town. And rather than read of
UNIA activities in "Cuba," or the "United States," readers would learn about
the UNIA's divisions in Banes, Cuba; Colón, Panama; Puerto Cabezas, Nicaragua; or Limón, Costa Rica. Thus, through the *Negro World*, readers could
situate themselves within the community of "Negro Peoples of the World," not
merely in distinct nation-states, but rather in specific localities.[42]

Unlike Afro-Cuban associations, and most African American organizations, the UNIA's explicit projection of an Afro-diasporic imagined community skillfully drew from the diverse histories of its transcultural membership.
Garveyite parades and meetings almost always featured the flags of the different nationalities of UNIA members. At the closing ceremonies of the UNIA's
First International Convention of the Negro Peoples of the World in August
1920, Liberty Hall was decorated with the "flags of various countries [and re-
gions], as England, Africa, the United States, Haiti, Panama, Central America,
San Domingo, and other world empires, and nations."[43] One can also note the
UNIA's embracing of its membership's diversity in the ways in which Garveyites routinely situated themselves as descendants of black revolutionary heroes
from different parts of the diaspora. Garvey's Black Star Line ships were named
after such prominent historical figures as Frederick Douglass, Phillis Wheat-
ley, and Antonio Maceo. Highlighting the exploits of military figures such
as Maceo and Toussaint L'Ouverture was a routine rhetorical strategy in the
Garveyite repertoire of speeches. During a speech to Garveyites in May 1920,
UNIA leader Edward Smith-Green reported his desire to honor the memory
of black soldiers who served in the War of 1898 during his trip to Cuba. He
went to the "Peace Tree" in Santiago de Cuba, the monument to the "Rough
Riders," because "I thought it would have been a sin not to visit the spot where
members of my race had made such a glorious past." During the same trip, he
commemorated the achievements of Antonio Maceo. Like the African Ameri-

can soldiers who were stationed in Cuba in 1898, Smith-Green paid tribute to Maceo, because he was "a man who shed his blood so that Negroes should be liberated."[44]

Garveyism's aggressive program of black enterprise also made it stand out from other black organizations in Cuba. Central to the UNIA's effort to establish transnational linkages was its pursuit of the "free and unfettered commercial intercourse with all the Negro people of the world." The centerpiece of this project was the BSL, the steamship company begun by the UNIA in 1919. As Garvey himself stated during his mail fraud trial in 1923, the purpose of the BSL was to "carry on commercial relationships with the Negro peoples of the world and take their produce from one section of the world to the other . . . by ships, like from the West Indies to America and America to the West Indies and from America to Africa, and at the same time to bring people into closer business and spiritual touch."[45]

To Garveyites, black enterprises such as the BSL would pave the way for "universal improvement." The point of comparison for UNIA leaders was the United Fruit Company, the corporation that epitomized white economic power in Central America and the Caribbean. If white people could successfully engage in multinational commerce, so too could the "Negro peoples of the world," Garveyites argued. Eduardo Morales, UNIA high commissioner to Cuba in 1921, highlighted the United Fruit model of commercial organization in a UNIA meeting in Havana:

> Today the Negroes, through Marcus Garvey are realizing that they are the greatest nation on the face of the earth. Not that we undervalue other men, but just as the United Fruit Company started forty-five years ago with a little yacht today they have thousands of floating palaces, so we started three and one-half years ago and today we have four steamships. Now, let us reason that United Fruit Company started with a yacht and today they have thousands. We started four years ago and we have four now; in forty-five years we shall have many thousands. We are going faster than the United Fruit Company; the reason is that they started in the days of [the] candle; we have started in the days of electricity.[46]

Despite the ultimate financial failures of the Black Star Line, the UNIA's black capitalism program generated enormous enthusiasm among Afro-descended peoples in the early years of the movement. It was this enthusiasm for black enterprise that enabled Garveyism to make inroads into Cuba. As UNIA members from the parent body in New York sought to attract members on the island, they utilized their full arsenal of performance practices to convince Cubans of the worthiness of their cause.

The Emergence of Garveyism in Cuba

While Cuba's transcultural black population was the primary social basis of Garveyism on the island, UNIA organizers from abroad, specifically African American and West Indian Garveyites arriving from Harlem, played a decisive role in the association's emergence in Cuba. Organizers from the parent body in Harlem sought out local West Indian immigrants, as well as elite and aspiring class leaders of Afro-Cuban associations. Just as the UNIA tapped into the expanding black markets in new urban centers of the United States, it also reached out to aspiring investors, black and white, in other parts of the U.S.-Caribbean world. Cuba was a logical place to look for potential investors. As a Cuban-based writer in the *Negro World* reported in August 1920, "many colored Americans of wealth are inquiring of conditions here, and it appears that they are looking toward this Edenland with a desire to invest and for recreation."[47]

One of these African Americans who looked toward Cuba was none other than R. M. R. Nelson, the black American entrepreneur who had been doing business in Cuba since 1898. While Nelson was unable to persuade Booker T. Washington to invest in his land scheme in 1904, he steadfastly continued his business activities in Cuba and sought to convince other African Americans to follow his example. The economic upturn of the late 1910s led some African American entrepreneurs to listen to Nelson's claims. African American beauty-culturalists, including Madame C. J. Walker's burgeoning hair-product empire and representatives of the Poro College beauty school, sought to establish markets in Cuba. In 1920, Nelson worked to convince the UNIA and other black businesspeople to invest in the "Edenland" ninety miles away from Key West. He attended the National Negro Business League's annual convention that year "with the hope of encouraging many of them to visit this free man's land."[48]

Entrepreneurial fever was at its height in Cuba in 1920, the year of the "Dance of the Millions." Sugar production, the mainstay of the Cuban economy, generated huge profits, thanks to the disruptions to Cuba's European competitors caused by World War I. Sugar prices skyrocketed during the latter part of the 1910s, and industry watchers gushed with enthusiasm when prices reached an all-time high in May 1920.[49] Black entrepreneurs in the United

States and in Cuba tried to cash in on this era of apparent prosperity. The small Afro-Cuban elite that had emerged as a result of the sugar boom, including those who were members of the Club Atenas, were virtually excluded from the island's commercial sector. Thus, it is not surprising that Afro-Cuban professionals, politicians, and the tiny number of entrepreneurs would have found Garveyism's black capitalist program attractive, even if they were less interested in leaving Cuba for a future black republic in Africa.[50]

When Garvey announced his plans to launch the Black Star Line in October 1919, Cuba's geographic proximity, its reputation for being a friendlier place to people of African descent, and its large black population, not to mention its booming economy, made it an attractive place for trade and investment. The first of his fleet of ships was the *Yarmouth*, a thirty-four-year-old ship that was ill-prepared for commercial transport. The Black Star Line unwisely purchased the ship and immediately rechristened it the SS *Frederick Douglass*, naming it after the famous black abolitionist. In December 1919, the *Yarmouth* made its maiden voyage under the flag of the BSL. Cuba was the first stop on the ship's Caribbean tour, which was marred by constant breakdowns of the less-than-seaworthy vessel. Nevertheless, the ship eventually made it to Cuba. Its first port of call in the Caribbean was Sagua la Grande, a town on the northern coast of Cuba that had economic ties to the northeastern United States since the early nineteenth century. Joshua Cockburn, the ship's captain, insisted in a letter to Garvey that "the people at Havana are mustering in [the] thousands to see the ship and I have no doubt it would be the means of collecting a Hundred Thousand of Dollars in quick time f[ro]m them because wherever you go it seems to be the same cry for freedom as in New York." While Cockburn might have exaggerated Cuban interest in the Black Star Line, it is clear that his letter highlights the enthusiasm the company had generated among some business-men in Cuba.[51]

Anticipation increased when the *Yarmouth* returned to Cuba from New York in February 1920 with a cargo of whiskey, which was shipped out just before the implementation of Prohibition in the United States. Although the ship's second voyage was even more turbulent than its first because of mechanical failures and confrontations with U.S. officials enforcing Prohibition, the vessel eventually chugged into the Havana harbor after a few weeks at sea. Hugh Mulzac, the ship's chief officer, remembered that the "*Yarmouth's* arrival had been heralded by Cuban agents of the UNIA." Local Garveyites and "sympathizers flocked from all parts of the island toward the docks to greet the first ship they had ever seen entirely owned and operated by colored men. They came out in boats when we arrived, showering us with flowers and fruit, but we couldn't let them aboard."[52]

The fanfare generated by the *Yarmouth*'s monthlong stay in Havana stimulated the founding of the first UNIA division in Cuba. Edward Smith-Green, the BSL's secretary, told a Garveyite audience in New York a few months later that when he arrived in Havana, he got "in touch with members of the UNIA down there; and I can assure you that they are going strong." Soon after the arrival of Smith-Green and the crew of the ship on 17 February 1920, the UNIA submitted its petition to the Cuban government for legal recognition as a society in Cuba.[53] Interestingly enough, article 10 of the UNIA's constitution stipulated that if the association dissolved, its remaining funds would be given to the Hermanas Oblatas de la Providencia (Oblate Sisters of Providence), a Catholic order of Afro-diasporic nuns who established mission schools in Cuba. While the exact connection between the UNIA and the Hermanas Oblatas is not clear, their appearance in the division's bylaws illustrates yet another linkage between the association and preexisting Afro-diasporic institutions in Cuba.[54]

The enthusiasm generated by the BSL's arrival in Cuba among Afro-Cubans is clear upon an examination of the activities of its crew in Havana, where Afro-Cuban associations welcomed the BSL and the UNIA to the island. One week later, the Havana division president met with the ship's crew at "54 Revilla-gig[e]do" Street, the address of the Unión Fraternal, the Afro-Cuban society located in the predominantly black Jesús María neighborhood.[55] Founded in 1890 by aspiring and working-class Cubans of African descent, the Unión Fraternal was one of the oldest Afro-Cuban societies in the city. After the Club Atenas, it was the most well-known Afro-Cuban society in the Cuban capital. While the details of that meeting do not appear in the historical record, the Unión Fraternal's decision to let Garveyites meet in their headquarters illustrates a pattern that would reappear in subsequent years: Afro-Cuban societies hosting Afro-descended visitors from abroad, particularly from the United States. The UNIA visit not only enhanced Unión Fraternal's visibility as a black institution but also played a key role in facilitating Garveyite inroads into Havana's Afro-Cuban community.

The UNIA also made contact with two other prominent black leaders, Primitivo Ramírez Ros, a journalist and representative in the Cuban legislature, and Pablo Herrera, president of the Club Atenas. Ramírez was one of the more visible Afro-Cuban intellectuals in late 1910s and 1920s. A poet and director of two major Afro-Cuban publications, *Labor Nueva* and *Atenas*, the latter being the organ of the Club Atenas, Ramírez was a well-known intellectual who also had some political clout, serving as a representative from 1913 to 1917. As historian Alejandro de la Fuente has shown, universal manhood suffrage in Cuba enabled Afro-Cuban men to have a modicum of political influence, resulting in a small number of black representatives in Cuban legislative bodies.[56]

The UNIA contacted Ramírez and Herrera not only because of their stature among Afro-Cubans but also because of their relationship to Cuban president Mario García Menocal. Ramírez was a member of Menocal's Conservative Party. Moreover, as a prominent Cuban planter who had previously managed the Central Chaparra, one of the larger sugar mills in Cuba, Menocal had the reputation of being friendly to business interests. By pursuing these connections with the Cuban government, UNIA leaders sought to legitimate the association on the island and in the United States. It was through these contacts that Smith-Green and the BSL crew met with Menocal at the presidential palace, where Menocal reportedly "expressed his great pride in seeing colored men make their own opportunities in the field of commerce," according to Mulzac, and pledged his support for the BSL.[57]

The precise form of support Menocal offered is not clear. It is likely that he chose to meet with the BSL delegation to solidify electoral support for his party from black voters in Cuba in an upcoming election year.[58] Ultimately, his motivation and his exact pledge are less important since the BSL was never able to carry out sustained commercial relationships with Cuba or any other country. What are important here are the ways that UNIA leaders sought to convey the significance of the encounter with the Cuban president. In a speech Smith-Green gave to the New York membership that was subsequently published in the *Negro World*, he proudly claimed that Menocal told him: "As long as you are in Cuba, and whenever you go away and return—you or any representative of the UNIA, or Black Star Line—you are welcome here, and as long as I am President of this Republic, see me for anything you want (Loud Cheers)." The *Negro World* editor apparently felt that the audience's response to this good news—that a white head of state pledged support to a black-owned steamship company—warranted not just "cheers," but "loud cheers."

From a publicity standpoint, the *Yarmouth*'s trip to Cuba was a success. While the ship's voyage to Cuba and other Caribbean ports turned out to be a financial disaster for Garvey's company, the UNIA generated further interest on the island, not only from the local West Indian migrant community, but also from the Cuban political and business circles, as well as the Afro-Cuban societies. Furthermore, the BSL's promise of black entrepreneurship paved the way for Marcus Garvey's more elaborate introduction to Cuba one year later.

The "Provisional President of Africa"
Meets the Afro-Cuban Elite

The UNIA's influence in Afro-Cuban cultural life and its role as a transcultural agent among Cuba's Afro-diasporic population is evident upon a close reading of Marcus Garvey's visit to Cuba in March 1921. It was the first stop in a Caribbean-wide tour designed to generate more money for the fledgling BSL. Garvey's visit was supposed to coincide with the arrival of the SS *Kanawha*, which the BSL had purchased after the demise of the *Yarmouth*. Tellingly, the company rechristened the ship the *Antonio Maceo*. However, like Smith-Green the previous year, Garvey did not travel on a BSL ship, perhaps because he was leery of traveling on a boat that he believed was less than seaworthy.[59] Showing up in Cuba on a broken-down vessel would destroy his effort to present himself as a "race leader" and successful businessman. Instead, he took the more reliable railway route from New York to Key West before boarding the SS *Governor Cobb* from Key West to Havana. The UNIA leader was welcomed at the San Francisco pier by Primitivo Ramírez Ros, who hosted the self-proclaimed "Provisional President of Africa" at his Central Havana home. Ramírez's gesture was inspired by the contacts generated by the BSL's trip the previous year. In fact, the local press reported that Garvey was recommended to Ramírez by "some American financiers who are friends with the local congressman." From there Garvey began giving speeches and staging the association's Afro-diasporic nation for the Cuban public.[60]

The main source historians have consulted on Garvey's visit to Cuba is an article published in the *Heraldo de Cuba*, one of the major Havana daily newspapers of the 1920s. The piece aimed to introduce Garveyism to the Cuban public and to profile his activities during his three-day stint in Havana. At first glance, it seems to present key evidence of Afro-Cuban rejection of the UNIA's Pan-African program. Particularly convincing is the reported encounter between Garvey and Miguel Angel Céspedes, the president of the Club Atenas, who seemingly affirmed Afro-Cubans' loyalty to the Cuban nation by telling Garvey that they "do not share the pan-African ideal" of the UNIA. For the *Heraldo* writer the significance of the moment was crystal clear: "Garvey's visit to the Club Atenas has the greatest importance: it has served as a reason for Cuban negroes to declare publicly through their brightest institution that they feel Cuban first and black second, and that they espouse no aims related to Garvey's Africanist propaganda." This moment seems to confirm a "nation-first" narrative that Cubans of African descent, unlike West Indians and African Americans, identify with their "nation" first and their "race" second.[61] However, a closer examination of the *Heraldo* piece and bits of evidence from other sources yield a more nuanced reading of the Garvey visit, one that highlights less an ideological clash between the UNIA and Atenas leaders and more a competition between Garvey and Céspedes as they jockeyed for race leadership on a public stage.

A latent anxiety permeates the *Heraldo's* portrait of Garvey's visit.[62] The unease is clear in the writer's attempt to assure readers of Garvey's aims with respect to "Cuba's affairs." In response to a question on this point by the *Heraldo* correspondent, the UNIA leader affirmed that he had "no intention of meddling in the internal affairs of this country." Such a declaration echoes the anxieties surrounding Afro-Cuban autonomous activism since the dawn of the Cuban republic. Indeed the memory of the repression of the Partido Independiente de Color (Independent Colored Party) was never far from the minds of observers of the "Negro problem" in the Cuban public sphere.[63] Moreover, the *Heraldo* writer was keenly aware of the different streams of African American activism and the place of Garveyism within the "three theories" of African American racial uplift at the time. One was the vision of economic uplift inspired by Booker T. Washington and its continuing personification by his successor "Roberto Morton" [Moton]. The second was the equal rights activism of W. E. B. Du Bois and the NAACP. To the *Heraldo* journalist, Garvey was "the most radical of all Negro American leaders," in short, "Morton [*sic*] plus Du Bois, plus the dignity of Negroes."[64]

The characterization of Garvey as a "Negro American" leader highlights the writer's utter disregard for the UNIA leader's Jamaican heritage. In fact, the writer never mentions Garvey's Jamaican roots, perhaps out of a willful disdain for the West Indian presence in Cuba. West Indian immigrants were routinely subjected to virulent Cuban racism, which was manifested in the derogatory label *jamaiquino*, as opposed to the more appropriate Spanish term for Jamaicans—*jamaicano*. During the 1910s, many Afro-Caribbean migrants were victims of racial violence. Only one year before Garvey's visit, José Williams, reportedly a Jamaican immigrant, was lynched by a white mob in Regla, an incident that was part of an antiblack *brujería* (witchcraft) scare.[65] Moreover, the correspondent's disregard for Garvey's West Indian identity also highlights the hegemonic position of African American leaders in the articulation of the African diaspora in this period. The UNIA leader's fame in the United States obscured his Caribbean roots and enhanced his stature—making him a "Negro American" not only among Afro-Cubans but also among many Cuban observers of U.S. affairs.

Despite the limitations of the source, the *Heraldo* article provides important details on Garvey's visit to Havana. For example, it is one of the few non-Garveyite sources on the UNIA's performance culture in Cuba. The UNIA staged a rally at the Santos y Artigas Park in Old Havana, where they charged the audience fifty cents to hear Garvey speak. The "Honorable Provisional President of Africa" spoke in the park for two hours. "There, up on the stage," the journalist reported, "a man of pure African race and dressed in a broad red robe adorned in green and black which reached down to his shoes, delivered a fiery speech in English, which was interrupted constantly by the applause and the enthusiastic screams of a multitude of Jamaicans and Americans who crowded the place." Here we encounter Garvey in his academic regalia, speaking to an audience that actively responded to his declarations. The rally also illustrates the way the UNIA brought the street corner public-speaking phenomenon of Harlem to Havana. Moreover, Garvey's speaking ability was duly noted by the *Heraldo* reporter, who wrote: "Marcus Garvey speaks with singular eloquence. It can be said that he has mastered the art of the word and that he exerts a strange fascination over his audience, who he makes laugh, scream or be moved at his whim." As Garvey spoke to the audience, he was accompanied on stage by a group of "colored ladies who wore a dress identical to the 'Red Cross' but with a black cross on their caps." These women were of course the Black Cross Nurses, the UNIA's women's auxiliary organization. Garvey's performance seems to have successfully promoted stock purchases for his steamship line. According to the *Heraldo* writer, Garvey's visit, described as "a true [grand] event," generated tremendous energy among Havana's transcultural black population. The UNIA leader's arrival had "served as a pretext for the foreign black colony of this capital to show signs of enormous vitality and enthusiasm."[66]

Like Smith-Green and the BSL officers the year before, Garvey's itinerary took him to the social and cultural institutions of the Afro-diasporic population on the island.[67] He sold stock and gave another speech at the Abraham Lincoln Club, located at 8 Blanco Street in Central Havana, the same address as the Havana offices of the UNIA and the BSL. While neither the founders nor the function of the Abraham Lincoln Club appears in the historical record, it was most likely a black association inspired by the U.S. president's abolitionist legacy. While the membership of this group is not clear, the group's very existence suggests that it was probably an Afro-diasporic cultural institution similar to the Instituto Booker T. Washington.

Garvey and his entourage continued to be entertained by other Afro-Cuban societies, including the Unión Fraternal, the same Afro-Cuban society that had hosted the BSL crew the previous year. The association's board of directors, as well as Ramiro Neyra, the editor of *La Antorcha*, another Afro-Cuban publication, welcomed Garvey. Neyra, Garvey, and Andrés Muñoz, the Unión Fraternal's president, met one evening. While the archive is silent on precisely what was discussed at the Unión Fraternal, it seems likely that Garvey visited the Afro-Cuban institution to enhance his own prestige on the island, as well as to seek out funds for his fledgling steamship company.

That same evening Garvey made his well-publicized visit to the Club Atenas. The Havana press underscored the reception in their coverage of the Garvey visit. The *Heraldo* writer reported there was a great excitement to "witness the exchange between the most important of the American leaders and the brilliant representatives of the Cuban colored race that belong to the 'Club Atenas.'" Garvey was welcomed to the club by its president, Miguel Angel Céspedes, who, along with his brother Emilio Céspedes, founded the Instituto Booker T. Washington in 1905. Céspedes personified the emergence of the Afro-Cuban elite and aspiring classes in the 1910s. He was one of the few black lawyers in Cuba during this period. Like Ramírez and other Afro-Cuban elite men, he surged to prominence through the ranks of journalism and electoral politics. His stature was further enhanced by his position as one of the founders of Atenas. At the time of Garvey's visit, he had just begun the first of many terms as president of the association. While Céspedes never ceased to assert his loyalty to the Cuban nation, his hosting of the UNIA leader was just one of many instances when he highlighted his connections to black leaders from the United States. Thus, to Céspedes, the Garvey reception was an opportunity for him to solidify himself as one of the stars of the Afro-Cuban elite. Welcoming the internationally renowned leader of the "colored race" to Atenas would only enhance his stature as one of the more "cultured" Afro-Cuban leaders.

With Atenas members at his side, Céspedes began his "race leader" performance by officially welcoming the UNIA leader.[68] He was quoted as saying that the club was honored to have Garvey in their midst, not only because of his noteworthy personality, but because the club admired the "great progress made by the colored element" in the United States. The Atenas leader informed Garvey that "Cubans belonging to the colored race enjoyed the same privileges as Cubans of the white race." According to Céspedes, despite this significant victory, the still-recent history of slavery resulted in "differences between the races in the state of progress," but "with continuing efforts toward their moral, intellectual, and material improvement [*mejoramiento*] those differences would disappear."[69] Such claims would not have disturbed Garvey, whose association was also dedicated to the "improvement" of the "colored race" worldwide. Hence Céspedes and Garvey were speaking the same language, employing the shared discourse of racial improvement, or *mejoramiento*.

While the *Heraldo* article illustrates Céspedes's and Garvey's similar vision of racial improvement, it also highlighted a moment of tension between the two men. After the UNIA leader reportedly said he was surprised when blacks who had fought for the independence of various countries viewed his goal of Pan-African nationhood with indifference, he stated that the liberation of Africa would require the same efforts that it took to liberate Cuba. Garvey's declaration about blacks in the abstract was a veiled criticism of Cubans of African descent. One wonders if Céspedes felt that Garvey put him on the spot. After the repression of the Partido Independiente de Color in 1912, Afro-Cuban leaders were frequently compelled to perform the delicate balancing act between fighting for racial equality while never giving the impression that they were disloyal to the Cuban nation. Forced to respond to the tactless Garvey in this public setting, the Atenas's president responded by predictably affirming Afro-Cuban loyalty to the Cuban nation and employing the national ideology of racial equality. The newspaper article quotes Céspedes as saying with "great eloquence" that "the Negro Cuban endeavored to create a Republic where he could live with dignity and exercise all of the rights of free and civilized men, thus he cannot conceive of having a motherland other than Cuba." Moreover, "he does not share the pan-African ideal because he has a cosmopolitan concept of the human spirit." After his tactful but firm answer to Garvey's challenge, Céspedes reportedly went right back to the common ground of racial improvement: "However, we believe that your ideas, Honorable Garvey, are truly plausible if viewed in their fundamental aspect, which is its civilizing mission toward the African continent, which occupies a very low plane in the order of universal civilization, and considering them from this perspective, they deserve all sorts of support."

Thus, to Céspedes the "fundamental aspect" of Garvey's program was the "civilizing mission" toward the African continent—in other words, the larger of goal of racial uplift, for the "Negro race" as a whole and for the African continent in particular. Certainly Garvey would have agreed with his counterpart, since "African redemption" was a central component of the Garveyite program. In 1921, the redemption of Africa was part of the latest Garveyite scheme—the Liberian Construction Loan. Perhaps this is why Garvey reportedly replied "with great emotion" to Céspedes: "The cultural development and the great harmony that exists here between whites and negroes has impressed me deeply. The Club Atenas is an institution that honors Cuba, and with an organization of this kind, it can be said that without a doubt this land is saved."[70] The *Heraldo* reporter explained the significance of the event as the fact that Cuban blacks "declare[d] publicly through their brightest institution that they feel Cuban first and black second, and that they espouse no aims related to Garvey's Africanist propaganda."

Despite the triumphant nationalist claims of the Havana press, the response of the Club Atenas to the Garvey visit was not as straightforward as the *Heraldo* reporter suggested. Soon after the visit, an article on Marcus Garvey appeared in *Atenas*, the organ of the Afro-Cuban association. The magazine, which was edited by none other than Primitivo Ramírez Ros, called Garvey "uno de los *leaders* más importantes de la raza negra en los Estados Unidos" (one of the most important leaders of the Negro race in the United States). It is worth noting the usage of the English word "leaders" here, which was italicized in the original. It highlights Cubans' tendency to incorporate English words into their vocabulary during the neocolonial era.[71] However, it also reveals the *Atenas* editor's understanding of the English term for an important figure and perhaps the desire for the club to demonstrate its comprehension of the hegemonic language in Afro-diasporic formations. The piece highlighted the banquet Atenas held for the UNIA leader, as well as Céspedes's "admirable speech," which "perfectly outlined the ideal of the Negro Cuban, the differences between his problem and the Negro American's, as well as the warm support [*simpatía*] that the struggles of Negro Americans have aroused among Cubans." Hence Céspedes was not offering an outright rejection of the Garveyite message, but rather an articulation of the perceived similarities and differences between the conditions facing Afro-Cubans and African Americans.

Along with their summation of the Garvey visit, Atenas published a sheet music version of the Garveyite national anthem that the UNIA leader had given to the club. The publication of the song reveals the club's desire to use music to communicate elements of the Garveyite vision. Even if the Afro-Cubans in Atenas did not fully agree with Garvey's ideas, they nevertheless invited readers to play and listen to the UNIA's message in musical form. Thus, the *Heraldo* reporter's claim that Afro-Cubans espoused "no aims" related to the

Garveyite project is misleading—more indicative of the long-standing anxieties surrounding Afro-Cuban autonomous activism than proof of Afro-Cuban rejection of the UNIA. The notion of a "clash" between the "black nationalism" of Garvey and the patriotism of Céspedes overlooks the extensive contact between Afro-Cuban associations and the UNIA, as well as their common visions of racial uplift. The tension that emerged between Garvey and Céspedes reveals a moment of competition between two self-identified leaders of the "colored race." Forced to confront Garvey's questioning of Afro-Cuban allegiance to the African diaspora in front of the press and interested spectators, the Atenas leader skillfully performed Afro-Cuban loyalty to the Cuban nation and the larger project of racial improvement at the same time. In the process, Céspedes managed to fashion himself as a leader on equal footing with the self-proclaimed provisional president of Africa.

Although Garvey never returned to Cuba, his movement continued to flourish on the island. UNIA divisions continued to pop up on the island during the 1920s. His mail fraud trial and eventual incarceration in an Atlanta penitentiary in 1925, along with the financial failure of the BSL, did not curtail Garveyism's appeal in Cuba.[72] By the middle part of the decade, Cuba was home to fifty-two divisions of the UNIA, the highest number outside the United States.[73] The UNIA's staying power in Cuba and other parts of the Americas illustrates that Garvey's own failures cannot be used as a way to gauge the success of the movement. Even if BSL investors lost their meager funds on Garvey's faulty business scheme, they could still feel connected to the larger world of the UNIA by participating in Garveyite activities. Garveyism remained a part of the Afro-diasporic social life on the island in part because of its seductive performance culture.

Performance and the UNIA's Movement Culture

On Sunday, 24 July 1927, members of the UNIA and interested spectators packed the Liberty Hall in Ciego de Avila, Cuba, to witness a special visit from Henrietta Vinton Davis, the prominent UNIA leader from the association's parent body in New York City. Davis was in the middle of an islandwide tour that was designed to generate support for the organization during Garvey's imprisonment. As the association's international organizer, Davis frequently found herself traveling throughout the U.S.-Caribbean world to rally support for the movement. In the hours leading up to her visit, news spread throughout the town that illness would keep the UNIA leader from attending the meeting held in her honor. Undeterred, she managed to arrive at 8:15 P.M., fifteen minutes after the appointed hour of most UNIA meetings. Davis was escorted into the local Liberty Hall by the Black Cross Nurses and the African Police, two UNIA auxiliary organizations, as the "congregation pealed forth the hymn 'Shine on Eternal Light,'" the customary hymn sung at the beginning of UNIA meetings. Davis, who was known as one of the association's most charismatic speakers, often drew from her own theater background to give rousing speeches at UNIA gatherings. However, her illness forced her to give a shorter address than usual on this particular day. Soon thereafter Rafaela Thomas, Davis's "private secretary," took over, giving a "stirring" speech in English and Spanish. Thomas's oratory inspired the *Negro World* reporter who attended the event to write: "Miss Thomas is one of the rising geniuses of our race and in an oratorical manner she kept the huge gathering spellbound for thirty-five minutes."[74]

This report of the Ciego de Avila meeting in the *Negro World* reveals the performative character of the UNIA's movement culture. The singing of "Shine on Eternal Light" during Davis's entrance into Liberty Hall illustrates the centrality of music and especially religious hymns in Garveyite meetings. The participation of the Black Cross Nurses and the African Police highlights the prominence of uniformed auxiliary groups in UNIA rituals in Cuba.[75] Moreover, the account of Rafaela Thomas's "stirring" address in English and Spanish shows the emphasis Garveyites placed on oratorical performance practices at UNIA events. Transcultural subjects like Thomas, whose bilingualism makes it difficult to identify her as either Cuban or West Indian, played key roles in communicating the Garveyite message to the island's diverse Afro-descended population.

Mundane *Negro World* accounts of UNIA meetings such as this one provide glimpses of the performative world of Garveyites. Within the context of the Garvey movement, the performances emphasized here include singing, praying, elocution, parade marching, and uniform wearing—in short activities that were designed to create meanings and provoke responses from spectators. The association's performance culture comes through in the reports of contributors and editors of the *Negro World* as they sought to translate it onto the page. Many of the transcriptions of the speeches of UNIA leaders published in that paper contained inserted comments like "cheers," "loud cheers," or "laughter" to communicate the approval of audiences and to underscore the significance of a particular point. These insertions, evocative of theatrical scripts with stage directions, highlight the performative nature of Garveyite events. The recording of audience participation conveys the interactive character of UNIA meetings between performers and spectators, even as it sought to project absolute unanimity of opinion among Garveyites. Despite their limitations, the division reports in the *Negro World* provide glimpses of UNIA men and women *in performance*. They offer accounts of Garveyites giving speeches, carrying out UNIA rituals, and singing songs. In short, we get a hint of how these Garveyites performed their membership in the African diaspora.

An analysis of UNIA performances in the *Negro World* enhances our understanding of the messy process of transculturation among African descendants in Cuba. Reports from divisions on the island contain numerous examples of Garveyite reporters trying to make sense of speeches or recitations made by Cuban participants in Spanish. For example, a *Negro World* report of the UNIA archbishop Alexander McGuire's visit to Cuba in March 1921 illustrates the linguistic challenges that occurred at Garveyite meetings. After detailing the rituals that opened the meeting, the reporter identified "the next speaker being a Cuban by the name of Elacio Espino who delivered himself most eloquently in Spanish." While the writer noted that "each and every word of his address were not understood by the audience," Espino's "warm feeling" was evidenced by "the impression that his address made on the several other Cubans present and the cheers given by them." Such accounts show how Garveyites sought to manage the challenges of establishing connections across linguistic differences by relying on bodily gestures as a means of translation. One can imagine Spanish-speaking listeners similarly stretching their limited knowledge of English to the limit in their attempts to understand West Indian and African American speakers at UNIA Liberty Hall events.[76]

The UNIA's role as a transcultural agent in Cuba was in part due to the fact that its performance culture appropriated preexisting performance traditions. As Robert Hill has pointed out, UNIA parades and royalty rituals were clearly inspired by carnival processions in the Anglophone Caribbean. Moreover, the UNIA's emphasis on elocution is also reminiscent of what Roger Abrahams has called the "man of words" tradition.[77] Such patterns of performance are not only prevalent among West Indians, however; in fact similar patterns are found in other parts of the African diaspora. One can argue that the UNIA's appeal to non-Anglophone Afro-descended peoples was also based on its ability to draw upon preexisting cultural practices. Afro-Cuban societies, like the UNIA, put a huge premium on elocution as a way to demonstrate their vision of Afro-Cuban racial uplift. To speak eloquently was to illustrate mastery of the tools of modernity. Indeed, Afro-Cuban associations often showcased their own "men of letters" by organizing readings and lectures. The *Heraldo de Cuba*'s report on Miguel Angel Céspedes's ability to speak with "great eloquence" highlights the Club Atenas's oratorical culture. Such practices were not dissimilar to the UNIA's emphasis on elocution.[78]

Indeed, mastering elocution, oratory, and singing were central activities of UNIA members. As was stipulated in the association's bylaws, Garveyites were expected to recite UNIA prayers and hymns at every meeting. Following the lead of Garvey himself, UNIA members, both male and female, were encouraged to engage in the art of speech giving. Division reports in the *Negro World* always highlighted members' ability to give "stirring" speeches and recitations. Oratory practice was one way the UNIA tried to bring members together across cultural and linguistic differences in Cuba. A report from a UNIA meeting in Cuba, for example, highlighted a recitation given by "J. Parris," one member of the association. Parris's recitation was a direct call for the island's black population to unite across its cultural and linguistic differences:

Africa's sons and daughters, we
Cubans, Jamaicans, small Islanders we be,
Cast in your lot with us and tell me not nay,
For your destiny is enveloped in our UNIA.[79]

If the Garveyite emphasis on elocution resonated with Afro-Cuban gendered understandings of racial uplift, the practice of wearing UNIA uniforms was a significant departure from the traditions of black-identified organizations in Cuba. UNIA auxiliaries had their own uniforms, and members were required to wear them at major association functions.[80] The uniforms of the Universal African Legion (UAL) and the African Motor Corps, two of the more prominent UNIA auxiliaries, were patterned after military attire worn by British and U.S. military officials. Garveyite uniforms, as historian Robert Hill has persuasively argued, reflected Caribbean folk traditions of mimicry that simultaneously emulated and satirized Euro-American symbols of power.[81] For many Garveyites, wearing the uniforms was a transformative experience. "We wore this uniform everywhere," Virginia Collins, a former UNIA member from New Orleans, declared to interviewers for the 2001 documentary *Marcus Garvey: Look for Me in the Whirlwind*. "That was a physical statement . . . that we are Garveyites, and proud of it!" Similarly, Frances Warner, the daughter of former UNIA member Jacob Samuel Mills, echoed the empowering effects of the uniform. After getting off work from his job as a janitor, Warner recalled, Mills would put on his uniform. "He felt very proud when he would wear that uniform," she told the filmmakers, "he would wear it on the trolley car.

Garvey Women's Brigade, 1924. Photograph by James VanDerZee;
© Donna Mussenden VanDerZee.

People would look at him and talk if they wanted to talk, but that was Captain Mills!"

The transformation of Jacob Samuel Mills from janitor to "Captain Mills" was experienced by other UNIA men. Mariamne Samad, another observer of UNIA parades, commented on the transformation of black male Garveyites once they donned their UAL attire: "You would almost see them metamorph into something else," Samad recalled for the documentary. "You would see it. They would suddenly get very tall, because even the smallest man in a uniform would still look like a giant." As Samad's comments show, observers could identify a transformation in the physical appearance of men in the legion. The act of marching in uniform enabled black male Garveyites to exhibit "manly" attributes of military officers: erect posture, discipline, and composure.

The sight of black men and women in uniform not only inspired people of African descent to feel a sense of belonging to a diasporic collective, but it also alarmed governments throughout the U.S.-Caribbean world. On a number of occasions, government officials expressed concerns about the presence of uniformed black men marching in UNIA parades and engaging in militaristic practices.[82] While there are few available images of uniformed Garveyites in Cuba, *Negro World* accounts hint at the reactions of Cuban authorities to UNIA members in organizational attire. One account reported that UNIA male members were "interested in the Legions of Honor, and are anxious to wear the uniform of the Legion, but dare not do so on account of the Cuban officials, who frown down upon anything savoring of drilling or military training." Although the Cuban government generally tolerated the UNIA throughout most of the 1920s, this report indicates that it was probably less than enthusiastic about the prospect of Afro-descended men mimicking state power in a uniform that did not belong to the Cuban army or police.[83]

Like Garveyites elsewhere, members in Cuba derived pleasure in recounting the responses of non-UNIA members (usually whites) when they wore their UNIA regalia. During his March 1921 speech to the Havana division, Eduardo Morales described the reactions of others to the sight of him wearing the UNIA African Cross on his lapel. "This evening I was coming on the train and there were a number of spectators looking at me in amazement," Morales claimed. "They were at a loss to see a black man wearing a medal (pointing to African Cross)," he concluded. With typical Garveyite flourish, Morales proclaimed to his listeners: "As England has her cross and Germany have [*sic*] this cross, so have we got our medals."[84] While Morales's speech underscores the desire of the UNIA to mimic the symbolism of European nations, it also illustrates the power Garveyites placed in their paraphernalia, echoing Virginia Collins's claim that wearing Garveyite uniforms was "a statement." Moreover, the division reporter's reference to Morales's gesture "pointing to the African Cross," illustrates the UNIA's textual attempts to capture their bodily movements and their effects.

Aside from the uniforms and other paraphernalia, the most dramatic symbol of the UNIA's viability was the presence of Black Star Line ships at Cuban ports. By all accounts of the *Yarmouth*'s voyages, frenzied crowds converged at ports throughout the U.S.-Caribbean world to see the ship "entirely owned and operated by colored men." During the *Yarmouth*'s monthlong stay in Cuba in March 1920, UNIA leaders used the physical presence of the ship to stage their notion of a powerful commercial diaspora-in-the-making. The fact that the *Yarmouth* was an aging vessel that barely survived its voyage to Cuba did not matter once the ship pulled into the Havana harbor. As the ship lay at anchor for five days due to a longshoreman strike, Mulzac remembered how Cuban Garveyites and sympathizers "came out when we arrived, showering us with flowers and fruit." When the ship finally docked at the port, it was "overrun with visitors from dawn until sunset," recalled Mulzac. The black seaman underscored the symbolic power of the *Yarmouth* when he recalled with awe at how the decaying ship had "become such a symbol for colored citizens of every land."[85]

Photographic evidence of the BSL delegation in Havana captures how the UNIA used embodiment to enact their vision of diaspora. One of the many visitors to the *Yarmouth* was Pablo Herrera, president of the Club Atenas. A photo of Herrera on the deck of the ship with BSL officials illustrates the staging of masculine Afro-diasporic power. The photo also demonstrates the viability of a black steamship line with its own captain (Cockburn), stockholder (BSL secretary Smith-Green), and potential black male investors (such as Herrera) for all to see. Cockburn is seated in his captain's uniform surrounded by Smith-Green, Herrera, and another unidentified man clad in their own uniforms: suits, ties, and hats. Herrera's accessories include a walking stick, which further enhances his male authority and class standing. The photograph of Afro-descended men in seafaring and civilian attire stages an Afro-diasporic commercial empire while obscuring their diverse backgrounds: Cockburn (British Virgin Islands), Herrera (Cuba), the unidentified man, and Smith-Green (British Guiana).

The spectacle of the ship, uniformed crew, and members and sympathizers in sharply dressed business attire was further legitimized by a reception given to the BSL by the Cuban government. Another photograph, which Smith-Green had taken to publish in the *Negro World*, portrays the uniformed BSL officers with Herrera and other, unidentified Afro-descended men in civilian attire with Cuban president Mario García Menocal at the spanking-new presidential palace. Here, the "colored" delegation stands alongside "white" state power embodied by Menocal. The visit with the Cuban president reveals the UNIA proclivity for the "spectacle of state fetishism," which sought to project the masculine power of "colored men" in the manner of statesmen and military leaders at Garveyite parades and conventions. But the UNIA not only mimicked and poked fun at dominant Euro-American models of state power in their own events when white statesmen were absent. Assembling a delegation of black men around Menocal enabled them to put themselves on the same level as the president of a recognized republic. It is for this reason that Smith-Green made a point of highlighting in detail his visit with "the President of the

Captain Joshua Cockburn (*seated*) surrounded by (*left to right*)
Pablo Herrera, an unidentified man, and Edward Smith-Green.
Courtesy of the Marcus Garvey Papers Project.

The Black Star Line delegation with Cuban president Mario García Menocal (*sixth from right*). To Menocal's right is Joshua Cockburn. To his left are (*left to right*) Edward Smith-Green, Hugh Mulzac, and Pablo Herrera. Courtesy of the Marcus Garvey Papers Project.

great Republic of Cuba" in a UNIA rally in New York weeks after his trip to the island.[86]

The skillful use of paraphernalia and symbolism allowed Garveyites to do more than stage an Afro-diasporic imagination for the public. These embodied practices were also central to the ways the UNIA engaged in politics. In Cuba, UNIA performances were designed by African American, West Indian, and Cuban leaders to convey the organization's legitimacy to the wider Cuban public. This was a difficult task, since Garveyites needed to contend with the banning of race-based political parties and a history of repression of Afro-Cuban collective mobilization.[87] For example, on 31 August 1924, the UNIA division in the town of Camagüey organized a "Negroes' Day" to commemorate the conclusion of the association's annual International Convention of the Negro Peoples of the World in Harlem. The fact that this event took place in Camagüey is not unimportant. Aside from being the location of extensive West Indian settlement, the city was one of the more notorious centers of racial segregation during this period. Since the dawn of the Cuban republic in 1902, Camagüey's central park was divided into "white" and "black" zones. People of African descent were not allowed to walk and socialize in the center of the park, the space reserved exclusively for people defined as white. This was a "custom" that required no signs to communicate its meaning. The movements of Afro-Cubans were routinely policed by Cuban authorities and white citizens during social hours at the park, and at times, they encountered violence when they crossed into the designated "white" spaces.[88]

How did the UNIA confront this practice of racial segregation? They did not hold a rally demanding that local authorities put an end to racial segregation. Instead, they organized their "Negroes' Day" march to the city's central park. In fact, somewhat remarkably, the Camagüeyan division secured permission from the local authorities to hold its ceremony in the park. All of the UNIA's auxiliaries were present in the procession, including the Black Cross Nurses, the Motor Corps, and the UNIA Juveniles. "For the first time in Cuban history," the *Negro World* reported, "an assembly of Negroes, united under the one, true, and sublime cause of the UNIA, paraded the principal streets of the city." The division then held a meeting in the plaza where the mayor and governor were in attendance. In an act that highlights the UNIA's multilingual membership, A. Corbin, a local UNIA division leader, gave an address in Spanish. Corbin's speech was followed by "rousing cheers" of "*Viva Cuba Libre*" from the audience on behalf of the governor and mayor. According to Ernest Provost, the *Negro World* reporter, UNIA local leaders spoke and held the audience "spellbound." Provost's claim of a "spellbound" audience reveals the criteria Garveyites often used to gauge the success of their movement. While the UNIA's stated objective was Pan-African nationhood, the primary criteria they often used to gauge their effectiveness was how well their members spoke, sang, and marched at their events.

The ceremony concluded with the UNIA band playing the Cuban national anthem and the Garveyite Ethiopian national anthem. Provost reported that he "felt proud when our National Anthem was played for the first time on the platform of the historical park of Camaguey." To Provost, the procession "left a great impression on the minds of the Cuban public" and brought "greater respect to our race in Camaguey then ever before."[89] Thus, to Garveyites themselves, this performance, which featured the participation of the transcultural, multilingual members, and the audience's reaction to it, was clear evidence of the "greater respect" accorded to their race. Here we can see Diana Taylor's notion of performance as an "act of transfer" that can transmit social knowledge, cultural memory, and identificatory practices. The acts of marching and shouting "*Viva Cuba Libre*" alongside UNIA chants and songs illustrate the ways these rallies could communicate meanings across linguistic differences. At the same time, the insertion of Cuban nationalist rituals also highlights the ways such performances were never simply carbon copies of the originals conceived of by the parent body in Harlem precisely because of the agency of the historical actors who participated in these codified scenarios. The procession allowed spectators and participants to declare their loyalty to both the Cuban nation and the UNIA. Here we can see the stuff of transculturation, in which UNIA performance practices were enacted alongside Cuban public rituals.[90]

The *Negro World* account of the UNIA parade in Camagüey illustrates the centrality of music to Garveyite movement culture. UNIA members were expected to engage in musical practices, and the UNIA constitution stipulated that each division was required to have "a band of music or orchestra which shall be used at all meetings or gatherings of the organization in whole or in part, as also a well-organized choir."[91] Like UNIA divisions elsewhere, branches in Cuba had their own bands that were responsible for playing Garveyite anthems and hymns at every meeting. Programs from the UNIA's Division 24 in Havana seized by the Cuban government in 1929 document the music performed at their meetings. "*De Heladas Cordilleras*" (From [Greenland's] icy mountains) was played at the beginning of every session, while the "Himno Etiópico Nacional" (Ethiopian national anthem) was performed at the end of meetings. Another program documents the playing of a "classical selection" by the "Universal Trio," which featured O. Pérez de Galindo, the wife of division president Rogelio Galindo, on the piano; A. Rivera on the violin; and A. N. Bustamante on the flute. These documents, along with the division reports published in the *Negro World*, show how music was part of every Garveyite activity, from their weekly meetings to their mass parades. Music occurred not only at public events, but also at their private *veladas* for the edification of members.[92]

Music's centrality to UNIA functions emerges in subsequent accounts of Garveyite activities on the island. This is clear in María "Reyita" de los Reyes Castillo Bueno's memoir, *Reyita*. In the narrative recorded by her daughter Daisy Rubiera Castillo, Reyita describes her participation in Garveyite activities as an adolescent woman growing up in Oriente Province on the eastern end of the island. Reyita learned about the movement from Molly Clark and her husband Charles, who were the leaders of the UNIA local. After listening to Clark's speeches and getting acquainted with Miss Molly, Reyita concluded that the UNIA presented an opportunity to go back to Africa and escape the racism that victimized her family in Cuba. The Garveyite message of African redemption resonated with her grandmother's stories about Africa.

Soon thereafter she began to recruit other Cubans of African descent into the movement.[93]

Not surprisingly, Reyita's recollections of her experience with Garveyites centered on the music and performances at UNIA meetings. "The parties were great fun, lots of people came," Reyita recalled. These parties were significant because "there weren't very many places where poor—and especially black—people could go to enjoy themselves." Moreover, she remembered the music at the division's parties: "The music they played to liven up the atmosphere was from both countries; for this they had to reach an agreement: as the Cubans wanted their music and the Jamaicans wanted theirs, they decided to draw lots and play the music of the winners. And what commotion from whoever won!"[94]

Reyita's comments not only highlight the role of music in UNIA gatherings but also reveal the process of translation, negotiation, and cultural exchange that was embedded in these Afro-diasporic encounters. Her recollections of UNIA parties suggest a competition between multiple Afro-diasporic peoples, one that acknowledged the cultural distinctiveness of West Indians and Cubans of African descent. At the same time, her testimony also reveals a moment of congregation, created in part by the limited opportunities for leisure for all poor persons of African descent in Cuba, irrespective of their national and cultural backgrounds. Thus, the UNIA provided an important space of congregation for people of African descent on the island, one that they used to fulfill their desires for socializing and belonging.

This space was especially important for black women in particular. Such positions as "Lady President," the Black Cross Nurses, and the African Motor Corps gave women official roles within the organization, even within the UNIA's patriarchal structure. For Afro-Cuban women who participated in UNIA rituals, this was particularly crucial, given that most Afro-Cuban associations relegated women to a secondary status. In Cuba, women were central players in the formation of local divisions. A member of the UNIA division in Guantánamo named Frederick recounted the local branch's history in the *Negro World*. He credited UNIA leader Theodora Thomas for getting the division off the ground, in spite of male opposition. "When Theodora Thomas came from across the seas and preached the doctrine of the UNIA and ACL [African Communities League] on the streets and corners," he wrote, "these men were all here and possessed the knowledge of this movement; but they never attempted to start this work, and now that this good lady has established the UNIA, they feel that she should not have had that fame."[95] The reporter's claim that Thomas "preached" is intriguing. It seems to suggest that even with male opposition to her activities, Thomas had the prestige of a preacher (at least in this reporter's mind), and thus, the status of a leader within the local division of the UNIA. The glimpse of male opposition to Thomas in Guantánamo echoes other debates about women occupying religious forms of leadership in the UNIA in the United States.[96]

The prominence of women Garveyite leaders is clear in *Negro World* accounts of Garvey's trip to Cuba in March 1921. After his visit with the Afro-Cuban elite, he traveled to the eastern part of the island to raise money for his fledgling steamship company. One of the last stops on his tour was at the Guantánamo UNIA division, which organized a reception for him at the Club Moncada, the headquarters of one of the local Afro-Cuban societies. According to the *Negro World*, *guantanamero* UNIA members carried out the meeting with the usual Garveyite attention to performance and spectacle, performing UNIA anthems and giving "splendid" speeches and recitations in English and Spanish. During the meeting, Luisa Raymond, secretary of the Cuban Auxiliary Division, gave a speech, prompting "scores of applause" from the audience. After Raymond's speech, she walked over to Garvey and presented him with a bouquet of roses. At that point, John Daniels, a bilingual division member, shouted, "Three cheers for Hon. Marcus Garvey! Three cheers for the Universal Negro Improvement Association! Viva Antonio Maceo! Viva Cuba! And viva la raza Negra!"[97]

This account of a UNIA meeting in Cuba highlights the ways in which Garveyites from different backgrounds performed an Afro-diasporic imagination. Luisa Raymond's speech and presentation of roses to Garvey stimulated Daniels's bilingual salute to Garvey and the UNIA, to the Cuban republic, and to Antonio Maceo. Here we see the association's attempt to create an Afro-diasporic identification while acknowledging the distinct national backgrounds of its membership. Raymond's speech and presentation of roses to Garvey, along with Daniels's response, once again illustrates performance as an "act of transfer" by which Garveyites negotiated and at times overcame language barriers. Furthermore, this moment underscores the ways that female Garveyites could use the UNIA's performative stage to become public figures in their community and thus Afro-diasporic subjects of their own making.

Transculturation Causing Trouble

Despite Garveyism's remarkable success in Cuba, a series of national and local conditions were paramount in shaping the direction of the movement as the decade of the 1920s came to a combustible close. If the decade began with hopes of economic prosperity, it ended in the midst of an unforeseen economic and political crisis generated by the onset of the Great Depression. The island's economic fortunes drastically deteriorated, as the price of sugar, its most important trading commodity, continued to drop throughout the decade, from the all-time high of 22.5 cents a pound during the "Dance of the Millions" in 1920, to 3.7 cents in 1930.[98] The passage by the U.S. Congress of the Hawley-Smoot Tariff Act, which increased duties on Cuban sugar one year later, provided concrete evidence that Cuba's most important trading partner was unable to rescue the island's economy from its downward spiral. Politically, the luster of President Gerardo Machado's administration had long since disappeared. Elected in 1924, Machado came into office promising jobs and a lessened dependency on sugar. After pledging not to run for reelection, he reneged on his promise and engineered his own reelection in 1928. Soon thereafter, Machado increasingly turned to violent repression to stem the growing strength of a burgeoning opposition movement. It was within this context of domestic and transnational economic and political upheaval that the Cuban government began to look more closely at the UNIA, even though it had largely tolerated the association since its emergence on the Cuban scene. As Machado went out of his way to gain the support of Afro-Cuban associations such as the Club Atenas, his government began to place Garveyite groups in Sagua la Grande and other nearby towns under close surveillance. Of particular concern to the Cuban government was the increasing visibility of Cubans of African descent in Garveyite activities.[99]

The fact that the Sagua division was singled out by the Cuban government is in some ways not surprising. Although the history of the town has yet to be written, as we have seen Sagua had already been a site of Afro-Cuban engagement with African descendants abroad. After all, Afro-Cubans from Sagua were particularly numerous among the students who attended Tuskegee Institute a decade earlier. As a port city, Sagua had long possessed economic links to the United States. The prevalence of Afro-Caribbean migrants in a town that was far removed from the eastern sugar mills illustrates once again the great mobility of Afro-diasporic migrants in Cuba.

In 1929, under the slogan of *Un Dios, Un Fin, Un Destino*, the translated version of "One God, One Aim, One Destiny," the UNIA renewed efforts to mobilize people of African descent in Havana, Sagua, and other towns throughout the island. Their latest membership campaign was geared toward galvanizing support for the UNIA's upcoming international convention to be held in Jamaica later that summer. Afro-Cubans were at the forefront of these efforts. In June 1929, Division 24 in Havana, led by its Afro-Cuban president Rogelio Galindo, held weekly meetings designed to publicize the organization's objectives. As usual, the meetings featured speakers visiting from the United States and other parts of the island, along with speeches and musical performances. The UNIA's attempts to harmonize Cuban national sentiment with its Pan-African ideas is evident in the following slogan printed on one of its manifestos:

> ¡Viva la República de Cuba!
> ¡Dios Bendiga al Hon. Marcus Garvey!
> ¡Viva AFRICA y la AUARN!

> *[Long live the Republic of Cuba!*
> *God bless the Hon. Marcus Garvey!*
> *Long live Africa and the AUARN! (Asociación Universal*
> *para el Adelanto de la Raza Negra, Universal Association*
> *for the Advancement of the Negro Race)]*[100]

But the UNIA's attempts to harmonize Cuban nationalism with their vision of diaspora no longer evaded the suspicions of the Cuban government. In the summer of 1929, local authorities sent informants to report on UNIA activities. It was through their spies that they became aware of the themes discussed at Garveyite meetings on 28 July of that year. Following this gathering, local and provincial branches of the *machadista* (President Machado's) state intensified their surveillance of the UNIA. A few weeks later, the provincial governor asked Luis Vega, mayor of Sagua la Grande, and the chief of special police to carry out a "thorough investigation" of the UNIA in the city.[101]

As we have seen, what was most disconcerting about the 28 July *velada* was the attendance of Afro-Cuban activists who had an established track record in Cuban racial politics. "The meetings held by that society," wrote Police Chief Joaquín Caballero Milanés, "are attended by a certain native element who are known racists." Among these known "racists" was Sierra Acosta, the Sagua UNIA's vice president, described by one official as an "unruly and disrespectful man who is an agitator and enemy of the white race."[102] As we have seen, it was Sierra Acosta, the employee of the United Railways of Havana, who voiced the most vehement charges against the company's employment practices, arguing that the company did not hire blacks for its private guard positions. In addition to Sierra Acosta, Cuban government officials were especially concerned about the UNIA's connection with Abelardo Pacheco and Domingo Thorndike, two figures who had been prominent members of the Partido Independiente de Color (PIC) nearly two decades earlier. Pacheco had indeed been one of the party's leaders in the region, and scattered evidence suggests that he continued his antiracist activism after the demise of the PIC. During Machado's drive for reelection, Pacheco became a vocal critic of the president's campaign and his attempts to court Afro-Cuban leaders associated with the Club Atenas. Thus, to government officials, the presence of Pacheco, Thorndike, and Sierra Acosta, all three of whom had "taken an active part in the Revolution of May 1912," led them to conclude that the UNIA posed a potential threat of another "racist" uprising.[103]

In late August 1929, UNIA leaders Antonio Sierra Acosta and Simón Taylor complained to Luis Vega, the mayor of Sagua la Grande, that their meetings were being disrupted by threats from "unknown persons," who claimed that they would "end their meetings with gunshots." Fearful of future harassment, Sierra Acosta and Taylor asked for the mayor's protection while they complied with the government's order to suspend their activities during the investigation.[104] However, Sierra Acosta and Taylor did not find a sympathetic audience in Mayor Vega's office. In his reply, Vega retorted that he found no evidence of threats made to the organization. Moreover, he reminded the Sagua UNIA leadership that they were in danger of violating the laws of the republic. "I believe it is my duty," wrote Vega, "to call your attention to the fact that meetings held by only one race for direct or indirect political and religious objectives are not permitted in this country." He warned the group that "the highest authorities" of the country were reviewing their constitution. Not surprisingly, the mayor conveyed his disapproval of UNIA performance rituals and paraphernalia when he informed them that "certain practices and certain disturbing insignias" were also being "carefully reviewed" by the government. And for good measure, Vega confidently informed the group that "not even the native element of your own race is in agreement with the theories in your Constitution." While the investigation had not yet concluded, Vega reiterated his admonition to postpone any meetings until further notice because he had already concluded that they carried out "exotic practices that were foreign to our laws and customs."[105]

Mayor Vega's mind was made up about the UNIA in Sagua la Grande because his administration had already concluded its rapid investigation. In a letter to the provincial governor, Vega privately admitted that he had always ordered the local police to keep an eye on the group despite its legal status because it used "symbols of a racist character." According to Vega, such dangerous slogans articulated by the group were "The Negroes before the League of Nations" and "The Negro Is without Fear." The mayor expressed his concern that the activities of the UNIA in Sagua would "give an example . . . to the Cuban Negro element."[106]

By early October, the Machado regime had seen enough. Armed with the information supplied by its intelligence-gathering operation, the government came up with its official explanation for eliminating the organization from the island. The cornerstone of the Machado regime's justification for shutting down the UNIA in Sagua and other towns was the Morúa Law, the legislation that had banned political parties organized along racial lines. Manuel J. Delgado, Machado's Afro-Cuban secretary of the interior, provided the official explanation for the government's decision to shut down the UNIA. He argued that the association had "an essentially racial character." To Delgado, the organization's protest against the absence of Afro-Cubans in railway and government jobs was direct evidence of the group's involvement in politics. Thus, the secretary of the interior argued that the group was in violation not only of the Morúa Law, but also of the UNIA's own constitution, which prohibited members from involving themselves in political activities. Delgado also argued that while the Cuban constitution permitted the republic's inhabitants to associate peacefully with one another, "it is no less certain that Article 11 of the same constitutional text prescribes that all Cubans are equal before the law and that the Republic recognizes neither exemptions nor personal privileges." And since the principle of racial equality was an established fact in Cuban society, according to Delgado, there was no need for groups such as the UNIA because they disturbed "the public peace with propaganda designed to establish conflict between the distinct ethnic elements of the Republic." Thus, the secretary instructed the local and provincial authorities to close down the UNIA.[107]

In the weeks that followed, the governor and local officials dutifully carried out their orders. In late October, Simón Taylor, the secretary of the Sagua Division 55, informed the governor that the organization had "closed its doors."[108] In November, word came from Placetas, another town where the UNIA was active, that the organization had suspended its activities as well.[109] Government reports represented the dissolution of the UNIA in the region as a voluntary act. Perhaps sensing that the tide was totally against them, the UNIA divisions in the province agreed to cease their activities with little protest.[110]

The Cuban government's decision to act against the UNIA in Sagua la

Grande and other towns on the island was rooted in its attempt to neutralize all sources of discontent in a politically charged period. In the polarized atmosphere of the late 1920s, the Machado government perceived the UNIA as a threat to the president's carefully constructed image as a friend to Afro-Cubans. As Machado sought to keep the Club Atenas and other Afro-Cuban associations in his corner, he was deeply concerned about the UNIA's potential compatibility with historic Afro-Cuban grievances. This is apparent in the government agents' almost exclusive concern with the presence of native Cubans in the UNIA in comparison with their minimal attention to the role of non-Cubans in the organization. Afro-Cuban Garveyites' complaints about racial discrimination in employment practices, which are evident in the reports on UNIA meetings in Sagua, reveal the influence of native Cubans in the organization. Furthermore, the presence of organized workers such as Antonio Sierra Acosta, a stoker for the United Railways of Havana, indicates that the UNIA provided a structure to articulate their grievances in a period when many Afro-Cuban associations were effectively controlled by Machado. This imperative becomes evident upon an examination of the government's actions toward the UNIA the following year. Shortly after Garvey was banned from entering the country in early 1930, the government suddenly reversed its position and permitted the association to reopen some of its divisions, presumably because the UNIA had been effectively neutralized.[111]

Conclusion

Garveyism in Cuba was a transcultural phenomenon that was driven by the participation of Afro-diasporic subjects from a wide range of cultural backgrounds. While the association was rooted primarily in Anglophone Caribbean cultural practices, it drew upon a diverse array of Afro-diasporic cultures and histories, including those of Afro-Cubans. Part of its success was due to the ability of its members to perform its vision of the African diaspora. Whether it was by staging black enterprise with its less-than-functional ships, or by marching in UNIA processions, or by giving speeches, the UNIA's presence within the associational lives of black people in Cuba was based on its ability to move (literally and metaphorically) black people across borders. An account of Afro-Cuban participation in the UNIA revises our understanding of the "radical" Afro-diasporic subject. Recounting the experience of Spanish-speaking Afro-Cubans in the UNIA challenges the assumptions in Anglophone-centric versions of Afro-diasporic history that English-speaking blacks possessed greater racial awareness than their Spanish-speaking counter-parts. To focus on the supposed failures of Garveyism as a political project would not only discount the material effects of UNIA's performance culture but also ignore how Garveyites themselves evaluated the effectiveness of the movement. For Garveyites, mastering elocution and performing UNIA rituals were just as important as investing their meager resources in the Black Star Line. Taking the power of performance seriously, on the other hand, would allow historians of the African diaspora to widen their understanding of the making of Afro-diasporic linkages across cultural differences.

After 1930, Garveyism continued to have a place, albeit diminished, in the social and cultural life of people of African descent in Cuba. The Machado government's repression coupled with the wider crisis of Garveyism through-out the diaspora facilitated its decline on the island. But while one black trans-national movement faded away in Cuba in the early 1930s, another one emerg-ing out of the same Harlem-Havana axis would have an even more profound effect on the ties that bound Afro-diasporic communities in Cuba and the United States together.

CHAPTER THREE

Blues and *Son* from Harlem to Havana

Readers of the November 1930 issue of *Opportunity*, the magazine of the National Urban League and the leading review of "New Negro" writers and artists, encountered an article written by Langston Hughes, the famous "Blues Poet" of the Harlem Renaissance. The piece, entitled "A Cuban Sculptor," was a profile of Teodoro Ramos Blanco, whom Hughes had met during his recent trip to Cuba. "Among the sculptors of the darker world," Hughes informed readers, "Ramos Blanco is most certainly deserving of your sincere attention." Hughes praised the Afro-Cuban artist's recent sculptures, particularly his white marble statue of Mariana Grajales, the Cuban patriot and mother of Antonio Maceo. Ramos Blanco's works of "great dignity and simple strength" signaled to Hughes "the arrival of a new and interesting personality in the field of American art." The Blues Poet's article not only chronicled Ramos Blanco's emergence as a formidable artist but also issued a challenge to the magazine's African American readership. "The fact that the first great figure by this dark Cuban sculptor is that of a Negro heroine makes it not without significance to the readers of this magazine," Hughes insisted, "we who have so few memorials to our own racial heroes in this country, so few monuments to Sojourner Truth or Frederick Douglass or Booker Washington or any of the great figures in our own perilous history." Hughes went on to ask, "Is it that we have no artists, or no pride?"[1]

Hughes's profile of Ramos Blanco exemplifies his role as a promoter of Afro-Cuban artists and writers in the United States during the era of the New Negro movement. Although Hughes's legend was built on his own poetry, plays, and prose, he was also a skillful proponent of Afro-Cuban artistic production. Hughes's advertising of Afro-Cuban artists and writers in the leading publications of the Harlem Renaissance situated the cultural movements in Harlem and Havana within part of a larger "darker world." His travels to

Cuba, his profiles of artists such as Ramos Blanco, and his translation of the poetry of Nicolás Guillén and Regino Pedroso made him the leading authority on Afro-Cuban art and literature in the United States. By touting Ramos Blanco as an emerging presence "in the field of American art" Hughes sought to position him as a figure relevant not just to Cuban art but also to the art scene in the United States. To Hughes, Ramos Blanco's sculpture of Grajales, the "Negro heroine," exposed a conspicuous absence of parallel monuments of African Americans, which Hughes somewhat disingenuously attributed to either a lack of artists or insufficient pride among them and not, as one might expect, to racism. Hughes's discussion of Afro-descended monuments in both countries reveals a rhetorical strategy of comparison employed by a number of observers of the New Negro movement in Cuba and the United States during this period. To publicize Negro artists and writers at home or abroad was to invariably stake larger claims about the state of cultural production in the African diaspora as a whole.

This chapter analyzes the pivotal role of promoters and audiences in the making of Afro-diasporic linkages between the Harlem Renaissance and the concurrent black cultural movement in Cuba known as *afrocubanismo* (Afro-Cubanism) in the 1920s and 1930s. While Hughes and Guillén became central figures in the Harlem-Havana cultural nexus, it was their readers who played decisive roles in connecting the two movements. Not unlike "The Six" influential figures in the Harlem Renaissance identified by historian David Levering Lewis, self-styled promoters such as José Antonio Fernández de Castro, Gustavo Urrutia, Arturo "Arthur" Schomburg, and Hughes himself were the central figures who built the bridges between the cultural movements in Havana and Harlem.[2] They shared a commitment to showcasing writers and artists from both movements while insisting that they were part of a larger New Negro phenomenon. Thus, even if the writers and artists themselves denied or downplayed this cultural exchange, the audiences and promoters of their work actively linked the two movements together. This chapter interprets the traffic between the cultural movements in Harlem and Havana as evidence of diasporization, rather than as mere background information for two distinct national movements.

The Harlem-Havana link was part of the larger cultural revolution that enveloped the Americas and the Atlantic world during the 1920s and 1930s. The popularity of tango, jazz, and "Negro" literature and the "enormous vogue for all things Mexican" were in part products of white fascination with "folk" and "primitive" cultures. While the movements in Paris, Havana, and Mexico City all contributed to this broader cultural transformation, the Harlem Renaissance became in many ways the most influential. African American intellectuals touted the emergence of a "New Negro" whose art and literature would work in the service of the goal of racial equality. U.S. imperial hegemony and the hegemonic position of African Americans in the African diaspora made the Harlem Renaissance central to the Atlantic and American-hemispheric fascination with Afro-diasporic cultural production.[3] Likewise, Afro-Cubanism was pioneered by poets, painters, sculptors, musicians, and dancers who highlighted what they saw as the African roots of Cuban culture. Afro-Cubanism, unlike the Harlem Renaissance, was a more thoroughly cross-racial movement that featured not only the participation of Afro-Cuban poets and musicians like Nicolás Guillén, Regino Pedroso, and Teodoro Ramos Blanco, but also many white poets and artists, including José Tallet, Emilio Ballagás, Alejandro García Caturla, and Ernesto Lecuona. While the movement was clearly shaped by white primitivist fantasies about black culture, it nevertheless resulted in greater recognition of the African roots of Cuban culture. The new *mestizaje*-infused (mixed-race) nationalism was epitomized by Guillén's prologue to *Sóngoro Cosongo*, in which he argued that the intermixture of Cuba's European and African roots led to the creation of "Cuban color." Although Guillén was at times critical of the vogue of blackness, he himself benefited, even if indirectly, from the heightened attention Afro-diasporic writers received in this period.[4]

To historicize the linkages between the cultural movements in Harlem and Havana is to build upon the voluminous comparative literature scholarship that is largely responsible for our understanding of these movements.[5] However, for all of their contributions, nation-based comparative models tend to inscribe an a priori notion of difference on the past informed by contemporary understandings of national and racial identity that obscure the ways historical actors understood similarities or differences themselves. As a result, the transnational traffic in ideas and cultures that made these movements possible gets overlooked in most studies of these movements. Havana's relative proximity to Harlem allowed for a greater frequency of interaction between artists, writers, musicians, and their audiences in these communities. Even if the formal musical structures of the quintessential Afro-Cuban song and dance style known as *son* were fundamentally different from those of the blues, and even if the content and style of Langston Hughes's verses differed from those of Nicolás

Guillén's, these distinctions did not prevent many participants in these movements from viewing them as parts of a larger cultural phenomenon.[6]

As was the case in the Tuskegee and Garveyite encounters with Cubans of African descent, the cultural diasporization of the 1920s and 1930s was partially shaped by racialized imperial structures and their attendant ideologies. The popularization of Afro-diasporic cultures was influenced by the emerging tourist economy dominated by U.S. and European steamship companies and hotels. The emerging transnational entertainment industry, pioneered by U.S. record companies, commercialized the music of African American and Afro-Cuban musicians. Moreover, Afro-Cuban and African American artistic interaction was influenced by white philanthropic organizations, such as the Harmon Foundation, which sought to capitalize on the Negro vogue for white consumption. Finally, individual intellectuals racialized as white (or as non-black Latin American) such as Miguel Covarrubias and José Antonio Fernández de Castro, or like Carl Van Vechten, played crucial roles in popularizing Afro-diasporic cultures, often within an exoticizing, primitivist perspective that catered to self-styled vanguard intellectuals.

But the political economy of primitivism overdetermined neither the forging nor the outcomes of Afro-diasporic linkages in this period. The Harlem-Havana cultural nexus was also produced by the ways Afro-descended writers and artists took advantage of the racialization of leisure and cultural production in both countries. As in the past, the Afro-diasporic institutions played a crucial role in the forging of these connections. Afro-Cuban poets, including Guillén and Pedroso, like their African American contemporaries, emerged not from a raceless artistic world, but rather from within the confines of the literary cultures that were shaped by the racialization of leisure practices in 1920s republican Cuba.[7] The publications of the Afro-Cuban "colored societies," such as *Atenas*, *Alma Joven*, and *Castalia*, among countless others, operated very much like African American periodicals such as the *Crisis* and *Opportunity* by providing venues where young black writers and artists could publish their work. Moreover, it was in the racialized clubs and dance halls of Havana, like those of Harlem, where the Afro-Cuban *son* and the rumba flourished, entertaining white audiences who desired to immerse themselves in the "low" cultures of Havana.

The cultural movements in both Harlem and Havana popularized previously denigrated cultural practices even as they were shaped by primitivist fascinations. A younger generation of writers and artists viewed the blues, spirituals, rumba, and the *son* as inspiration for a new cultural aesthetic. The popularization of these cultural forms had profound consequences. Although established black cultural elites in both countries rejected the celebration of what they deemed as the "low" cultural expression of black communities, the Harlem-Havana movement eventually triggered the gradual decline of racial uplift respectability that had shaped African American and Afro-Cuban interaction up to that point. Unlike the followers of Booker Washington and Marcus Garvey, Afro-Cuban and African American artists and writers in this period began to draw more confidently from what they saw as their common African cultural heritage in an effort to form a new self—a "New Negro." As the celebration of the blues and the *son* gave way to a radicalized art of social protest in the early 1930s, the poetry of Hughes, Guillén, and Pedroso reflected more diverse forms of Afro-diasporic politics that highlighted the plight of the black working classes in both countries.

The challenges to racial improvement ideology initiated by the cultural movements in Harlem and Havana had larger implications for the understanding of Afro-diasporic cultures. By linking these movements, artists, writers, and their promoters began to alter the hierarchical relationship between African American and Afro-Cuban cultures in this period. Afro-Cuban writers and artists and their white collaborators continued to view the cultural production of African Americans as evidence of the most modern people of the African diaspora. However, the views of African American observers of Afro-Cuban culture began to shift. While Hughes and Schomburg initially promoted the achievements of Afro-Cubans in art and culture in accordance with the logic of racial uplift, blacks in the United States ultimately came to valorize Afro-Cuban culture as more authentically "African" than their own. Hughes played a key role in this transformation. It was in the dance halls of Havana in 1930 where he discovered what he interpreted to be "true" blackness when he characterized Afro-Cuban percussionists as "those fabulous drum beaters who . . . somehow have saved—out of all the centuries of slavery and all the miles and miles from Guinea—the heartbeat and songbeat of Africa."[8] Rather than advocate for the civilization of the African continent in the manner of previous Afro-diasporic intellectuals, Hughes, Guillén, and many of their contemporaries helped inaugurate a new appreciation for the previously disregarded "heartbeat and songbeat of Africa" in the diaspora (Cuba) and, by extension, the African continent itself. In this way, the movements in Havana and Harlem played key roles in the reimagination of Afro-diasporic cultural production throughout the Atlantic world.[9]

Havana in New York's Transcultural "Black City"

The Anglophone Caribbean influence in the Harlem Renaissance and all aspects of the New Negro movement is well documented. In contrast, the influence of Afro-Cubans (and other Caribbean populations, black and nonblack) in Harlem cultural life is less clear, due in part to their smaller numbers in comparison to the Anglophone Caribbean immigrants in this period. Moreover, the presence of non–West Indian Afro-Caribbeans in Harlem is obscured by the complex ways their racial identities and linguistic differences were interpolated in the New York racial continuum. As Ira Reid and Irma Watkins-Owens, among others, have shown, linguistic and national differences shaped the experiences of English-, French-, and Spanish-speaking African descendants in the city.[10] Although the number of Spanish-speaking African descendants was smaller, their presence is evident not only in the emerging immigrant community that we define today as "Spanish Harlem" but also in the transnational linkages of artists, musicians, writers, and their audiences that connected the neighborhood to parallel cultural developments in Cuba.

Harlem's exposure to Afro-Cuban culture stemmed from the fact that it was a stop on a transnational performance circuit that was shaped by the emerging recording industry. Pioneering these efforts were the record companies based in the northeastern United States, particularly the Victor Talking Machine Company and its rival, Columbia Records. Like many other U.S.-based companies, Victor and Columbia looked to Cuba and the Caribbean both as markets for their goods (records and phonographs) and as sources of "raw material" (i.e., musical talent) for recording purposes.[11] Almost simultaneously, these companies began to record African American and Afro-Cuban bands during the mid- to late 1920s. *Son* groups such as the Sexteto Habanero and the Septeto Nacional began to record with the Victor and Columbia labels in New York. During these record dates, *son* bands seem to have performed in Harlem's most popular nightspots. According to *son* historian Jesús Blanco, the Sexteto Occidente, a band organized by Columbia Records that featured the bolero vocalist María Teresa Vera and the bassist Ignacio Piñeiro, performed at the Apollo Theater in 1926. In 1934, Antonio Machín, an Afro-Cuban vocalist, also performed at the Apollo. Moreover, a photograph of the Sexteto Habanero taken by James Van der Zee in his Harlem studio in 1926 indicates that the band might have also participated in the Harlem music circuit during a recording trip to New York. These bits of evidence suggest that Afro-Cuban musicians were part of the traffic of black artists who performed in Harlem in this period.

They indicate that Mario Bauzá, the trumpeter and pioneer of "Latin Jazz" who got his start with the Chick Webb Orchestra at the Savoy Ballroom, was only one of a number of Afro-Cuban musicians who were part of the Harlem music scene. Thus, Afro-Cuban music was likely familiar to Harlem audiences during this period, a moment that predates the emergence of the more well-known Cubop movement pioneered by Dizzy Gillespie, Chano Pozo, Bauzá, and "Machito" (Frank Grillo) in the 1940s.[12]

While Harlem audiences were exposed to Afro-Cuban music at local performance venues, Harlem readers encountered Afro-Cuban literature and art at the 135th Street Library (the roots of today's Schomburg Center for Research in Black Culture). This was largely due to the efforts of Arturo "Arthur" Schomburg, the Puerto Rican–born bibliophile who was one of the major figures in the emergence of Afro-diasporic history as a field of study.[13] Although Schomburg's career as a bibliophile and historian is well known, his effort to publicize Afro-Cuban writers and artists remains obscure. A transcultural Afro-diasporic subject whose multiple identities have tended to bedevil historians more than do his contemporaries, Schomburg was well-positioned to document and publicize the histories of Afro-descendants in the Spanish-speaking Americas and Europe. His position as curator in the Division of Negro History, Literature, and Prints at the 135th Street Library, a division bolstered by the library's purchase of his own personal collection, enhanced his ability to publicize the culture and history of Afro-Cubans. Moreover, his relationship with Charles Spurgeon Johnson allowed him to publish numerous articles on African descendants in the Spanish-speaking Atlantic world in *Opportunity* during the 1920s and early 1930s. His association with Evaristo Estenoz, the leader of the ill-fated Partido Independiente de Color, enabled him to inform African American readers about racism in Cuba.[14]

Schomburg's articles on Afro-Cubans, like all of his writings, exhibit his desire to present African descendants as modern subjects with their own history and culture. His 1933 article "My Trip to Cuba in Quest of Negro Books," published in *Opportunity*, exemplifies his own version of the contributionist model of black history writing that sought to combat racism by documenting the contributions of African descendants to the history of the West. The piece, which was inspired by his trip to the island the previous year, presented Afro-Cubans as rightful contributors to the history of Cuba and the West in general. The essay was a sweeping portrait of the cultural achievements of the "colored race" in Cuba since the colonial era, according to the precepts of racial uplift ideology. It underscored the activities of Afro-Cuban educators and writers of the colonial era, including Lorenzo Meléndez, Juan Gualberto Gómez, Juan Francisco Manzano, and Plácido. After extolling the achievements of Afro-Cubans in the past, Schomburg enthusiastically described his encounters with current Afro-Cuban writers and artists in the halls of the Club Atenas, including Guillén, whom he described as a "person of culture and refinement." His glowing portrait of Guillén and his poetry ignored the disdain that some members of the Afro-Cuban elite had for the poet's *son*-poems. Schomburg was clearly enamored with a black community that seemed to exemplify his own vision of racial uplift. He concluded the essay by conveying his awe of the activities of the Afro-Cuban artistic community in Havana, testifying to readers: "To American Negroes interested in the cultural development of their race, a trip to Cuba would be an inspiration and a revelation that might astound them."[15]

In addition to Schomburg's writings in the publications associated with the Harlem Renaissance, his most important contribution to the making of the Harlem-Havana connection came in his roles as collector and publicist. The bibliophile was clearly astounded by what he saw in Cuba, leaving the island with "trunks full of books and pamphlets by and about the Cuban Negro."[16] Schomburg took his role as a promoter of Afro-descended cultures in the Spanish-speaking world seriously, calling himself in a 1932 letter to Guillén "a good soldier in the renaissance of writers of the colored race." The bibliophile used the 135th Street Library as the space to showcase Afro-Cuban writers and artists. Throughout the 1930s, Schomburg displayed the work of Afro-Cuban artists, including the paintings of Pastor Argudín, who eventually contributed a portrait of the bibliophile that still hangs in the Schomburg Center to this day. Schomburg also added portraits of Claudio Brindis de Salas, the nineteenth-century Afro-Cuban violinist, as well as other pieces of artwork by Afro-Cubans. Shortly after his return from Cuba, Schomburg informed Guillén: "Next week I will put in the display cabinet the works of Cuban writers, including *Sóngoro Cosongo*, a portrait of Guillén, as well as one of the Club Atenas." The bibliophile assured the poet that soon enough "we are going to see Guillén, Argudín, Ramos and the rest coming to America so that this community will know the artists of their sister republic."[17]

Schomburg made good on his promise. Within a few months of his trip to Cuba, he used his connections with the Harmon Foundation, the white philanthropic institution that promoted black art and literature in the late 1920s and 1930s, to set up Teodoro Ramos Blanco for the foundation's annual exhibit of "Negro art." Ramos Blanco, the former policeman turned sculptor, was one of the leading Afro-Cuban artists of the period. After studying at the famous San Alejandro Art School in Havana, Ramos Blanco continued his development as a sculptor in Italy in the late 1920s, where he made his prize-winning white marble statue of Mariana Grajales, the iconic Cuban patriot. Overshadowed in Cuban art historiography by the more famous painter Wilfredo Lam, Ramos Blanco's art explicitly represented Afro-Cuban contributions to the nation's history. Among the pieces included in the Harmon exhibit were Ramos Blanco's *The Slave, Country People,* and *Head of Langston Hughes,* a piece he made after befriending the poet during his 1930 trip to Havana. Schomburg seized upon the Harmon's interest in "Negro art" and convinced them to contact Ramos Blanco, and the artist took advantage of the opportunity. He had displayed his work in Europe and in Cuba in an exhibition held by the Club Atenas, but he had not yet showcased his art in the United States. Thus, the Harmon exhibition was a potential boost to his career. This is why the sculptor expressed his sincere gratitude to his publicist for giving him "the opportunity to exhibit my modest works in such an important exposition of artists of our race."[18]

The importance of the Ramos Blanco's sculptures was not lost on the foundation either. The exhibition, held at a midtown Manhattan gallery in February–March 1933, was the fifth such event that showcased "new happenings in the field of Negro art." According to the exhibition catalog, the 1933 exhibit was significant because "in previous years work of artists from continental United States only has been shown." However, thanks to the labors of Schomburg, "the Foundation has learned of artists not only in our own island dependencies but among our neighboring countries in the West Indies." The foundation judged Ramos Blanco's eight pieces of sculpture to be a "real contribution" in light of the absence of non-American black artists in previous years.[19] Alain Locke expressed similar sentiments, predicting to readers of his introduction to the exhibit that Ramos Blanco's work would serve the purpose of "uniting for purposes of comparison the work of Negroes separated by differences of cultural background and artistic tradition." Locke argued that the inclusion of the Afro-Cuban artist's sculptures would, in a line that unintentionally exposed his own primitivist gaze, stimulate interest in the "little known but increasing contemporary art work of the native African."[20] The Howard University professor and self-styled promoter of New Negro art and literature did not explain how exposure to the Afro-Cuban artist's work would lead to greater interest in the artwork of the "native African." It is likely that his prediction reveals the imagined continuum of Afro-diasporic art, in which

African American cultural production held up the modern side and the "native African" pulled down the other. In Locke's schema, Afro-Cuban art would be situated closer to the primitive African.

The appearance of Ramos Blanco's sculptures in the Harmon exhibit highlights the material benefits black artists attained from Afro-diasporic connections between Harlem and Havana. These linkages were facilitated by a racialized transnational cultural economy, a structure that contained narrow avenues made available by white-dominated foundations, publishers, and the transportation industry that linked Havana to New York. The process by which Ramos Blanco's sculptures were included in the Harmon exhibit illustrates this point. The sculptor received his invitation to participate in the exhibition only one month before the opening. With little time to prepare and without the funds to send his artwork to New York, he called upon his friend in the Cuban government, Manuel Capestany Abreu, the undersecretary of justice and president of the Club Atenas, and another friend who worked for the Ward Line, who managed to get permission to send the artist's work to New York on the company's ship, the SS *Morro Castle*, free of charge. Thanks to these connections, Ramos Blanco was able to get his artwork to Schomburg in time for the opening on 20 February 1933.[21]

The 1933 Harmon exhibition was the first of a number of instances when Ramos Blanco's work was displayed in the American, especially the African American, art world. His *Head of Langston Hughes* became a permanent part of Schomburg's collection, where it remains up to the present. His sculptures were displayed in the American Negro Exposition in Chicago in 1940 and at Howard University's thriving art scene in the early 1940s. His show at Howard introduced him to the African American intelligentsia in Washington, D.C. Ramos Blanco became a close associate of Ben Frederic Carruthers, Howard's specialist on Afro-Cuban poetry, who later helped Hughes translate Guillén's verses into English. As we shall see, these relationships enabled Ramos Blanco to figure prominently in the hosting of Rayford Logan and representatives of Mary McLeod Bethune's National Council of Negro Women trips to Cuba in the early 1940s. As was often the case in the forging of Afro-diasporic linkages, one set of contacts begot another, shaped by the necessity of aspiring Afro-descended writers and artists to exploit openings in the racialized imperial structures that governed the world of the arts in both countries.[22]

Whether it was at the 135th Street Library, the Apollo Theater, the Savoy Ballroom, or in the growing community that became known as "Spanish Harlem," Afro-Cuban cultural forms were an inextricable part of Harlem's vast array of Afro-diasporic cultures. Langston Hughes's "My Early Days in Harlem," written in the early 1960s, eloquently underscores how the movement of people and cultures made Harlem a unique mix of diverse black cultures:

> Harlem, like a Picasso painting in his cubist period. Harlem—Southern Harlem—the Carolinas, Georgia, Florida—looking for the Promised Land—dressed in rhythmic words, painted in bright pictures, dancing to jazz—and ending up in the subway morning rush time—*headed downtown*. West Indian Harlem—warm rambunctious sassy remembering Marcus Garvey. Haitian Harlem, Cuban Harlem, little pockets of tropical dreams in alien tongues. Magnet Harlem, pulling an Arthur Schomburg from Puerto Rico, pulling an Arna Bontemps all the way from California, a Nora Holt from way out West, and E. Simms Campbell from St. Louis, likewise a Josephine Baker, a Charles S. Johnson from Virginia, an A. Philip Randolph from Florida, a Roy Wilkins from Minnesota, an Alta Douglas from Kansas. Melting pot Harlem—Harlem of honey and chocolate and caramel and rum and vinegar and lemon and lime and gall.[23]

Hughes's recollections of Harlem eloquently convey the community's diversity and its multiple connections to the various parts of the African diaspora in the United States and the Caribbean. While his poetic prose might romanticize his youth in Harlem, it nonetheless reminds us of the scope of the community's diverse black population as it emerged in the early part of the century. The Harlem that Hughes evokes is not an "African American" space; it is not just one that was home to peoples from different nations, but one populated by black peoples from different localities and regions: Missouri, California, Virginia, Florida, Jamaica, Cuba, Puerto Rico, and Haiti. In this sense, Harlem was translocal. The "magnet Harlem" was a site of multiple migrations, of people flowing in and out and returning to the homeland and going back again. Harlem became a place of "tropical dreams and alien tongues" in part because of its connections to the cultural revolution developing in Havana during the 1920s and early 1930s.

The Colored Societies and the Lettered Man of the Colored Race

If Afro-diasporic institutions such as the 135th Street Library anchored one end of the Havana-Harlem cultural nexus, the Afro-Cuban "colored societies" anchored the other. The role of Afro-Cuban societies in the formation of black literary culture has tended to be obscured by the fact that many Afro-Cuban leaders sought to distance themselves from the Afro-Cubanist movement. But Afro-Cubanism was not simply a phenomenon generated by primitivist white Cuban intellectuals and a few Afro-Cuban fellow travelers. In fact, like the New Negro movement in Harlem, it was a product of a younger generation of writers and artists who began to challenge the tenets of racial respectability touted by black cultural institutions. And like Langston Hughes's generation in the United States, young Afro-Cuban writers foregrounded precisely the cultural practices and the material conditions of the working classes shunned by aspiring-class and elite blacks. Perhaps this generational shift is what Schomburg was obliquely referring to when he classified *Sóngoro Cosongo*, Nicolás Guillén's second book of *son*-poems, as "a novel change [that] has come to the old established school."[24] Gustavo Urrutia, one of Guillén's erstwhile supporters, was certainly referring to this tension when he divulged to Hughes soon after the appearance of the poet's *Motivos de son*, "Of course there is a bunch of high-life negroes which condemns this kind of literature, same as in the states."[25] But to highlight Afro-Cuban elites' rejections of Afro-Cubanist poetry need not create the illusion that Afro-Cuban writers, artists, and musicians emerged from a world that was defined more by class than race, in contrast to the supposedly more racist United States. Instead, the reality of Cuba's subtle form of racialized leisure practices required aspiring Afro-Cuban artists to work within the limits imposed by the racialization of cultural production on the island. This meant working within the confines of the centers of Afro-Cuban cultural life in this period—the Afro-Cuban colored societies.

As we have seen, a key component of Afro-Cuban understandings of racial uplift was the emphasis on education, and more specifically, the mastery of literature. While recreational activities were a primary function of the Afro-Cuban societies, they made efforts to promote literacy both for members and for the public at large.[26] Most societies had libraries and night schools to teach members and associates to read. They also organized literary readings as part of their leisure activities. These *tertulias* (gatherings) were designed to expose members to classics in Western literature, such as the works of Aristotle and other Greek philosophers. For example, the Club Atenas regularly held "Tardes Literarias" (literary afternoons) and conferences that they promoted as "parties of intelligence." These literary gatherings resembled the activities promoted by African American literary societies in the same period. Nicolás Guillén recalled these literary festivities organized by the Maceo Society in his hometown of Camagüey in a poem "Elegía camagüeyana," included in his memoir:

Y mi compadre Agustín Pueyo
Que hablaba de Aristóteles
En las tertulias de "Maceo."

*[And my godfather Agustín Pueyo
who would speak about Aristotle
in the gatherings of "Maceo."]*[27]

While these "parties of intelligence" sought to make Afro-Cubans into "cultured" subjects schooled in the Western canon, they also exposed readers to the works of black writers at home and abroad, including Nicolás Guillén and Regino Pedroso, as well as Booker T. Washington, Langston Hughes, and a host of other African American writers. As we shall see, Afro-Cuban elites did not foresee that their literary parties would eventually create spaces for a younger generation of writers who would look for alternative sources of "intelligence" in the less "respectable" urban cultures of the black working classes.[28]

The formative influence of the "colored" societies on Afro-Cuban writers can be seen in Nicolás Guillén's early career. Guillén's own self-positioning as a communist dedicated to a mixed-race *cubanidad* (Cubanness) and the oft-cited disdain of members of the Afro-Cuban elite for his *son*-poems has obscured his roots in Afro-Cuban cultural institutions. His status as Cuba's national poet after the triumph of the Cuban Revolution further camouflaged his connections to the Afro-Cuban elite of the republican era. Despite its limitations as a historical source, Guillén's memoir provides evidence of his activities in Afro-Cuban societies, even though the poet simultaneously sought to distance himself from this history in the same narrative. Reading his memoir against the grain enables us to gain glimpses of the literary worlds of the Afro-Cuban societies that shaped his early career.

Indeed Guillén's family was part of the Afro-Cuban artisan class in the province of Camagüey, a region known for its particularly overt forms of racial discrimination. His road to notoriety was facilitated by his being the son of Nicolás Guillén y Urra, a prominent politician, silversmith, and journalist who was one of the few black or mulatto senators during the early years of the Cuban republic. From his father, young Nicolás was exposed to journalism, printing, and politics. In the early 1920s, he edited a local publication titled *Lis*, a publication indicative of the style of many magazines published by urban blacks and mulattoes at this time. According to Guillén, *Lis* "had partially a literary character, and the other part was dedicated to outlining the activities of the societies 'of color,' as they were then called."[29] *Lis* was one of a plethora of Afro-Cuban publications that showcased Afro-Cuban writers and journalists. Continuing a trend that began in the postemancipation period, Afro-Cuban periodicals appeared throughout the island for the first few decades of the Cuban republic and in some cases beyond. Publications such as *Lis* in Guillén's hometown of Camagüey, *Castalia* in Cienfuegos, and *Alma Jóven* in the town of Trinidad, among other publications, all profiled Afro-Cuban writers and documented literary gatherings. Thus, like African American periodicals, these publications were an important way literate Afro-Cubans conveyed to the public their aspirations for cultural advancement.[30]

As a child in Camagüey, Guillén attended the night school of Tomás Vélez, an Afro-Cuban teacher. During his adolescence, Guillén began his literary writings in the headquarters of the Sociedad La Victoria, one of the local Afro-Cuban societies, "where my contacts with black Camagüeyans began."[31] Guillén's connection to the society was his friend Félix Nápoles, whose position as the society's secretary of communications gave him access to a typewriter. "Every Sunday," Guillén recalled, "from nine to midday, we would work putting together those short lines that would appear under the title 'Cerebro y Corazón' [Brains and heart]."[32] Hence, Guillén was able to continue his education, and ultimately his development as a poet, thanks in part to his connection to Afro-Cuban associations. In this sense, Guillén's early career reflects a larger pattern for young males who sought to demonstrate their "culture" by becoming men of letters. Guillén was following the model of Afro-Cuban manhood personified by Juan Gualberto Gómez, Martín Morúa Delgado, and Lino D'ou, the prestigious Afro-Cuban patriots who demonstrated their elevated status through their mastery of letters.

The gendered promotion of male literary figures obscured, and continues to overshadow, the work of Afro-Cuban women writers. This is clear when one encounters the paucity of documentation on the life and work of María Dámasa Jova. A poet, teacher, and social activist for children and for racial and gender equality, Dámasa Jova was a product of the racialized worlds of the island's literary culture. Yet she also managed to transcend the racial and gender boundaries imposed on her by Cuban society. Details of Dámasa Jova's career are difficult to reconstruct, due in part to the silencing of Afro-Cuban women's history. However, she was a prominent figure on the local level during the 1920s and 1930s. Born in Ranchuelo in 1890, Dámasa Jova was the beneficiary of parents who put together their meager resources to send her to school until she was orphaned at the age of seventeen. Like some of her black female contemporaries in the United States, Dámasa Jova combined her literary aspirations with a career as a teacher, one of the few professions available to Afro-Cuban women at the time.[33] She began her remarkable teaching career at the age of thirteen and four years later became the director of a rural school. Soon thereafter she relocated to the town of Santa Clara, where she taught elementary school classes and began her social work for children. Dámasa Jova published *Arpegios intimos* in 1925, a book of verse that was praised by Cuban critics.[34] In the 1930s, she was part of a cohort of Afro-Cuban women whose work among poor youth brought the abuses of impoverished children to light. Her essay "La situación de la mujer negra en Cuba" (The situation of the Negro woman in Cuba), an essay on the conditions facing black women in that country, has eluded the grasp of historians. Dámasa Jova's virtual absence from the Afro-Cubanist movement of the late 1920s shows that black women were systematically excluded from Cuban literary cultures. The promotion of the black man of letters by the Afro-Cuban societies further obscured the work of Dámasa Jova and her contemporaries.[35]

The national and international visibility of Afro-Cuban male writers and artists was enhanced by the emergence of Gustavo Urrutia, the architect-turned-journalist who created the "Ideales de una Raza" (Ideals of a race) column in the *Diario de la Marina*, perhaps the most prominent Havana daily at the time. Like Luís Delfín Valdés, the Tuskegee alumnus and designer of the Club Atenas building, Urrutia was a successful black architect during the 1910s. However, despite his individual success, he remained dissatisfied by the persistence of racial inequality in Cuba, convinced that José Martí's vision of "Cuba with All and for All" had failed to come to fruition. By his own account, Urrutia's journalistic career began with a conversation he had on a Havana streetcar with Miguel Angel Céspedes, the lawyer and cofounder of and former teacher in the Instituto Booker T. Washington; fellow lawyer Ramiro Cuesta Rendón; and Agapito Rodríguez in 1927. After lamenting what they saw as inadequate public forums for Afro-Cuban rights, Urrutia decided to approach José "Pepín" Rivero, the editor of the conservative newspaper the *Diario de la Marina*, with the idea of contributing a few articles on Afro-Cuban issues. Remarkably, Urrutia convinced the editor to accept his articles even though he had no background in journalism.[36]

Urrutia's periodic contributions eventually turned into his weekly "Ideales de una Raza" page, which was published from 1928 through early 1931. What Urrutia created was not only the most important forum for public debates on racism in Cuba, but also a space where Afro-Cuban artists and writers were publicized, including Guillén, Pedroso, Ramos Blanco, and many others.

Gustavo Urrutia. The photograph
is signed: "To Mr. Langston Hughes,
the poet of the Negroes. With admiration, G. E. Urrutia, March 7, 1930."
Courtesy of Yale Collection of
American Literature, Beinecke Rare
Book and Manuscript Library.

Urrutia was especially proud of the role of his page in bringing Cuban writers of color to the public. Shortly after Guillén's *Motivos de son* poems appeared on Urrutia's "Ideales" page in April 1930, he proudly reported to Langston Hughes that the editors of the predominantly white periodicals such as *La Semana* and *Social* were "anxious to get poems of this kind from Guillén." Urrutia privately revealed a keen racial attitude that one might call "black nationalist" when he informed Hughes that white publications were "indignant because our poet did not give them the preference to start in their papers with this new literary style; they don't want to understand that a negro poet, loyal to his race, should prefer a negro paper or page to give his negro poems." In Urrutia's opinion, Guillén's poetry "should be a specialty of our negro page and bring the reader to look for it in our page." However, he concluded that it was best to "be cour-teous and friendly to all" by reluctantly letting the white literary press have access to Guillén's poems.[37]

The impact of Urrutia's "Ideales" page and his subsequent journalistic work for the *Diario de la Marina* throughout the 1930s on Cuban racial politics is undeniable. Yet it is also clear that Urrutia's page was a space where Afro-Cuban intellectuals articulated their understanding of their relationship to the broader African diaspora. As in previous years, Afro-Cuban notions of diaspora in this period continued to be framed in relationship to African

Americans. In virtually every column during the more than two-year run of "Ideales," Urrutia featured a news item on an aspect of the "negro americano" experience.[38] His desk at the *Diario de la Marina* offices received a steady flow of news about African Americans. Articles routinely appeared not just on racial oppression in the United States, but more frequently on the efforts of African Americans to overcome racial discrimination, usually by featuring black leaders from Booker T. Washington to Oscar DePreist. The "Ideales" page also translated articles from a gamut of African American publications, including the *Chicago Defender*, the *Pittsburgh Courier*, and, of course, *Opportunity* and the *Crisis*. After Urrutia met Langston Hughes in 1930, his columns began to feature the work of African American writers and artists. Thus, Urrutia's "Negro page" illustrates the continuing belief of Afro-Cuban intellectuals that the situation facing African Americans, more than any other Afro-diasporic population, was most pertinent to the Afro-Cuban condition. Urrutia's work in his "Ideales" page made him one of the key figures of the Harlem-Havana cultural nexus.

It was on Urrutia's page where Guillén became known to Cuban readers. In 1928, the architect-turned-journalist published a number of Guillén's journalistic pieces, including the well-known "El Camino de Harlem" (The road to Harlem), which condemned the persistence of racism in Cuba. As the article clearly demonstrates, the Afro-Cuban writer was not interested in celebrating the black cultural "renaissance" in New York's famous black neighborhood. Instead, Guillén portrayed Harlem as a manifestation of the U.S. model of racial segregation that he feared would take root in Cuba. If racial discrimination continued, the day would soon come when every Cuban town had "its 'Negro neighborhood' like our neighbors to the North. And that is the road that all of us, those of Martí's color and those who have the same color as Maceo, must avoid. That is the road to Harlem."[39]

As we shall see, the "road to Harlem" that ultimately linked Cuba to the "barrio negro" in New York was not the one-way street that terminated at the imagined U.S. model of racial segregation. Instead, it was a two-way street of cultural exchange that, ironically, was created by the transnational structures of racialization that shaped leisure and artistic practice in Cuba and the United States. But the structures of racialization did not produce the Harlem-Havana nexus on their own. It took the work of a person with the cultural and linguistic facility, notoriety, and connections to black cultural institutions, not to mention access to the resources of white patrons and philanthropic organizations, to bring the two communities together. The person who played a decisive role in bridging the two movements was one of the most famous personalities associated with the Harlem Renaissance — Langston Hughes.

The "Blues Poet" Finds the "Heartbeat and Songbeat of Africa" in Havana

Of the four figures who linked Havana and Harlem together, Langston Hughes was perhaps the most important. His roots in the African American culture of the Midwest and his experience living in Mexico with his father gave him a unique transcultural background in Latin American and U.S. cultures. While his role as a translator of Afro-Cuban poetry has been thoroughly documented, there is more to learn from his well-known but little-studied travels to Cuba in 1930 and 1931 about the forging of the linkages between the movements in Harlem and Havana, as well as the racialized and gendered social spaces that produced them.

In 1930, Hughes was undergoing a period of transition. After achieving enormous success through his "blues poems" in *The Weary Blues* (1926) and *Fine Clothes to a Jew* (1927), and having just completed *Not without Laughter*, a novel about a black family in Kansas, Hughes now looked to Cuba as a potential source of inspiration for a new folk-opera project. He was interested in working with Amadeo Roldán, the Cuban classical composer known for incorporating Afro-Cuban themes into his symphonic compositions. Going to Cuba in many ways would be a logical progression for Hughes, having already transferred the blues into poetry. The southern United States and the Caribbean had one thing in common: they were both viewed as repositories of more "primitive" Afro-diasporic cultural forms. Encouraged by Charlotte Mason, his then patron and enthusiast for all things "primitive," Hughes went to Cuba hoping to spark a creative synergy between Afro-diasporic music and poetry. As he related to Mason, "I am to go to Havana for rest, new strength and contact with the song."[40]

But why go to Cuba in particular? The country had been on Hughes's mind since he was a child. As we have seen, his father, James Nathaniel Hughes, was among the African Americans who went to Cuba looking for a better life during the first U.S. occupation. Langston's father's experience ran through his mind during the first few hours of his trip to Havana. After settling into the very untouristy Hotel Las Villas, Hughes wrote: "So here I am at 'Las Villas,' Avenida Bélgica 20 — which is certainly native enough. . . . I don't suppose another American has ever stopped here (unless it was my father 25 years ago)."[41]

A few years before, Hughes had also written "Soledad: A Cuban Portrait," one of the poems published in *The Weary Blues*. In it, the subject of "the Cuban portrait" is a person saddened by years of pain:

The shadows
Of too many nights of love
Have fallen beneath your eyes.
Your eyes,
So full of pain and passion,
So full of lies.
So full of pain and passion,
Soledad,
So deeply scarred,
So still with silent cries.[42]

Hughes's decision to go to Cuba to look for "the song" might have also been informed by the fact that he likely encountered the sounds of the *son* in New York. As we have seen, Afro-Cuban *son* groups such as the Sexteto Habanero and the Septeto Nacional began to perform in New York and record with the Victor and Columbia record labels. Other Cuban musicians, such as Xavier Cugat and Alberto Socarrás, were also performing in other venues in New York. Thus, Hughes was likely aware of Cuban musical genres before he departed for Cuba in February 1930.[43]

When Hughes arrived in Havana, he encountered a vibrant and politically active intellectual community. As we have seen, the 1920s was a time of dramatic change and turmoil in Cuba. Cuban intellectuals were becoming a major force in island politics, emerging as critical voices against corrupt Cuban governments. This in turn led to a resurging nationalism that was based on strident anti-imperialist critiques of the U.S. presence on the island. This was the era of the *minoristas* (Grupo Minorista, the influential intellectual and artistic vanguard group), Julio Antonio Mella and the emerging Cuban Communist Party, the Federation of University Students, and labor organizations such as the National Confederation of Cuban Workers. Periodicals such as *Revista de Avance*, *Revista de la Habana*, the *Revista Bimestre Cubana*, and *Social* were some of the publications that expressed their views. Although these intellectuals came from diverse political tendencies, they found common ground in their calls for Cuban nationalism and anti-imperialism. By 1930, these calls for change grew louder under the increasingly authoritarian regime of Gerardo Machado.[44]

While Hughes encountered a country on the verge of political upheaval, he also discovered Havana's vast array of cultural institutions that were propelling the emerging Afro-Cubanist cultural revolution. His journals provide rare glimpses of the social spaces where the musical aspects of the cultural transformations in Havana were taking shape. During his stays on the island, the poet immersed himself in the city's bustling nightlife. While images of tourist casinos and prostitution from the 1950s overshadow Havana's cultural history, the city possessed a diverse cultural scene that extended beyond American tourist sectors of the city.[45] The Cuban capital's recreational and literary societies, along with its plethora of dance halls and bars, were the locales for the cultural transformations that took shape in Havana in the 1920s and 1930s. To be sure, Havana's nightlife was as robust as Harlem's in this period. Although a cultural history of Havana has yet to be written, the existing scholarship on Afro-Cuban cultural production has highlighted the importance of specific neighborhoods in the production of Cuban popular culture. Barrios such as Jesús María, Cayo Hueso, and Pueblo Nuevo were the neighborhoods that produced famous Afro-Cuban musicians. The district of Marianao on the outskirts of the city was also a zone where Afro-Cuban musicians and dancers performed for local audiences. *Sonero* musicians also played in *academias de baile*, or ballroom dance halls that existed in Havana during this period. Although these halls were technically "dance schools" where men could learn how to dance, in reality they became centers of prostitution where men, mostly white, sought the sexual services of women. The fact that the *son* was frequently the music of choice at the *academias* led it to be associated with the supposed "low" elements of urban life. Thus, it had a reputation similar to the one jazz and the blues had in the United States in this period.

It was at the *academias de baile* that Hughes initiated his quest for Afro-Cuban music. On his first night in Havana, Hughes somehow found his way to the "Habana Sport" *academia de baile* on Galiano Street in the Central Havana district. Whether he knew it or not, he had stumbled onto one of the primary sites of the *son* revolution in Havana. His observations of the *academias* provide rare bits of evidence on these well-known but still understudied institutions. Hughes took note of "the many lovely madura girls in wine-colored dresses," along with the preponderance of white male patrons. He also couldn't help but notice "the black orchestra but no black dancers."[46] The absence of the black dancers signifies the complex forms of racial segregation that operated in the *academias*. The patrons at these dance halls were almost always white men while the women were white or mulatto. As in other leisure spaces where music was performed, such as the *retreta*, Afro-Cuban men could participate only as musicians, not as consumers of leisure practices.[47]

Although it is unclear how Hughes entered an *academia de baile* that tended to bar nonwhite patrons, many of his evenings were spent at the Club Occidente, a dance hall that catered to Afro-Cuban men at 125 Galiano Street, a block away from "Habana Sport" (98 Galiano) and a stone's throw away from Guillén's apartment (103 Galiano). Perhaps Guillén's proximity to these dance halls was one of the reasons why he wrote about the practices and the complex interplay between race and gender in these spaces in his "El Camino de Harlem" piece:

> Nowadays there are dancehalls for Negroes operating in Havana in op-position to the schools where only whites dance, a totally natural phenom-enon when one bears in mind that the first dancehalls that were founded excluded men of color. (Some women are able to attend). What was the Negro going to do if he wanted to dance, since he likes to dance so much? Join together with his own, accept the separation imposed by his "white brother," as he accepted it in the park and the barbershop and try to live and dance with those who have the same skin pigmentation.[48]

Guillén's discussion of the *academias de baile* highlights not only the persis-tence of racism in republican Cuba, but also the ways Afro-Cuban men were able to construct their own forms of leisure. If they could not enter the Ha-vana Sport, they could simply create their own *academias* where the dancers were, as Hughes wrote in his journal, "all mulatto or black." Indeed, in a letter Guillén wrote to Hughes after the Blues Poet returned to the United States, he implored Hughes to return to Cuba so that he could "learn to dance the *son* at the Club Occidente, or wherever you want."[49]

While Hughes began his investigations of Afro-Cuban culture in the dance halls of Central Havana on his own, it was José Antonio Fernández de Castro, a Cuban defined as white, who played a critical role in facilitating his con-tacts with Afro-Cuban writers and artists, as well as a more extensive exposure to Cuban nightlife. Years later, Hughes described Fernández de Castro as a person "extraordinary in this world or any other world" for his intense interest in Afro-Cuban culture and his relationship with the "Negro drummers" in the Marianao district. "Although he was a white Cuban of aristocratic back-ground, he knew and loved Negro Cuba," Hughes wrote years later.[50] Born in 1897, Fernández de Castro followed the path of many upper-class Cuban men—studying in the United States, which allowed him to learn English, and

Rare visual evidence of racial segregation in leisure practices in Cuba. The banner announces a dance in Pinar del Río: "Grand dance for white people, 14 December, with the Military Band at the A-Fo-Ruíz." This photograph was probably given to Hughes during his 1931 trip to Cuba. Courtesy of Yale Collection of American Literature, Beinecke Rare Book and Manuscript Library.

getting a law degree from the University of Havana. However, the political and cultural transformations on the island during the 1920s pushed him in a different direction. In the early part of the decade, he was active in the Grupo Minorista after his participation in the "Protest of the Thirteen" against the corrupt presidency of Alfredo Zayas in 1923. He began editing the literary page of the *Diario de la Marina* and eventually became a prominent journalist. The energetic Fernández de Castro also wrote for other magazines and became a historian of Cuban literature. Thus, his travels to the United States and his position as a journalist enhanced his awareness of the New Negro movement in Harlem.[51]

Fernández de Castro was one of the four major figures who linked the Harlem Renaissance to the Afro-Cubanist movement and the first to introduce Hughes's poetry to Cuban readers. He became familiar with the work of Hughes after reading Countee Cullen's anthology *Caroling Dusk*. The renegade intellectual performed the first translations of Hughes's poetry into Spanish, translating "I, Too, Sing America" and publishing it as "Yo, También,

Honro a América" in 1928 in the magazine *Social*. Fernández de Castro found Langston's poetry inspiring, helping stimulate his own interest in Afro-Cuban poetry and music. While his love for "Negro Cuba" was clearly influenced by the dominant primitivist currents of the day, it was also shaped by his own political activism against Cuba's corrupt neocolonial system.[52]

Hughes sought out Fernández de Castro because of their mutual relationship with Miguel Covarrubias, the Mexican caricaturist. Born in 1904, Covarrubias came to New York in 1923 and soon thereafter became one of the major artists of the Harlem Renaissance.[53] Hughes met Covarrubias through Carl Van Vechten, and all three were part of Alfred Knopf's circle of writers and artists. The Mexican caricaturist sketched the cover of Hughes's *The Weary Blues*. Covarrubias's own contributions to Harlem Renaissance art were compiled in his *Negro Drawings*, a collection of sketches of people of African descent in Harlem and Cuba published by Knopf in 1927. Most of the book's sketches sought to represent African American nightlife in Harlem, featuring images of black people dancing the Charleston and the Cake Walk, musicians playing jazz and singing the blues, and supposed everyday folks, such as the "Lenox Avenue Type." The collection was acclaimed by both white and black critics in the United States and Cuba.[54]

Almost totally unnoticed by critics of *Negro Drawings*, however, were his sketches titled "Three Cuban Women." Covarrubias must have developed the ideas for the "Three Cuban Women" sketches during his 1926 visit to Cuba. It was during this trip that he met Fernández de Castro and Alejo Carpentier. A comparison between the Cuban and the Harlem sketches reveals Covarrubias's vision of the African diaspora in Cuba and the United States. While the portraits of Harlem nightlife connote the image of a people at a crossroads between modernity and primitivism, the Cuban sketches were much more rooted in a primitivist gaze. One of the "Cuban" women portrayed by Covarrubias seems to come straight out of an African village. Other sketches by Covarrubias highlight his vision of black expressive culture in Havana. These sketches illustrate the emerging notion that Afro-Cubans were closer to the roots of African cultures than African Americans. Ultimately, Covarrubias's artwork and writings provide key evidence of the imagined connections between the black cultural movements in Harlem and Havana.

Armed with a letter of introduction by Covarrubias, Hughes proceeded to Fernández de Castro's office the day after his arrival in Havana. It was Fernández de Castro who put Hughes in touch with "the Negro Poet Guillén." For Guillén this was an excellent opportunity, because, as he noted in his memoir,

One of the three sketches of Cuban women by Miguel Covarrubias published in his *Negro Drawings*. Courtesy of the Harry Ransom Humanities Research Center, The University of Texas at Austin.

"I was unfamiliar with the work of Hughes because of the very important reason that I did not know English."[55] Fernández de Castro also called up Gustavo Urrutia, and the three of them were the African American poet's companions for the remainder of his stay in Havana. Hughes's journal also illustrates Fernández de Castro's effort to introduce the Blues Poet to other influential members of the Cuban intellectual elite, including Conrado Massaguer, the famous caricaturist and publisher of a number of magazines, including *Social*, which had published Fernández de Castro's translation of Hughes's "I, Too, Sing America." Although Hughes socialized with members of the white Cuban intelligentsia, he spent most of his time with Guillén, Urrutia, and the Afro-Cuban sculptor Teodoro Ramos Blanco.[56]

Hughes's understanding of Afro-Cuban culture was undoubtedly influenced by his relationships with Fernández de Castro and Covarrubias. Although he went to Cuba in search of a classical composer for a folk-opera idea, he instead wound up spending most of his time immersing himself in Afro-Cuban expressive culture and meeting emerging Afro-Cuban writers and artists thanks to Fernández de Castro. Moreover, because of Covarrubias's previous trips to the island, it is likely he encouraged Hughes to spend time in the Havana dance halls. After all, Covarrubias himself had been taken by his Cuban hosts to local nightclubs that "rocked with rumba and the *son*" during his 1926 trip to Cuba. In short, Hughes's understanding of "Negro Cuba" was

"Untitled" by Miguel Covarrubias. This sketch of rumba dancers and musicians was likely inspired by Covarrubias's trips to Havana in the late 1920s. Courtesy of María Elena Covarrubias.

largely shaped by the primitivist-inflected representations he gathered from Fernández de Castro and Covarrubias. Herein lies one of the paradoxes of the Harlem-Havana cultural nexus.[57]

But the fetishization of the primitive was not the only factor informing the making of Afro-diasporic linkages during this period. If gender and sexuality shaped the making of the Harlem Renaissance and Afro-Cubanism, they also influenced the forms of interaction that took place among those individuals who linked the two movements together.[58] Diasporization was predicated on an economy of desire that was based on the objectification of women. As an attractive male celebrity in Havana, Hughes was expected to partake in the supposed delights of male heterosexual living. In their correspondence with Hughes, both Guillén and Fernández de Castro sought to bond with the Blues Poet over an assumed common sexual orientation. In a 1931 letter to Hughes, Fernández de Castro wrote: "I feel in heaven now boy; [I] have three and a half girls—if you care about the names I'll send them to you in my next letter."

However, he admitted to Hughes that he was "still in love with the little Mexican dancer and another Mexican you haven't met. You should come to Cuba to know them." Fernández de Castro's belief that Hughes would empathize with his conundrum echoes the ways in which the Blues Poet was introduced to numerous "pretty girls" on his trip, particularly Afro-Cuban women. During his stays in Havana, he frequently ate at the restaurant of Lalita Zamora, "said to be the loveliest black girl in Cuba," Hughes noted in his diary, a view that he clearly learned from his Cuban male hosts. Hughes's references to "pretty girls" in his diary and autobiography throughout his stay are as much a reflection of the sexual energy he received from his male Cuban counterparts as it was of his own opinion of their attractiveness.

Hughes's Havana itinerary illuminates the homosocial worlds that shaped Cuban leisure culture in general and the Afro-Cubanist movement in particular. His recollections of the rumba parties he attended in Havana highlight the intersection between gender, race, and sexuality in Cuban leisure practices as well as the sexual expectations placed on him by his Cuban hosts. On one occasion, the Blues Poet was thrown a *cumbancha*, an impromptu evening feast by "a group of young business and professional men." As the guest of honor at the party that was held in the courtyard of a private home, Hughes watched couples dancing the rumba while "a few lovely mulatto girls sat fanning in wicker chairs." As the *rumberos* tirelessly played "like a mighty dynamo deep in the bowels of the earth," he continued to watch as "glass after glass" of wine and Bacardí were thrust into his hands. As Hughes noted, parties such as these were affairs that men did not attend with their wives and girlfriends. Instead, the women in attendance were "friends and mistresses of the hosts, their most choice females invited especially for zest and decorativeness," according to Hughes.[59]

As the drumming and dancing continued unabated after supper, Hughes learned that it was time for him to perform the role prepared for him as the guest of honor. His male hosts proudly informed him that he could spend the night at the house in the company of some of the "pretty girls" at the party. "You are the guest of honor. Take your choice from any," Hughes recalled their telling him, "our women are your women, tonight." While Hughes did not inform his readers whether or not he accepted the invitation of his hosts, this moment from his memoir underscores the culture of male sexual privilege that pervaded the social spaces of the Afro-Cubanist movement. Here, Afro-diasporic bonding was predicated on the transaction of women as objects of male desire.[60]

It was during those nights at the rumba parties and *academias de baile* when Hughes discovered the "heartbeat and songbeat of Africa" in Cuba. Hughes's discovery is apparent in his famous interview with Guillén, "Conversación con Langston Hughes," held toward the end of his trip. The conversation, which was conducted in Spanish and published in the *Diario de la Marina*, shifts from a question-and-answer interview format to Guillén's account of Hughes at a Havana dance hall frequented by people of African descent, probably the Club Occidente, a few doors down from Guillén's home. According to Guillén, immediately upon hearing the pulsating rhythms of a *son* band, Hughes acted "as if possessed by the spirit of his own people, who are my people." At that point Hughes excitedly declared: "Mi gente! [My people!]."[61] Guillén gave the following description of Hughes at the conclusion of the article: "He stays for a long time next to the scandalous orchestra where the 'son' spreads its green smoke, following, with his breath faltering from emotion, the rhythm, new in his spirit. Afterwards, while watching the 'black as the night' bongo player, he declares with a dissatisfied sigh: 'I want to be black. Very Black. Truly Black!'"[62]

Guillén's account of Hughes at the dance hall raises a number of interpretive challenges. After all, the source is Guillén's representation of Hughes. In some ways, the Hughes that emerges from the piece resembles the classic tourist who viewed Cuba as an exotic land of dancing natives. However, Guillén may have accurately represented Hughes's primitivist perspective. To Hughes, to be "truly black" was to be "black like the depths of my Africa," as he wrote in the introductory poem in *The Weary Blues*. Indeed, in Hughes's *I Wonder as I Wander*, written more than two decades later, he characterized Afro-Cuban percussionists as "those fabulous drum beaters who use their bare hands to beat out rhythm, those clave knockers and maraca shakers who somehow have saved—out of all the centuries of slavery and all the miles and miles from Guinea—the heartbeat and songbeat of Africa."[63] If these Afro-Cuban musicians managed to preserve "the heartbeat and songbeat of Africa," Hughes by contrast "did not feel the rhythms of the primitive surging through me." He was, as he wrote a few years later, "only an American Negro—who had loved the surface of Africa and the rhythms of Africa—but I was not Africa."[64] Moreover, his own racialized position as a mulatto might have led him to conclude that an encounter with music played by darker-skinned people of African descent would enable him to gain a momentary taste of "true" blackness.

Yet despite Hughes's primitivist gaze, what is striking is the way in which he sought to forge a diasporic connection across difference. Even as he viewed the musicians through a primitivist frame of reference, he still imagined them as his *"gente"* (people). Furthermore, the Hughes that Guillén presents seems to be in an almost ecstatic state as he yearned to be "truly black." This is clear in Guillén's insistence that Hughes acted as if he were "possessed" by the music. His reaction to the performance led him to imagine that he could feel "true" black culture, in other words, "African" culture. What we can see in this Hughes-Guillén encounter was a central tenet of the Harlem-Havana cultural movement—that black music, art, and poetry could enable black people to "feel" part of the same *"gente"* regardless of the language they spoke or their cultural proximity to Africa.[65]

For all of the time Hughes spent with his *"gente"* in Havana's dance halls, the Blues Poet also made several visits to the Club Atenas, the mecca of Afro-Cuban cultural respectability. As Hughes pointed out in *I Wonder as I Wander*, "no rumbas were danced within the walls of the Atenas for in Cuba in 1930 the rumba was not a respectable dance among persons of good breeding. Only the poor and déclassé, the sporting elements, and gentlemen on a spree danced the rumba."[66] But Hughes's affinity for the cultures of the "poor and déclassé" did not stop him from visiting the "persons of good breeding" at Atenas. If Hughes had been taken with the rumba and the *son*, he was equally awed by Atenas, writing that he had been "astonished and delighted with its taste and luxury, for colored people in the United States had no such club." Neither did it prevent the club from entertaining Hughes. In the same way that the club rolled out the red carpet for Marcus Garvey in 1921, so it did for the "poeta de los blues." Moreover, the club was able to welcome their distinguished guest in their new headquarters designed by the Tuskegee-trained architect Luís Delfín Valdés, who was still a member of the club in 1930 and who was in attendance that evening.[67] In his journal, Hughes marveled at the new building located on Zulueta and Apodaca streets, a few blocks south of the Capitol building: "[A] marble palace, sumptuous drawing rooms, a basketball court, 250 members at $3 per month keep it going. A lovely library of hand carved cases, many books."[68] Hughes stopped at the club on more than one occasion during his trips to Cuba, highlighting yet again the association's role in the forging of Afro-Cuban and African American linkages.

Toward the end of Hughes's 1930 trip, the club held a reception for the Blues Poet, along with Edward H. Henry, Raymond P. Alexander, and their spouses, who were distinguished African American visitors from Philadelphia. Even though the Blues Poet had been in Havana for a few weeks, the Atenas reception marked his first formal introduction to the Cuban public. The event resembled the club's usual "respectable" literary gatherings. According to Hughes, there was "dancing, wine and cake." Those in attendance that evening were likely to have danced to the *danzón*, itself a musical genre that had once been associated with "low" culture but had become the dance of choice of the Afro-Cuban elite by 1930. As the audience gathered on the second floor of the Atenas building, surrounded by concrete and marble walls and under the crystal chandeliers, the club's leaders began their ritual for receiving distinguished guests. After an opening speech by Primitivo Ramírez Ros, himself a "man of letters" and the same person who hosted Marcus Garvey nine years before, and a brief performance by pianist Reynolds González, the stage was cleared for Hughes and his Afro-Cuban literary peers. As Hughes recorded in his journal: "Four of my poems read by myself in English then in Spanish by J. Villareal [*sic*]," followed by "champagne and music." The Club Atenas described the poetry reading in this way: "Juan Jérez Villarreal, the well-known and admired man of letters from Bayamo . . . read a fitting translation of various poems of Mr. Hughes, which was well received by the audience. Immediately thereafter, the poet Mr. Nicolás Guillén gave a reading of two of his own compositions, which were read afterwards in English by Mr. Hughes, who has produced an admirable translation of them for a great New York magazine."[69]

This fascinating account of the event highlights the ways Afro-diasporic connections can be made across cultural and linguistic boundaries. The reading took place before the widespread dissemination of Hughes's poems in Cuba, which did not occur until after the poet left the island. Thus, many of those who attended the reception encountered his poems for the first time that evening. Moreover, it is ironic that Atenas was hosting a reading for a poet who was popularizing the blues, a cultural form that many of their African American elite contemporaries rejected. Furthermore, the presence of Guillén at the reading is also noteworthy because he had not yet published the *son*-poems that the Atenas elite would shun just a few weeks later. In fact, Atenas documents show that Guillén was one of the club's members in 1930.[70] So why did the club host the Blues Poet who dared to declare his desire to be "black as the night" as he did in *The Weary Blues* and who boldly wrote about the physical abuse of black women by black men in "Beale Street Love"? It is possible that the association was largely uninformed of the content of Hughes's poetry, and therefore unaware of its subversive character. Regardless of their cognizance of the ways Hughes troubled the politics of respectability in the United States, hosting the poet was consistent with the Club Atenas's self-fashioning as an Afro-diasporic association. Indeed, the club took its self-perception as the representatives of the "colored race" seriously. Throughout its existence, Atenas routinely hosted foreign black travelers to Cuba, a fact that highlighted the club members' desire to present themselves not simply as the best of the Cuban "colored race," but also as members of the African diaspora. What is more, the club's decision to hold a reading for Hughes was based on the essential fact that he was a celebrity, the best poet from the vanguard of the global "colored race" in the United States. Therefore, hosting Hughes would enhance the association's prestige at home and abroad. What was most important to the club, as its publication indicates, was the presence of "distinguished visitors" from the "colored race" in the United States.

The club's decision to have Hughes share the stage with Guillén, González, and Jérez Villarreal is not insignificant. Simply by bringing together an assembly of black and brown bodies from Cuba and the United States, the event enacted a transcultural African diaspora. Not unlike the Garveyite ceremonies that drew upon the power of embodied activity to forge commonalities across difference, the Atenas reception highlights the symbolic power of embodiment in the formation of Afro-diasporic linkages. Even if the translators did not adequately convey the intricacies of Guillén's and Hughes's verses, spectators were able to witness the male poets in the act of reading in their native languages. Furthermore, by putting Guillén on the same stage with the famous Blues Poet, the event allowed the club to showcase their own versifiers for their African American visitors.

By the time Hughes boarded the *Essequibo* to return to New York, it was clear that his trip was a success on a level that he had not anticipated. While he was unable to find a composer because, as he wrote in *The Big Sea*, "Roldán said he wasn't a Negro," he managed to acquire a host of new admirers and potential artistic collaborators.[71] More important, he left Cuba with a cache of materials of Afro-Cuban culture, including "a bongo drum, various records of [Ernesto] Lecuona and the *sones* he learned in Marianao, as well as original paintings and drawings, Cuban books, and unpublished poems."[72] Along with Schomburg, Hughes became the most important promoter of Spanish-speaking writers of African descent in the United States. Not surprisingly, *Crisis* and *Opportunity* were the publications that showcased Hughes's translated essays and poems by Afro-Cuban writers. A few months after his return to the United States, they published some of Guillén's new poems and an essay written by Hughes on Teodoro Ramos Blanco, the Afro-Cuban sculptor. Over the next few years, these publications continued to periodically print essays translated by Hughes on the "Negro in Cuba," including articles by Gustavo Urrutia. For these reasons Elmer Anderson Carter, the editor of *Opportunity*, commended Hughes for taking "the first steps towards an intellectual rapprochement between the Negroes of the western world."[73]

Interestingly, Hughes's translations and essays presented Afro-Cuban artists and writers in a way that was more palatable for the respectable readerships of *Crisis* and *Opportunity*. Like the members of the Club Atenas, the African American cultural establishment probably would not have found published tales of Hughes's nights in the *academias de baile* very appealing. His translations of Guillén's poems that appeared in the *Crisis* sought to convey the latest "West Indian poetry" to African American readers. The pieces presented Guillén, Pedroso, and the Haitian poet Jacques Roumain as "young Negro poets" who were "doing much to free the poetry of their islands from out-worn foreign patterns." Even though he highlighted Guillén's success using "the dialect of the Cuban Negro," he chose to publish "Llegada" (Arrival), "Caña" (Cane), and "Propósito" (Proposition) instead of the poems that were more explicitly written in Afro-Cuban vernacular, such as "Negro Bembón" (Thick-lipped Negro), "Búcate Plata" (Go Get Money), or "Rumba" (Rumba). While it is likely that his selection was based in part on the poems that were easier to translate into English, his decision could also be read as an attempt to present a more recognizable Afro-Caribbean poetry for African American readers. Indeed, black readers in the United States would have been more likely to appreciate the portrait of black oppression in "Caña" than the aggressive critique of "high brown" women in "Mulata." To be sure, the translations from this period stand in stark contrast to Hughes's subsequent attempts to explicitly render the rhythms of the *son* and Afro-Cuban vernacular speech in African American vernacular.[74]

Audience Reception and the Harlem-Havana Link

In addition to the promotion and translation work of Hughes and others, audience reception was also critical to the forging of the connections between the cultural movements in Havana and Harlem. Glimpses of the process of audience reception can be seen by examining the initial reaction of Cuban readers to the poetry of Guillén and Hughes. While it is impossible to gauge how all readers interpreted their poetry, correspondence from some of their Cuban readers provides some clues. Such evidence indicates that observers responded to Hughes and Guillén as "Negro poets," or rather, as mulattoes who took up, rather than rejected, the cultures of the black masses. Thus, Cuban audiences reacted to their symbolism as much as they did to the actual content of their poetry.

The Hughes-Guillén comparison emerged almost immediately after Hughes's trip to Cuba in February and March 1930. In the weeks following his departure from the island, Guillén began to work on his *son*-poems. After he finished the verses, he gave them to Urrutia but asked him not to publish them without his permission. According to Guillén, Urrutia did just that, publishing them in his "Ideales" page on 20 April 1930, only a few weeks after Hughes's visit.[75] *Motivos de son*, as the poems were titled, propelled Guillén into the center of the Afro-Cubanist literary movement. The day after his poems were released, the Afro-Cuban poet happily wrote to Hughes that his verses had created "a real scandal" in the Havana cultural establishment.[76] Indeed, some literary critics disliked Guillén's poems about thick-lipped Negroes ("Negro Bembón") and black women lovers ("Mi Chiquita") written in Cuban vernacular. One year later, Guillén followed up his "scandalous" collection with *Sóngoro Cosongo*, in which the poet addressed critics by arguing that his "mulatto" poems represented the racially mixed essence of *cubanidad*.[77]

While much has been written about Hughes's influence on Guillén's poetry, such debates have tended to overlook the ways in which readers at the time understood the relationship between their work.[78] Although it is clear that Guillén had been writing about the *son* in his essays before Hughes's 1930 visit, there is no evidence of the music's influence on his poetry until immediately after the Blues Poet's departure. Perhaps this sudden presence of the *son* in Guillén's poetry is why, as some of his contemporaries argued, Hughes's impact on the Afro-Cuban poet was substantial. At the very least, the Hughes visit seems to have opened a space for Guillén to experiment with a new poetic form. Hughes's impact may have had less to do with the content and formal aspects of the poetry and more to do with inspiring Guillén by his example as a poet of African descent—a "*mulatico*," in the Cuban poet's words, just like himself—who was making a name for himself by popularizing a black working-class culture rejected by the black elite. A letter from Fernández de Castro to Hughes alludes to this potential influence. "I know that you like very much the '*Motivos de Son*,'" Fernández de Castro wrote Hughes shortly after they were published, "and I know also what he and Regino [Pedroso] owe to your poetry and your manner." Thus, Guillén was indebted not only to Hughes's artistic influence, but also to the Blues Poet's "manner," or the way in which he conducted himself as a public figure and, perhaps, as an Afro-descended writer. A year later, Fernández de Castro again highlighted Hughes's impact on the Afro-Cuban poet when he flattered Hughes in another letter by calling Guillén the *"Cuban Langston Hughes."*[79]

To Gustavo Urrutia, the link between Guillén's and Hughes's poetry was also quite clear. Urrutia enthusiastically informed Hughes of the success of Guillén's recently published *Motivos de son.* "I feel exceedingly happy in this moment on account of *eight formidable negro* poems written by our Guillén," Urrutia wrote. "They are real Cuban negro poetry written in the very popular slang. They are the exact equivalent of your 'blues.' The language and feelings of our dear negroes made most noble by the love and talent of our own poets."[80] Urrutia's distinction between "feelings" and "language" is instructive, referring to both the linguistic and the emotional power of Guillén's *son* poetry. Like Hughes's blues poems, the *son* poetry was something to be felt, not simply read. The assessments of Fernández de Castro and Urrutia illustrate the ways in which Cuban observers of the Harlem Renaissance and Afro-Cubanism saw them as comparable figures irrespective of the particular differences between the poetic structures of the two writers.

As Hughes learned about the critical reaction to Guillén's poems, he received similar communications from other Cuban readers of his own poetry and fiction. Lalita Zamora, the woman whose restaurant Hughes frequently visited during his trip, thanked him profusely for sending her copies of his poetry books. In a letter Zamora wrote to Hughes in English a few weeks after he left Cuba, she conveyed her admiration for the fact that Hughes's writing style effectively conveyed to "the reader the sensation and feelings of the desires, hopes, love and ambitions of our race."[81] Zamora's use of the words "sensation" and "feelings" conveys her belief that Hughes's poems authentically represented the emotions and aspirations of those of her "race" and perhaps even herself. A few months later, Zamora sent the poet another letter after reading Hughes's *Not without Laughter*, his recently published novel. She told him she was especially taken by the female characters in the story. Zamora's praise is particularly noteworthy because despite the cultural differences between herself and Hughes, she clearly felt that she understood the female characters as "types" with whom she could identify. Aunt Hager as a "good mother type" and Harriet as the "type of modern young black woman" were characters that resonated with her own understanding of black women. She seemed genuinely moved by his novel, claiming, "I do not have the words to express my joy in the great step forward that you have just provided. It is with great pride that the negro race can count on you as one of its poets and writers."[82] In a sense, Zamora's sentiments resemble Urrutia's excitement for Guillén's *Motivos de son.*

Zamora's letter is one of a few fascinating communications the Blues Poet received from Afro-Cuban women fans. While he received letters from many Cuban admirers, the most extensive and detailed that appear in his files are those from female Afro-Cuban readers. They provide us with rare glimpses of the reaction of Afro-Cuban readers to Hughes's poetry and personhood. Examining their letters as evidence of audience reception also shows that even if women of African descent tended to be excluded from Havana's intellectual circles, some still sought to engage with the writers they found appealing. These documents reveal the ways black women readers sought to penetrate the gender and class hierarchies that shaped the Blues Poet's exposure to Cuban readers. Hughes's stature as a successful black writer impressed Edelmira Linares, a barely literate reader from Marianao. In a letter she wrote to Hughes some years later, Linares informed Hughes that she learned about his life after reading his profile in *Ultra* magazine. She began her letter with an apology for her less than perfect Spanish. "It is difficult to read and write when one drops out of school in the third grade" (No es facil podel abler bien cuan se sale del colegio del tersel grado), she informed Hughes. "The way that you write and recount your life is marvelous," Linares wrote, "and the fact that you triumphed without the help of anyone" was even more impressive. The letter's imperfect Spanish did not prevent Linares from expressing her admiration for the Blues Poet in expressions of sentiment through which she sought to make a connection.[83]

Other letters from Afro-Cuban women express romantic feelings that infused their desire to connect with the attractive man from another part of the African diaspora. Some of his admirers clearly wrote with an intent to get to know the man whom Guillén described as a "*mulatico cubano*" a little better.[84] If they did not get a chance to see him in person during his stay, they certainly were able to read his poems and see the accompanying photo of him on Urrutia's "Ideales" page. A few weeks after Hughes's 1930 visit, Caruca Alvarez, a woman living in Vedado who described herself as a "romantic," wrote Urrutia in an effort to obtain the Blues Poet's address in the United States. "As one of the first admirers of his race and as a Cuban woman, I would very much like to be Langston's spiritual friend," Alvarez wrote. After informing the journalist that she was a frequent reader of his column, she admitted that she did not always adhere to the ideals espoused by "men of the pen" like Urrutia. "I read for comfort and to refine myself so as to see with clarity the brilliant ideas of yourself and those who, like you, work for the good of the Race."[85] Alvarez's comments illustrate both her admiration for "men of the pen" and her struggle to close the gap that separated them from some of their black readers.

Alvarez's embarrassment over her writing skills, however, did not stop her from sending a letter to Hughes. Urrutia passed on Hughes's address to Alvarez, who wrote to the Blues Poet a few weeks later. "I feel intense desires to know your verses in my adored fatherland," Alvarez wrote, "where we have not had the pleasure of reading them and to praise our brother of the Americas." Alvarez revealed to Hughes that the poet drew her interest with his "rebellious ideas against the color more or less white, those phrases of yours that are very personal for sure." It is not clear if Alvarez objected to Hughes's explicit identification with blackness. At the very least, her letter suggests that she found the idea of a light-skinned Afro-descended man embracing a black identification intriguing. As she did in her letter to Urrutia, Alvarez apologized for her "poorly crafted lines," possibly indicating her own working-class background. Nevertheless, she hoped that Hughes would remember "the dreams of a young woman who lives a life that is distinct from your ideas because they are little understood." Here we see Alvarez once again grappling with her inability to comprehend Hughes's racial assertiveness and perhaps the black vernacular language of Hughes's poems that could not be adequately conveyed in translation. And yet these class and cultural obstacles did not foreclose her attempt to forge a connection with the Blues Poet.[86]

A more aggressive series of communications came from Fara Crespo, another one of the Blues Poet's female "admirers" who hoped to be his "friend." A few weeks after Hughes's departure from the island, the determined Crespo tracked down Hughes by writing to Walter White, the secretary of the NAACP, for the Blues Poet's address. From her Puerta Cerrada apartment in Havana's famous black barrio of Jesús María, Crespo wrote Hughes to express her admiration for the "poet of the 'spirituals,'" as she called him, and to make a request. "I, a young Cuban woman admirer of one who is brave enough to exclaim: I want to be truly black, would like to be able to call myself the friend of the poet Langston Hughes!" Here, Crespo recited the aspirations Hughes had expressed in his interview with Guillén: "I want to be truly black." Like Alvarez, Crespo was drawn to Hughes's explicit identification with blackness. Yet, her attraction ran deeper. While acknowledging the boldness of her explicit request to ask for the "friendship of a man," she felt confident that Hughes would not be turned off because he "belong[ed] to this modern era free of all forms of prejudice and marked by material, intellectual, and moral freedom." Indeed, Crespo fashioned herself as a woman of the modern era. "When you arrived in Havana you attracted my attention," Crespo wrote, "because you were what I had been looking for and for this reason I write you with the hope of having [you] as a true friend."[87]

A few months later, Crespo received a response from Hughes, but it was not the one she was anticipating. While a copy of his letter does not appear in his papers, Crespo's response suggests Hughes sought to forestall Crespo's advances by claiming that he was unable to carry out a correspondence in Spanish. Crespo would have none of it, informing him that she understood enough English and reminding him that he himself admitted that he had a facility with Spanish. To prove her point, Crespo sprinkled her letter with a few phrases in the Blues Poet's native language. She assured him that it was "good enough for you to write me in English, because *I will comprehend*" (basta que me escriba en inglés, que yo *I will comprehend*). Crespo, who described herself in another letter as "a young woman teacher who is something of a romantic, but *very worthy*" (una señorita maestra algo romántica . . . pero *very worthy*), flirtatiously asked Hughes once again if he "want[ed] to be a friend of this young Cuban woman who has *interested* [sic] *for you?*"[88]

The Blues Poet apparently did not. Two months later, Crespo fired off another letter in frustration, wondering why Hughes had not responded to her advances. Dismayed and puzzled, Crespo feared that her third letter would wind up going, as the ones before, "to the basket of papers," she wrote in English. Hughes's admirer understood that "writers have odditys [sic] that the general population calls caprice." However, she informed Hughes that one of her own oddities "is the ability to bother you every month with a letter that offers my friendship to you." She warned Hughes that she was "a woman that when something is presented to me, I get it, and I have not failed yet!" Convinced that Hughes was actively ignoring her, she envisioned the Blues Poet smiling as he read her letter, believing that she had "found [her] Waterloo." Hughes's fan informed him that she was smiling as well, but then she angrily wrote that he "should thank God that there are many miles of water between you and I." Frustrated by Hughes's disregard for her, she still hoped that the poet would send her two autographed copies of his books.[89]

The letters from Alvarez and Crespo convey the complex motivations at work among those who expressed their admiration for the Blues Poet, including the desire to know a celebrity, romantic attraction, and intellectual curiosity. They also reveal how black women admirers of Hughes in Cuba sought to navigate cultural differences by relying on expressions of desire infused with a romantic attraction. His decision to ignore their letters could be attributed to a number of factors: his sense of propriety, his distraction due to the collapse of his relationship with his patron at the time, or his well-known tendency to dissemble about his own sexual proclivities, which is also made clear in his account of the Havana rumba party in *I Wonder as I Wander*.[90] Rather than dismiss these letters as little more than expressions of romantic interest, I suggest that they reveal the yearnings embedded in Afro-diasporic interaction—desires that ranged from Hughes's wish to be "truly black," to Crespo's yearnings to be "the friend of Langston Hughes." Crespo's and Alvarez's apparent inability to understand the intricacies of Hughes's poems did not matter to these women who, like many of his Cuban fans, sought to connect with the famous Blues Poet because they were attracted to his physical and symbolic personage as a "colored" man of letters from the United States. Perhaps most important, Crespo's and Alvarez's letters illustrate how black Cuban women could use the epistolary form to engage with the writers of the Harlem and Havana movements as agents, rather than as mere objects, of desire during this era.

Hughes's male collaborators, unlike his female fans, were more successful in maintaining a relationship with the Blues Poet after his departure from Cuba. These relationships deepened the connections between the cultural movements in Harlem and Havana. Perhaps the most important aspect of the linkages created by the Hughes connection to Cuba was the way in which it accelerated intellectual and artistic interchange between Harlem and Havana. In the early 1930s, Hughes, Urrutia, Guillén and Fernández de Castro kept the mail routes between New York and Havana busy. Hughes sent copies of his poetry to Urrutia and the Club Atenas, while Urrutia regularly sent him copies of his "Ideales" page. A few weeks after Hughes's 1930 visit, Urrutia wrote to the poet to thank him for sending him a number of books on African American life and culture. Urrutia was grateful to receive a wide range of academic and literary texts, including Hughes's *Weary Blues*, Walter White's *Rope and Faggot*, Victor Calverton's *Anthology of American Negro Literature*, Scott Nearing's *Black America*, Melville Herskovits's *American Negro*, and Alain Locke's *New Negro*. Urrutia was particularly captivated by Hughes's *Weary Blues*, which he reported to the latter that he almost knew by heart, as well as Locke's *New Negro*. Of Locke's text, he wrote: "This splendid book has made a deep inpression [*sic*] on my mind. I am unable to drop this book—it is so interesting in every aspect. You have given me a great help by supplying this series of books so enlightening on the American Negro. I have much to learn out of them."[91]

Urrutia's letters to Hughes illustrate the impact of the extensive traffic of literature between Harlem and Havana. The encounter with Hughes clearly invigorated Urrutia, who would go on to write extensively about the New Negro movement in the United States and its relevance to the conditions facing Afro-Cubans during the 1930s. This is not to suggest that Afro-Cuban literature and prose were simply derivatives of African American cultural production. Yet, it is to underscore the ways cultural production was the product of cross-fertilization through the linkages facilitated by promoters of the Harlem-Havana nexus.

Good Night, Blues and *Son*;
Good Morning, Revolution

The success of Hughes's 1930 trip to Cuba undoubtedly shaped his decision to return to the island the following year. In April 1931, he used the money he won from a Harmon Foundation award to go to Cuba and Haiti with his friend Zell Ingram, an artist from Cleveland, Ohio. Hughes sought to escape the heartache from the painful end of his relationship with his patron Charlotte Mason and his nasty dispute with Zora Neale Hurston over the authorship rights to *Mule Bone*. However, this time Hughes was not looking for an artistic collaborator but instead was "in search of sun." Upon his arrival in Havana with Ingram, he once again received a hero's welcome, drinking and dining with prominent Cuban intellectuals and artists. Hughes himself was struck by the warm reception he received from his Cuban admirers, remarking to Carl Van Vechten that he was "surprised at the amount of publicity our visit got—reporters and flashlights at the pier, with pictures and a front page story the next morning."[92]

But the Cuba Hughes returned to with Ingram in 1931 was in a bleaker state than it had been the previous year. During his time away from the island, conditions had continued to deteriorate. The ramifications of the 1929 economic depression were more evident as the sugar industry, the mainstay of the Cuban economy, was grinding to a halt due to collapsing sugar prices and U.S. protectionist tariffs. As a result, unemployment skyrocketed. On the political front, the Machado regime's repressiveness intensified. The president who had fraudulently engineered his own reelection three years earlier was showing his increasing intolerance for political dissent. A year of arrests, forced exiles, and assassinations culminated in a failed but violent uprising against his regime later that year.[93] Guillén conveyed the impact of the crisis to Hughes in a letter he wrote later that year in which he explained that Cuba "was a little dead," due to the "bad economic situation that the country is going through." For this reason, "there is no work, and therefore no money," he informed Hughes.[94] The crisis even darkened the mood of the normally ebullient Fernández de Castro, who had grown frustrated by the state of affairs on the island, informing Hughes that he planned to be "leaving this damn country as soon as I can."[95] Cuba's economic and political crisis began to change the character of the Harlem-Havana connection from one that celebrated the art and literature of the New Negro to a politicized transnational struggle against imperialism and racism.

If Cubans acutely experienced the catastrophes unleashed by the Great Depression, so too did people of African descent in the United States. The Depression devastated black communities in all parts of the country, north and south, and brought an end to the Negro vogue in Harlem.[96] Perhaps no one event symbolized the political and economic oppression of African Americans in the early 1930s more than the Scottsboro Case. On 25 March 1931, right before Hughes and Ingram left for Cuba, nine young black men were pulled off a train and arrested for allegedly raping a white woman in a small town in Alabama. What began as yet another routine episode of injustice by the Jim Crow racist machinery spiraled into a case that produced a massive international solidarity campaign to free the accused, propelled by the International Labor Defense's support for the young men. Scottsboro had a tremendous impact on African American intellectuals and clearly contributed to Hughes's political radicalization. After his return from Cuba and Haiti, he produced a number of poems and a one-act play (*Scottsboro, Limited*) inspired by the case.[97]

Scottsboro helped promote the emergence of a new, radicalized Afro-diasporic intelligentsia, not just in the United States, but also in Cuba and other parts of the Caribbean. It became one of a number of transnational reference points for a new cross-racial, antidiscrimination movement sparked by Afro-Cuban and white progressive activists. Throughout the 1930s, communist organizers launched protests throughout the island in support of the incarcerated young men in front of U.S. consular offices. In this way, the Scottsboro campaign merged with developing currents of anti-imperialism in Cuba that even had some influence among the Afro-Cuban elite. In the summer of 1931, the Club Atenas sent a telegram to the governor of Alabama characterizing the incarceration of the young men as an example of "racial prejudice and capitalist cruelty."[98] Thus, the Scottsboro episode marked an important shift in Afro-Cuban and African American interaction from the celebrating of Afro-diasporic cultures to a new set of politicized linkages between their parallel struggles against racism.

Regino Pedroso exemplifies this newly emerging politicized solidarity between Afro-Cubans and African Americans. Before the early 1930s, the Afro-Chinese-Cuban poet was already developing his own poetic voice, catalyzed more by his leftist political orientation and his Chinese heritage than a desire to turn black popular culture into poetry like Guillén. However, like Guillén's, Pedroso's poetry took on a more anti-imperialist tone in this period. Furthermore, like Guillén and other radicalized Caribbean poets such as Jacques Roumain, he seems to have been inspired in part by Hughes's example. Indeed, he was frequently at Hughes's side during the Blues Poet's 1931 visit to Havana. It seems likely that the celebration of Hughes in Havana facilitated his explicit embrace of blackness in his poetry. Like other poets and artists galvanized by the Great Depression and the growth of the global communist movement, Pedroso developed a transnational anti-imperialist perspective against racial and class exploitation. Such a vision was vividly articulated in "Hermano Negro" (Negro Brother), his 1934 poem that signaled the call for an Afro-diasporic movement against imperialism. Pedroso's poem shunned the primitivist celebration of black cultures and instead posited the notion that the ties that bound black communities together were not the Lindy Hop, the *son*, and the rumba, but rather the struggle against global racism. Like so many other Afro-Cuban intellectuals had before, Pedroso highlighted the relevance of the African American struggle to those of Afro-Cubans. As the closing stanza of the poem makes clear:

Negro, hermano negro
más hermano en el ansia que en la raza
Negro en Haiti, negro en Jamaica, negro en New York,
negro en La Habana—dolor que en
vitrinas negras vende la explotación,
escucha allá en Scottsboro, en Scottsboro, en Scottsboro
Da al mundo con tu angustia rebelde
tu humana voz
y apaga un poco tus maracas!

[Negro, negro brother
more brother in yearning than in race
Negro in Haiti, Negro in Jamaica, Negro in New York

Negro in Havana
Pain that sells exploitation in black shop windows
Listen there in Scottsboro, in Scottsboro, in Scottsboro
Give your rebellious cry to the world
Your human voice
And tone down your maracas a little!][99]

If Pedroso's poetry highlights the ways Afro-Cuban intellectuals were galvanized by the struggle against racism in the United States, Hughes exemplifies the ways Cuba radicalized African American activists in this period. His 1931 trip to the island gave him a heightened political awareness that allowed him to link his understanding of racism in the United States to racialized imperialism in the Caribbean. As his biographer makes clear, the end of his relationship with his white patron facilitated this political transformation. Yet it is also apparent that his perceptions of U.S. imperialism first in Cuba, then in Haiti, where he encountered the U.S. occupation directly, catalyzed his eventual embrace of communism in the early 1930s. As we shall see in the next chapter, his heightened anti-imperialist consciousness stemmed from both his encounters with racism in the U.S.-dominated tourist sector in Cuba and his exposure to Gerardo Machado's repressive regime during his 1931 trip to the island. During an evening spent at the home of Addison Durland, the Cuban American who would be an important figure in Hollywood's crafting of "Good Neighbor" films ten years later, Hughes got a taste of the increasing persecution of Cuban intellectuals by the *machadista* government when he noted that Fernández de Castro's brother Miguel hid for "2 months in [Durland's] house when the police wanted to arrest all the professors of the University as revolutionaries." On the same page of his journal, Hughes noted that even Cuban musicians were subject to the state's repressive policing, remarking that the police had driven off "a band of *soneros*."[100]

Indeed, Hughes's awareness of political repression in Cuba inspired "Little Old Spy," the short story centered on the theme of *machadista* surveillance. His poem "Ode to the Little Fort of San Lázaro," published in *New Masses* in May 1931, even more vividly highlights Hughes's emerging awareness of U.S. imperialism in the Caribbean—a theme he would pick up again in "People without Shoes," a critique of the U.S. occupation of Haiti. In this poem, Hughes, like many American tourist guides, evokes the region's history of piracy. Rather than use the buccaneer theme to construct a quaint history of the island, he links the old pirates to the new ones in Washington and Wall Street:

Watch tower once for pirates
That sailed the sun-bright seas—
Red pirates, great romantics.
    DRAKE
    DE PLAN
    EL GRILLO
Against such as these
Years and years ago
You served quite well—
When time and ships were slow.
    But now,
Against a pirate called
THE NATIONAL CITY BANK
What can you do alone?
Would it not be
Just as well you tumbled down
Stone by helpless stone?[101]

Hughes's 1931 poems about Cuba illustrate the beginning of his transition from Blues Poet to Revolutionary Bard before he began to write his Scottsboro-themed play and poems. "Ode to the Little Fort of San Lázaro" highlights the shift that eventually led him to embrace the communist vision of revolution that emerged most forcefully in the subsequent poems "Good Morning, Revolution" and "Goodbye Christ." Moreover, Hughes's personal transformation illuminates a broader African American political transformation vis-à-vis the rest of the African diaspora. Left-wing, black, communist, and more moderate organizations such as the NAACP would continually critique the U.S. presence in Cuba and the Caribbean throughout the decade and beyond. As Hughes and his Afro-Cuban colleagues waved good-bye to the blues and *son*, a new set of politicized relationships that drew upon the networks they themselves had created would transform the character of Afro-Cuban and African American diasporic linkages.

Conclusion

The promoters and audiences of the black cultural movements in Harlem and Havana played pivotal roles in the making of Afro-diasporic linkages in this period. Even while these interactions were marked by primitivist fascinations and black elite respectability discourses, they undeniably valued and popularized previously denigrated cultural forms such as the blues, jazz, rumba, and *son* in the United States and Cuba. Despite differences in content and form in African American blues and jazz versus Afro-Cuban rumba and *son*, promoters and audiences often constructed these works and the artists who produced them as integral parts of a larger cultural movement in the "darker world." Both Fernández de Castro's claim that Guillén was the "Cuban Langston Hughes" and Urrutia's assertion that his *son*-poems were the "exact equivalent" of the blues reveal how this diasporic "darker world" was forged through an emphasis on a shared black aesthetic produced by these two mulatto writers, regardless of their different artistic styles and forms. Moreover, the responses of Afro-Cuban women admirers of Hughes illustrate how feelings of desire (even if only propelled and romanticized by Hughes's celebrity status) animated diasporic connections within the Harlem-Havana nexus. Thus, an attention to the complex dynamics of promotion and reception, and not simply a focus on the differences in content and form within artistic products, enriches our understanding of the historical significance of these movements.

As the interactions among promoters, artists, and their audiences show, the black cultural movements in Harlem and Havana and the transnational networks that brought them together altered the relationships between Afro-Cubans and African Americans. This is clear in the popularization of Afro-Cuban culture in the United States less than a decade after Hughes's travels to Havana. The creation of Afro-Cuban or "Latin Jazz" by Frank Grillo ("Machito"), Mario Bauzá, Dizzy Gillespie, and Chano Pozo during the 1940s illustrates the merging of Afro-Cuban rhythms into African American musical forms. Indeed, Gillespie was prompted to collaborate with Pozo because of his mastery of African polyrhythms, leading the trumpeter to conclude that Pozo was "really African."[102] Rather than shun the "African" elements of their cultures, Afro-Cuban and African American artists, writers, and musicians valorized them, thereby challenging the precepts of racial uplift ideology that had previously informed Afro-diasporic linkages. Because of their perceived closer proximity to African culture, Afro-Cubans could occupy a new place of importance in the African diaspora. The altering of hierarchical understandings of African American and Afro-Cuban culture that were first evident in the late 1920s and early 1930s came to full fruition after the triumph of the Cuban Revolution in the 1960s. African American poets such as Jayne Cortez often celebrated "the heartbeat and songbeat of Africa" in Cuba, as a passage from Cortez's 1982 poetic tribute to Chano Pozo reveals:

Oye
I'm in the presence of ancestor
                    Chano Pozo
Chano connector of two worlds
You go and celebrate again with
the *compañeros* in Santiago
                    and tell us about it
You go to the spirit house of Antonio Maceo
and tell us about it
you go to Angola
and tell us about it
you go to Calabar
and tell us about it
you go see the slave castles
you go see the massacres
you go see the afflictions
you go see the battlefields
you go see the warriors
you go as a healer
you go conjurate
you go mediate
you go to the cemetery of drums
return and tell us about it.[103]

If the Great Depression did not completely curtail Afro-Cuban and African American diasporic practices, it did transform their scope and character.
At the same time that Hughes, Schomburg, Urrutia, and Fernández de Castro were promoting the works of their colleagues, another set of relationships
developed between African American and Afro-Cuban activist organizations
that were linked to, but expanded beyond, the networks that propelled the
Harlem-Havana cultural nexus. Within the context of unprecedented labor
activism and a burgeoning critique of U.S. imperialism in the Caribbean, the
Scottsboro campaign and the overthrow of the Machado dictatorship in Cuba
in 1933 helped stimulate the emergence of new movements against racial discrimination in both countries. One of those arenas of contestation focused on
an activity that Afro-Cubans and African Americans increasingly perceived as
a fundamental right—the ability to travel.

CHAPTER FOUR

Destination without Humiliation

Black Travel within the Routes of Discrimination

Go to the Black Countries
Cuba—Haiti—West Indies, Brazil, Africa
Rates and means
No passports to C[uba] & H[aiti]
Hotels
South by car
Spanish and French at your very door
Cultural and racial advantages
Invaluable contacts—to see one[']s own people in banks, shops, fine clubs,
*   high positions. Negro artists—exchange of ideas, musicians and painters,*
*   new rhythms, new colors and faces. Poets and writers new background and*
*   basis for comparisons. A paradise for a Kodak camera . . . strange dark*
*   beauties, and interesting (unknown) contacts in a world of color.*
Beer, wines, and liquors. Tropical fruits you've never heard of before.
—Langston Hughes, 1931

Langston Hughes issued the call to "go to the black countries" from the diary of his 1931 trip to Cuba. His entry highlights the desire of many African Americans to travel to see their "own people" abroad. It documents an emerging African American tourism in the early 1930s, one geared toward developing "invaluable contacts" and an "exchange of ideas," not to mention the pleasures of "new rhythms" and "beer, wines, and liquors." Cuba and Haiti were particularly appealing to black travelers since they did not require passports or visas for entry, due to their incorporation into the U.S. imperial order in the region. Moreover, the islands' geographic proximity made them close enough to be within easy reach by boat from south Florida. Traveling to Cuba and Haiti could provide educational opportunities for African American travelers while affirming the potentialities of African descendants in Cuba and the United States.

A central concern of Afro-Cuban and African American institutions from the early 1930s until the dawn of the Cuban Revolution and the civil rights movement in the 1950s was equal access to opportunities for travel. This chapter considers the importance of travel in the making of Afro-diasporic linkages in the mid-twentieth century. In this period, leisure travel was transformed from an exclusively elite activity to one that became more widely available to the expanding middle class. One ramification of the expansion and transformation of passenger travel service from steamships and railways to buses and airplanes in this period was an increase in the opportunities for Afro-Cubans and African Americans to interact. At the same time, black travel had to contend with persistent transnational structures of racialization that pervaded every corner of the transportation industry from Havana through the Jim Crow South to the northeastern United States. Instances of racial discrimination against black travelers helped propel the growth of civil rights activism in both countries, not only against the transit companies and state legislatures of the South, but also against the steamship lines that operated between Cuba and the United States. Yet Afro-Cuban and African American travelers did not wait for the abolition of racial discrimination to take their excursions. The de jure and de facto racial segregation of leisure and recreation in both countries created opportunities for black entrepreneurs to assemble a tourist network that relied upon segregated institutions and businesses that catered to African American travelers. Thus, what follows is not simply a tale of black bodies experiencing discrimination but a continuation of the theme of diaspora-making as a form of adaptation; of Afro-descended elites developing their own transnational strategies to counter persistent forms of racial exclusion within the imperial structures that governed travel and leisure between Cuba and the United States in this period.

Travel, like migration, has been central to the Afro-diasporic experience. From Olaudah Equiano to Mary Prince to Langston Hughes and beyond, the writings of black travelers have illuminated the complexities of Afro-diasporic identifications. This chapter analyzes the actual making of black tourist networks, rather than the texts of black travel narratives, as evidence of diaspora-making. From the interwar period until the early years of the Cold War, African American and Afro-Cuban institutions and entrepreneurs attempted to accommodate an expanding number of black travelers. In this period, the class of black travelers expanded beyond the category of the cosmopolitan itinerant intellectual. An increasing number of African American professionals and leaders of prominent black associations began to view themselves as "tourists" eager to visit other parts of the world, particularly countries with significant Afro-descended populations. The growth of tourism allowed more African descendants to see their "own people" in the flesh more frequently. The proliferation of different modes of transit between the two countries, along with Cuba's popularity as a North American tourist site, accelerated Afro-Cuban and African American encounters. By the late 1940s and early 1950s, increasing numbers of elite Afro-Cubans joined their African American fellow travelers on the black tourist network. Thus, the black excursions of the mid-twentieth century made tourism an inextricable part of diaspora-making long before the emergence of contemporary forms of "heritage tourism."[1]

An examination of black tourist networks reveals the struggles of African Americans for equal access to travel in the Jim Crow and post–World War II periods. Cuba's geographic proximity, attractive climate, and significant Afro-descended population presented an appealing option for African American travelers with means to travel. Taking an excursion to Cuba could also present the possibility of evading the Jim Crow transit system. Like African American baseball players who sought to play in Latin America and the Caribbean in order to escape the specter of Jim Crow, African American travelers viewed excursions to Cuba as a way to avoid the humiliation of racial segregation.[2] However, African American travelers found that they could not avoid the color line while journeying to Cuba. African Americans encountered difficulties when they tried to travel abroad by steamship as well. Racial segregation overseas could be in some ways even more invidious, because it was often enacted in an unpredictable manner. Black travelers might enjoy first-class accommodations on one trip and suffer discrimination on the next. Once they arrived in Cuba, they had to navigate the racially exclusionary practices of the U.S.-dominated tourist sector on the island. African Americans were often refused accommodations at hotels and were almost always prevented from entering Cuba's beaches. The right to travel to Cuba and other "black countries" abroad without the threat of mistreatment became an important civil rights issue for African American activist organizations such as the NAACP. Highlighting the struggles of African Americans travelers in Cuba against racial discrimination gives another perspective on a story that is often told from a U.S.-centered narrative of the civil rights era.

The history of tourist networks created by Afro-Cubans and African Americans also complicates our understanding of the history of tourism in

Cuba, a story that is dominated by the image of the island as a playground for white Americans. The disruption of transatlantic transit in World War I and then the onset of Prohibition made Cuba an increasingly popular destination for Americans. "So near and yet so foreign," as one tourist advertisement proclaimed, Cuba presented all of the benefits of exoticism, while also being familiar enough to make white Americans comfortable.[3] Yet the image of white American tourists going to Cuba for sun and fun overlooks the wide array of travelers to Cuba during the republican era. African American travelers also found Cuba attractive for some of the same reasons as their white counterparts: the island's agreeable climate, beaches, and "exotic" culture. African American travelers could also be seduced by the exoticism promoted by the tourist industry; however, they also found Cuba attractive because of its large population of African descent. Unlike white tourists who went to Cuba to experience a culture that they perceived to be fundamentally different than their own, African Americans traveled to the island to see their "own people" even as their understanding of Afro-Cubans was sometimes shaped by touristic gazes. As we saw in the previous chapter, Langston Hughes was drawn to Cuba partly because he viewed it as a place where African cultural survivals flourished. Indeed, the desire to study African-derived populations prompted a number of black scholars to conduct research in Cuba in this period. Others went to the island to see Cuban Negroes in high positions, including Fulgencio Batista, who was described by many African American journalists as a "Negro leader." Hence, African American travel to Cuba highlights the larger phenomenon of cultural tourism that emerged in the 1930s and 1940s in which black travelers sought to harmonize their desires for leisure with motives for cultural exchange.

But Cuba's tourist history need not be reduced to the activities of foreign travelers on the island. The emphasis on foreign travel to Cuba overshadows the fact that Cubans themselves were also traveling more frequently in this period. The opening of the much-ballyhooed Central Highway in 1929 and the advent of bus transit in the 1930s and 1940s enabled Cubans not only to migrate in search of better job opportunities, but also to visit families as well as the island's numerous recreational sites. Afro-Cubans embarked on excursions, visiting different Afro-Cuban communities in other parts of the island and going to the few available beaches for persons of African descent. Throughout the republican era, they continually pressed the government to grant them greater access to beaches. Moreover, in the late 1940s and early 1950s, they also traveled to the United States to visit relatives and sister Afro-Cuban and African American associations and cultural institutions. These "social and cultural excursions" strengthened diasporic connections between Afro-Cuban and African American cultural and educational institutions.

The emergence of tourism in this period was directly tied to the technological innovations in the international transportation industry. During the 1910s and 1920s, the number of steamship companies that operated between Cuba and the United States rapidly multiplied. At the turn of the twentieth century, most travel between the island and the U.S. mainland was dominated by the New York and Cuba Mail Steamship Company, also known as the "Ward Line." By 1931, the Ward Line was joined by the Vacarro Line, the United Fruit Company, the P. O. Steamship Company, and the Panama Pacific Line, among others. United Fruit's "Great White Fleet" expanded from a crew of 44 ships that transported 350 passengers to a fleet of 90 ships that carried 2,500 passengers.[4] Railways funneled travelers on their way to Cuba to Miami, Key West, New Orleans, and other southern ports where they boarded steamships to the island. The advent of air passenger service during the 1940s and 1950s further accelerated tourism to Cuba. As was the case with U.S. railway companies in the nineteenth century, U.S. American air transit companies made Cuba the place where they launched their international operations. In 1927, Pan-American Airways launched its first flight between Key West and Havana. As Pan-Am expanded in subsequent years, the company made Cuba a hub of its Latin American operations.[5]

The impact of the rise of tourism on African American organizations became evident at the end of the 1920s. In 1929, Marcus Garvey added a tourist component to his long-standing black capitalist project. His editorial in the 5 January 1929 issue of the *Negro World* declared: "American Negroes Must Travel." Part of his call to attend the UNIA's 1929 convention held in Jamaica attempted to entice African Americans to "spend their holiday in the tropics." Garvey promised his readers that "trips around the island will be arranged for all visitors so that they may see the beautiful tropics." Thus the convention would "be a wonderful chance for the Negroes of America to see the beautiful tropics and enter into closer relationship with the people."[6] African American businesses were thinking along the same lines by promoting the few available public accommodations for black travelers in the United States. Signs of an emerging black tourism in the United States can be found in the early 1930s, when a number of companies published tour guides for black travelers. One such guide was the *Hackley and Harrison's Hotel and Apartment Guide for Colored Travelers*. The Philadelphia-based company's guide advertised "board, rooms, and garage accommodations" in over three hundred cities in the United States and Canada. That same year, another tourist company advertised the benefits of automobile travel to "Negro travelers," enabling them to evade the humiliating experiences of Jim Crow railway cars.[7]

The emerging activism over the right to travel by African descendants in Cuba and the United States took shape in an age of heightened mobilization throughout the diaspora. The international Scottsboro campaign, the emerging anticolonial movement in Africa and Europe that coalesced around the Italian invasion of Ethiopia, and the explosion of militant labor uprisings in the Caribbean helped set in motion more aggressive challenges to ongoing practices of racial exclusion.[8] While black radical organizations were undeniably central to the forging of Afro-diasporic relationships in this period, the supposedly more "conservative" Afro-Cuban and African American associations also actively pursued Afro-diasporic connections. In the United States, elite organizations, such as the NAACP and the Associated Negro Press (ANP), and educational institutions, such as Howard University and Bethune-Cookman College, joined with Afro-Cuban societies in Havana, like the Club Atenas and the Unión Fraternal, to be the driving forces of these networks. African American and Afro-Cuban entrepreneurs schooled in the tenets of Booker T. Washington's gospel of black business also played decisive roles in the creation of black tourist exchanges. It was also in this period that black women's groups, including the National Council for Negro Women (NCNW) and the Asociación Cultural Femenina (Women's Cultural Association) formed their own linkages in an effort to highlight what they saw as the common interests of "Negro women" in Cuba and the United States. The participation of these self-styled elite organizations illustrates that diasporic relations were on the agenda of black associations across the political and social spectrum in this period. In fact, the creation of these vibrant exchanges between Afro-Cubans and African Americans was kick-started by a series of incidents against "reputable" African American travelers who visited Cuba in 1930.

The Perils of "Colored Travelers"

William Pickens was angry. On 27 August 1930, while en route to Havana on the maiden voyage of the *Morro Castle*, the Ward Line's new steamer, the field secretary of the NAACP fired off an angry letter of protest to Henry Stimson, the U.S. secretary of state. "There is a policy," Pickens fumed, "inspired and supported from some source to harass, hinder and discourage Negro citizens of the United States, when they seek to exercise their privilege of coming to the republic of Cuba, even as tourists for a week or a month seeking education and knowledge, or on business or pleasure."[9] In his letter, Pickens referred to a number of cases where African American travelers experienced humiliating treatment from Cuban and U.S. immigration officials and representatives of the steamship companies. Pickens's protest was an early manifestation of the NAACP's attempt to combat racial discrimination in the transportation industry. His skillful usage of the language of citizenship to force government action was a strategy that would be employed continuously by the NAACP and other civil rights organizations in subsequent decades. Such efforts focused not only on segregated transit in the southern United States but also on racial exclusionary practices of steamship companies and foreign governments.[10]

The NAACP field secretary was not exaggerating. In 1930 alone, several incidents occurred where African American travelers were discouraged from traveling to Cuba. Langston Hughes's experience was the first case of discrimination reported to the NAACP. As he prepared to depart for Cuba from New York in February 1930, he found steamship liners unwilling to sell him a ticket. The companies claimed that they could not sell him a ticket because the Cuban government banned "Chinese, Negroes, and Russians" from entering the country. When Hughes inquired about these restrictions at the Cuban consulate in New York, he was coolly told that they knew "nothing about this" while reminding the poet that the Cuban government "has the right to keep out whom they will."[11] After he was unable to buy a ticket from the Ward Line, United Fruit, and the Pacific Line, he took his concerns to his friend Walter White, chief secretary of the NAACP, who quickly fired off letters demanding an explanation from the U.S. State Department, the steamship companies, and the Cuban government. Eventually, Hughes was able to use his patron's money to buy a first-class ticket on the Cunard Line's *Caronia*. Meanwhile, Miguel Campa, the Cuban undersecretary of state, informed White that "no government ruling exists denying entry of aliens under race or nationality. Prohibition only deals against Chinese laborers enacted twenty-eight years ago—of course passengers not complying with immigration provisions will not be allowed to land."[12]

While the Cuban and U.S. governments denied responsibility for the supposed restrictions against black travelers, the Ward Line tried to provide White and Hughes with an explanation. William C. Campbell, the company's general passenger agent, insisted to Hughes that during the fifty years it had run ships to Cuba, the line had "never refused transportation to members of your race and have always extended all courtesies and taken necessary steps to protect their interests and feelings while guests on our steamers."[13] Nevertheless, Campbell felt that the line was compelled to comply with the Cuban government's new stipulation that "negroes, American citizens or otherwise, would not be allowed in Cuba." Campbell's claim that the Cuban government was responsible for the ban on black travelers seems plausible. As we have seen in the government's suppression of the UNIA and its decision to bar Marcus Garvey from entering Cuba in 1930, the increasingly authoritarian regime of Gerardo Machado was nervous about potential trouble from "Negroes." Still, Campbell assured Hughes and White that Cuban immigration officials had informed him that "members of the colored race of the prominent class, or reputable standing, coming to Cuba as tourists, would be admitted, but would be excluded the same as other races if they attempted to enter Cuba because of contract to perform labor." Campbell's assurance reveals the anti-immigrant backlash against Afro-Caribbean migrant workers in Cuba during this period. As the Great Depression crippled the Cuban economy, black migrants were targets of racist scapegoating that blamed them for the island's ills. In the early 1930s, the Cuban state deported thousands of West Indian and Haitian migrants who worked for U.S. sugar mills on the island. Still, as Campbell maintained, since Hughes and "reputable" members of the "colored race" were not going to Cuba for labor, they would not have to be concerned about the effects of the government crackdown on black immigrant labor.[14]

Campbell's prediction turned out to be wrong. Later that summer African American travelers "of the prominent class" continued to encounter troubles when they tried to visit Cuba. Sue Bailey, then national secretary of the YWCA, was detained by Cuban immigration authorities when she tried to visit the country. She was able to gain entry only after the intervention of local YWCA members.[15] Shortly thereafter, Mary McLeod Bethune, founder and president of Bethune-Cookman College in Daytona Beach, Florida, along with fellow educator Ronald P. Sims, president of Bluefield Institute in West Virginia, were unable to purchase tickets in Miami to board a ship bound for Havana. After obtaining passage from Key West, they received a hostile reception from Cuban immigration authorities upon their arrival in Havana, who detained Bethune while allowing the lighter-skinned Sims and his daughter to pass into the city. After a lengthy argument with Cuban and U.S. officials, who blamed each other's government for the policy against black travelers, they were eventually allowed to pass, but not before they were forced to forfeit their return tickets until their date of return to the United States. Bethune pointed out that while they were held up by Cuban officials, "scores of white men and women were passed in who had second and third class tickets."[16] A few days later, Pickens himself was spared the same treatment by Cuban immigration authorities at the pier because of the intervention of the Club Atenas, "which had forestalled the reenactment of the horror by applying directly to the Cuban Commissioner of Immigration, and then dispatching to the pier several of its own agents, among them Señor Belisario He[u]reaux," who Pickens pointed out was the "son of a former president of Santo Domingo."[17]

The NAACP field secretary's letter of protest to Secretary of State Stimson picked up where Walter White's efforts left off earlier that year. Pickens viewed these incidents of discrimination as an opportunity for the NAACP to publicize the concerns of African American travelers. He encouraged Bethune, Sims, Bailey, and other African Americans who were subject to the abuses of the steamship companies and Cuban authorities to make their stories public. "We have them on the defensive and might as well give it to them good and heavy," Pickens wrote to Bailey. In his letter to Sims, he expressed his desire to "pile up the evidence against them for future use."[18] Like White earlier in the year, Pickens worked with Gustavo Urrutia to publicize his protest in Cuba through the *Diario de la Marina*. Urrutia published Pickens's letter on his "Ideales de una Raza" page. Urrutia published the NAACP field secretary's letter to Stimson in Spanish. Within the context of other episodes of racial discrimination on the island at the moment, Urrutia viewed the cases of mistreatment of African American travelers as an opportunity to force the Cuban government to respond to the accusations and to address already existing practices of racial discrimination on the island.[19]

Predictably, both the Cuban and the U.S. governments disputed Pickens's protest. E. Francis White, acting secretary of state, curtly informed the NAACP "that the United States Government has in no way initiated or supported any policy of discrimination against Negro citizens of the United States."[20] Cuban officials, determined to maintain the image of Cuba as a raceless society, issued a number of denials in the Cuban press. Pedro Cartaya, the undersecretary of immigration, declared Pickens's accusations "false" in an article titled "Tourists of Color Are Well Treated." "All tourists have been treated equally," Cartaya insisted. The government's primary concern was to "avoid the importation of foreign *braceros* [sugar workers], the element most capable of competing with native workers."[21] Pickens and other African American travelers learned that the racialized structures that bound the United States and Cuba together did not distinguish between "reputable" and working-class Negroes. Cuba's national ideology, following José Martí's motto of "Cuba with all and for all," coexisted with ongoing practices of racial discrimination against people of African descent regardless of their class and national backgrounds. The onset of an economic and political crisis intensified the Machado regime's effort to police the movements of Afro-descended peoples on the island.

Although Pickens's attempts to pin down the roots of the racial discrimination in the transnational transit industry failed to produce concrete results, the publicizing of the discrimination cases that accompanied his trip generated greater interchange between the NAACP and Afro-Cuban associations. His decision to visit Cuba was prompted by his friend Margaret Ross Martin and her husband James Walter Martin, an African American couple who resided in Cuba at the time. The Alabama-born Margaret had met Pickens while he was on a lecturing tour in her home state in 1907. Before her arrival on the island, she followed the limited paths available to aspiring black women, studying stenography, typing, and nursing. After relocating to New York, where she worked at the 135th Street YMCA, she married James and relocated with him to Cuba.[22] By 1930, the Martins had been living in Cuba for five years. James managed to secure a job in Havana with the Simmons Mattress Company. Throughout their residency in Cuba, they plugged themselves into the social and cultural world of the Afro-Cuban elite in Havana. Both participated in the activities of the Club Atenas, evidenced by the fact that both appeared in the *Boletín Oficial del Club Atenas* that year. James was active in the club's sports activities, while Margaret was featured as one of the club's prominent "ladies."[23] Like R. M. R. Nelson, the entrepreneur, the Martins were part of the small community of African Americans who settled in Cuba after 1898. Their connections to Afro-Cuban and African American associations made them a key part of the networks that linked them together.[24]

Martin's numerous 1930 letters to Pickens from Cuba highlight both the privileged existence of herself and her husband and the tenuousness of their social position due to the transnational color line. Like all African descendants on the island, they were barred from entering the beaches controlled by white elite Cubans and Americans. "The Americans have bought over, improved and beautified, Havana's only beach," Martin informed Pickens that summer "and it would be just like them to say that it has become the private property of the Havana Yacht Club."[25] This shared experience of discrimination facilitated relationships with the Afro-Cuban *habanero* elite. Yet despite her intimate knowledge of Cuban society, Martin herself was not above employing stereotypes of Cubans. In her efforts to convince the NAACP leader and his secretary to visit the island, she asked Pickens to inform his assistant "that if he accompanies you when you make that trip to Cuba, I am going to see that he meets some of our charming señoritas, in whose sparkling eyes lies the romance of Old Spain. (I am assuming, of course, that he is a young chap just out of school)."[26]

Martin's letters also provide clues as to how "colored travelers" navigated the unpredictable dangers of moving through the transit system of the U.S.-Caribbean world. In one letter, she compared each steamship line's reputation regarding the treatment of "colored travelers." "The Ward Line is the choice of colored persons traveling between Cuba and the States, though personally I prefer the United Fruit," Martin wrote on 19 June 1930. "The United Fruit Line takes a day longer to make the trip, but the means are, in my opinion, better. However, I am told that they refused point blank to sell passage to some colored Cubans desiring to go to the States."[27] Martin's advice led Pickens to purchase a ticket on the Ward Line's *Morro Castle*, which was making its maiden voyage to Cuba. The NAACP field secretary's securing a passage on the ship highlights the more random nature of racial discrimination in steamship transit. Pickens bought his ticket only a few months after the Ward Line refused to sell Hughes a ticket.

For the ambitious Martin, Pickens's visit was a boost to her career aspirations. Aside from her enrollment in Spanish and stenography classes and her occasional contributions to Urrutia's "Ideales" page, Martin felt a bit stifled by her life in Cuba. Nevertheless, her relationships with Pickens and the Club Atenas and her ability to speak Spanish made her an important point of contact between the Afro-Cuban elite and African American "talented tenth." She followed the NAACP field secretary's advice to write articles on Afro-Cubans for the *Crisis*. As she prepared to send Pickens her essay titled "The Negro in Cuba," she wrote in her typically florid language: "Now here I've been languishing here in this tropical sunshine for the past five years wanting to 'tell the world' something about 'The Lord's Chosen People' in Cuba, and 'Behold, the angel of the Lord' appeared unto me in a letter from a very dear friend, saying, 'Write!' And straightaway she rose up (no, she sat down) and doth testify of those things." Her article described the particularities of racism in Cuba, while highlighting the achievements of "some distinguished Cubans," including María Teresa Ramírez, the daughter of the Afro-Cuban politician Primitivo Ramírez Ros (who died in 1930); Manuel José Delgado, the most prominent Afro-Cuban in Gerardo Machado's administration; and of course, Miguel Angel Céspedes, the lawyer, politician, and long-standing member of the Club Atenas.[28] Within a year, her relationship with Pickens and Mary McLeod Bethune facilitated her departure from the island to study in Europe. Hence, Martin's correspondence with Pickens provides rare evidence of an African American woman's experience in Cuba. Her role in the making of Afro-diasporic networks between the two communities in this period foreshadowed greater participation of black women in the forging of these linkages in subsequent decades.

The Origins of a Tourist Network

Pickens left Cuba inspired by the possibilities of hemispheric connections between Afro-descended populations. Like Langston Hughes, he helped Afro-Cuban writers such as Gustavo Urrutia publish pieces in the *Crisis*. Moreover, as the NAACP's field secretary, he saw possibilities for establishing new branches of the association on the island. Cuba seemed to present an ideal country for the association to expand its reach beyond the United States. In a letter he wrote to Percival Prattis of the Associated Negro Press a few weeks after his return from Cuba, Pickens insisted that the "Negro peoples of the Western Hemisphere are beginning to reach hands to each other and that those in the West Indies have great possibilities." Pickens liked Prattis's idea of sending two people to Cuba "for a special trip of investigation and excitement." He expressed his enthusiasm for the idea at the end of the letter where he scribbled, "Boy, we could wake 'em up!"[29]

Pickens's excitement at the prospect of "waking up" Afro-Cubans was an example of the long-standing elitism of the African American "vanguard." Like their predecessors of previous decades, African American members of the "talented tenth" in the 1930s charged themselves with the task of leading the supposedly sleepy branches of the "colored race" in the United States and abroad. And yet Afro-Cubans were in fact wide awake in 1930, keenly aware of the continuing struggles they faced in Cuban society, evidenced by their participation in politics and by their vibrant cultural and social institutions. Moreover, they too saw the potential material benefits of constructing relationships with African Americans. Not unlike the Afro-Cuban students at Tuskegee who cunningly tried to take advantage of Booker T. Washington's paternalism decades earlier, Afro-Cuban intellectuals and entrepreneurs sought to manipulate African American self-representations to extract benefits from members of the most advanced sector of the "colored race."

Soon after his departure from Cuba, Pickens sent numerous letters to Afro-

Cubans proposing the idea of a collaboration with the NAACP. Not surprisingly, he was especially impressed by the Club Atenas, the organization Martin called Cuba's "most exclusive cultural, social, and recreational organization among the colored people." In a letter Pickens wrote to Urrutia, he expressed his desire that "the colored leaders of Cuba and any of the other leaders who are interested in inter-racial justice will in some way attach themselves to our organization." It seemed to the NAACP leader that "the Club Atenas would be a fine organization to be affiliated with us, at least to receive our literature."[30] Pickens obtained a copy of the club's membership list and sent letters of inquiry to each one. One of the people he contacted was Luís Delfín Valdés, the Afro-Cuban Tuskegee alumnus. "I am also sending you a copy of my biographical sketch and a photograph," the field secretary wrote. "I am doing this because the Secretary who furnished me with a number of addresses specially checked your name and indicated that you would have that personal interest also."[31] While there is no record of a reply from Valdés, Pickens's note highlights the ways in which the architect's background at Tuskegee was known by his peers.

One person who did respond to Pickens's offer to "join hands" with the NAACP was the energetic José García Inerarity. Born in Placetas, Cuba, in 1892, García was the son of Severiano García, an Afro-Cuban general in the Liberation Army from Santa Clara, and Nicolasa Inerarity, who was possibly a former slave on the Inerarity plantation in Matanzas, Cuba. Like the Afro-Cuban students who studied at Tuskegee decades before, García was an alumnus of the "Hampton-Tuskegee Idea" of industrial education. In 1907, at the age of fifteen, García was sent to study at Hampton Institute, Washington's alma mater. The U.S. presence on the island undoubtedly influenced his parents' decision to enroll him at Hampton, which was facilitated by Lieutenant M. W. Day of the U.S. Sixth Cavalry during the U.S. occupation of the island from 1906 to 1909. According to records in the Hampton University Archives, García had aspirations to pursue an advanced degree in engineering at Howard University. However, he struggled academically during his three years at the school before finally leaving in 1910. From Hampton, he moved on to get a degree in engineering from the College of Agriculture in New Jersey. Despite his lack of academic success at Hampton, García proudly identified himself as a Hampton alumnus in his correspondence with African American intellectuals and entrepreneurs. Moreover, he maintained an active membership in the Hampton Alumni Association, which kept him in touch with the school and with former classmates.[32]

Like other Afro-Cuban alumni of Tuskegee, García was a firm believer in Booker T. Washington's vision of black entrepreneurship. In the decades following his years as a student, García became a successful businessman. In the 1930s, he established his own fruit and vegetable exporting company and he sought to sell his produce to African American venders through the National Negro Business League. Years later, he moved into the field of engineering and held various posts in the Cuban government during the first Fulgencio Batista regime (1940–44). His business ventures carried him frequently to the United States, Haiti, and Panama. Despite his pro-business outlook, the resourceful García even managed to establish ties with the Cuban revolutionary government soon after Fidel Castro's regime took power in 1959.[33] García's activities illustrate that he was a rarity: a Cuban of African descent who became a successful businessman in an era when most Afro-Cubans were shut out from the island's business circles.

Thus, when Pickens proposed the idea of establishing relations between the NAACP and Afro-Cuban institutions, García jumped at the opportunity. However, they had different ideas about the nature of such a collaboration. While Pickens likely saw it as an opportunity for advocacy and cultural exchange, García saw it as a potential travel service for black tourists visiting Cuba. A branch of the association in Cuba would, García thought, "take care of all Colored people that want [to] come to Cuba so we meet at Depot and fix Hotel accommodation[s] for them and give any information they want to [do] business in Cuba and South America." A branch staffed by his brother and cousin, both of whom were lawyers, García proposed, would prevent "any immigration trouble when the Colored people want to come to Cuba." All that was required to launch the venture, according to the Afro-Cuban entrepreneur, was a "small amount of money every month [to] help any office here." The amount need not be large, he assured Pickens, since his goal was simply to "do some service to my race."[34] However, Pickens informed García that the association's headquarters could not supply such funds. "The National Office does not pay the expenses of the local branch," Pickens explained, "inasmuch as the local branch is allowed to keep one-half of all membership dues." Nevertheless he felt confident "that a good branch in Cuba would be well supported if it were led."[35]

Undaunted, García sought out other opportunities to forge linkages with African American institutions. He convinced Pickens to introduce him to Claude Barnett, a Tuskegee graduate and head of the ANP, a news service that supplied stories to African American newspapers. García offered to become the Cuban correspondent for the ANP even though he had no apparent experience in journalism. "I have been in States over 6 years and I went to Scool [*sic*] in Hampton Inst. in Virginia, so I know well the Colored condiction [*sic*] in there and also in Cuba so I can be very useful to the Negro Press in Cuba," he wrote. He pitched the same idea of developing a travel service to Barnett. "What we must have," García suggested, "is somebody that will take care of American colored people when they come to Cuba so nothing will happen like [what] happen[ed] to Mrs. Bethune." In the same letter, García enhanced his credentials as a host for African American visitors to the island when he told Barnett that he had "take[n] care of all colored people from U.S. to Cuba every winter."[36] The Afro-Cuban entrepreneur's repeated business propositions to African American leaders and businessmen illustrates his Afro-diasporic vision of race entrepreneurship.

Although Barnett did not take up García's proposal to form a black tourist organization, he did maintain a relationship with the Afro-Cuban entrepreneur for two decades. During that time, García continually kept the ANP informed of his various entrepreneurial achievements. In Barnett, García found a fellow traveler—a black entrepreneur who believed black business was the salvation of the race. In the 1940s and 1950s, Barnett played a role in the forging of black tourist linkages between African American institutions and Cuba and Haiti. García and Barnett shared a similar outlook that they both acquired as disciples of Booker T. Washington. Barnett attended Tuskegee Institute in the early years of the century, graduating in 1906. It was at Tuskegee where he not only learned Washington's gospel of black entrepreneurship, but where he also met the Afro-Cuban students who enrolled at the school, including Juan Eusebio Gómez, the son of Juan Gualberto Gómez, who graduated with Barnett in 1906, and Luís Delfín Valdés, the Afro-Cuban architect. Like Gómez and other Afro-Cuban male students, Barnett was one of the Tuskegee principal's "office boys" who were close to Washington. Years later, after flipping through the pages of the Club Atenas's magazine, Barnett asked Valdés if he was the same person "who was at Tuskegee Institute at the time I was there and who occupied with his brother, Julian, the room next to mine in Thrasher Hall."[37] Hence, García and Barnett illustrate the ways the legacy of the Tuskegee-Cuba connection shaped the making of the Afro-diasporic linkages in the 1930s and 1940s.

While Barnett, like Pickens, informed García that his organization did not have funds to support the entrepreneur's travel service, the idea of such an endeavor was clearly the subject of discussion in Afro-Cuban and African

American encounters in the early 1930s. As the opening epigraph of this chapter demonstrates, Langston Hughes's 1931 trip to Cuba, which he took with the young artist Zell Ingram, seems to have been motivated in part by a desire to promote black tourism in the Caribbean as much as it was by his own desire for sun and relaxation. He gave the impression to a Cuban journalist writing for the *Diario de la Marina* that his stop in Cuba was the beginning of a tour of the Caribbean. Revealingly, Hughes and Ingram traveled by car from Ingram's home in Cleveland to Miami before boarding a ship from Key West to Havana. The car, which they dubbed "Nazimova," was on loan from Ingram's mother. "And this detail of the car is not superfluous," the *Diario* journalist reported. "It is the evasion of the humiliations that Jim Crowism inflicts on people of color, making conditions on the railway intolerable." "The automobile," the writer proclaimed, "has solved an annoying problem for the Negro traveler."[38]

While the *Diario* writer seems to have overlooked the fact that owning an automobile was a virtual impossibility for the vast majority of African Americans at this time, nevertheless his article reveals the perceived possibilities automobile travel presented to people of African descent in the United States.[39] Such enthusiasm was rooted in African American motives to travel abroad to countries with Afro-descended majorities. To Hughes, Cuba and Haiti possessed the advantages of geographic proximity—"South by car"—and distinct black cultures—"Spanish and French at your very door"—which could provide black travelers with a "new background and basis for comparisons." Hughes's travel diary also indicates that the Club Atenas gave him materials, including a collection of photos of their new building, to promote their organization for black American travelers, or as he wrote, "to see one's own people in banks, shops, fine clubs, high positions."[40]

The idea of promoting African American travel to Cuba was also discussed by Arthur Schomburg and Atenas leaders during his 1932 trip to the island. "I find your idea of bringing 100 or 125 Americans and representatives from Puerto Rico and Panama to Cuba to hold conferences and conventions to be a magnificent and beneficial one," Conrado Thorndike, then Atenas president, wrote to Schomburg. However, the Atenas leader felt that the unstable political situation on the island did not permit such a venture.[41] Schomburg also conferred with Claude Barnett, who had experience organizing excursions for black travelers. "The plan which the Cubans talked to you of, we have had up with folk in the Virgin Islands and Haiti also," the ANP editor informed Schomburg. In previous years, he had worked "with a railroad on an all expense tour. These are railroad people whom I know well and can go a long way with." However, the Depression had forced Barnett to postpone the idea. "We here think that it will be necessary to wait until times improve before launching the effort," Barnett concluded.

Barnett's view that black tourism to Cuba needed to await better economic conditions highlights the Great Depression's impact on both countries. What is more, the political upheaval that accompanied the overthrow of Cuban president Gerardo Machado in August 1933 further forestalled the development of an Afro-Cuban and African American tourist network. Yet even in this moment of economic and political crisis, African Americans continued to travel to the island. In fact, the historian Rayford Logan went to Cuba to promote tourism to the island for the *Baltimore Afro-American*, only to find himself in the middle of the moment when Machado was overthrown in August 1933. The *Afro-American* editors proclaimed the purpose of his mission:

> If there is any country, close to ours, which we ought to know intimately, it is Cuba, just one hundred miles from Key West, Florida. No passport is needed to visit it. The only barrier is the Spanish language, which should be taught in every public school instead of French or German. The AFRO, with the help of its readers, begins the task of making our country Cuba-conscious, and to this end has sent Rayford Logan to Havana.[42]

As we shall see, more sustained tourist linkages would not emerge until Cuba and the United States pulled out of the economic and political malaise of the Depression era. Meanwhile, African Americans continued to face obstacles when they tried to travel to Cuba. Seven years after the episodes of 1930, another discrimination incident achieved public attention. If the discrimination cases against African American travelers to Cuba in the early part of the decade stimulated activism by the NAACP, another incident against one more "reputable" black traveler to the island helped galvanize Afro-Cuban efforts against racism in Cuba.

El Caso Mitchell and the Antidiscrimination Movement in Cuba

On 16 November 1937, the Sociedad de Estudios Afrocubanos (Society of Afro-Cuban Studies), the newly formed scholarly and advocacy organization founded by Fernando Ortiz and a number of prominent Afro-Cuban intellectuals, organized a lecture by the Puerto Rican intellectual Tomás Blanco. The lecture, titled "El Prejuicio Racial en Puerto Rico" (Racial prejudice in Puerto

Rico), juxtaposed what Blanco viewed as mild Puerto Rican racism with the stringent racialized practices of the United States. Indeed, this talk formed the basis of what was to become a foundational text in the study of racialization in Puerto Rico.[43] Blanco's textbook case of American racism was an incident involving Arthur Mitchell, an African American congressman who was forced out of a first-class "white" railroad car on a train traveling through the state of Arkansas, in April 1937.[44] His reference to the discrimination case involving Congressman Mitchell was ironic, for it was only one month after his lecture that Mitchell would again be embroiled in a racial discrimination incident, this time in Cuba.

The Cuba that Mitchell encountered in 1937 was in the midst of a political transition from authoritarian rule to a new political system under a new constitution that would be implemented a few years later. The political transformations of the 1930s had an enormous impact on antidiscrimination activists. The fall of the Machado regime in 1933 helped stimulate a renewed movement for racial equality on the island. During the 1930s, a younger generation of male and female activists with roots in the Afro-Cuban societies and the Cuban Communist Party waged a battle for the citizenship rights belonging to Afro-Cubans. Younger activists such as Salvador García Agüero and Nicolás Guillén, among others, challenged the Afro-Cuban leadership class that was associated with the hated Machado, including some of the more prominent leaders of the Club Atenas. They insisted that more active measures be taken to attack the persistence of racism on the island. As a result, in the late 1930s and the 1940s Atenas-style "respectable" leaders were compelled to collaborate with their more radical challengers. Like activists in other parts of the African diaspora at this time, these younger Afro-Cubans and their progressive white allies sought to combat practices of racial discrimination by more forcefully incorporating the interests of the often-overlooked sectors of the Afro-Cuban population, namely, working-class blacks and mulattoes and Afro-Cuban women. They argued that the national ideology of a raceless nationality meant little if there was no corresponding effort to actively contest persistent practices of racial discrimination on the island. It is within this context that one must situate the outburst of activism generated by the visit of Arthur W. Mitchell to Cuba in late 1937.[45]

African American political leaders also took a leftward turn during the 1930s. Arthur Mitchell's career illustrates the political trajectories of a number of African American leaders during this period. Born in Alabama in 1883, he was a disciple of Booker T. Washington and rose to prominence as an educator in his home state before he decided to enter into politics. After working in President Herbert Hoover's 1928 campaign, Mitchell moved to Chicago and switched over to the Democratic Party. He learned the rules of Chicago machine politics and quickly rose through the ranks of the Chicago Democrats. In 1934, he made an unsuccessful attempt to capture the Democratic nomination for representative of the First District, finishing as the runner-up to the longtime white politician Harry Baker. After Baker's unexpected death shortly thereafter, Mitchell suddenly became the Democratic candidate for the congressional seat held by popular black incumbent Oscar DePriest. Mitchell, who had been a virtual unknown in local politics, unexpectedly defeated DePriest in 1934 and replaced him as the only African American in Congress. As the first African American elected to Congress as a Democrat, Mitchell's victory signified the beginning of the shift of African American loyalties to the Democratic Party after decades of loyal support for the Republicans.[46]

During his tenure in Congress, Mitchell was an unpopular figure among a number of African American leaders who saw him as little more than a political opportunist. However, during the 1930s his status as the only African American serving in the U.S. Congress automatically placed him in the role of race leader, a position that he strategically embraced. Mitchell's conflicts with other African American leaders meant little to Afro-Cuban observers of U.S. domestic politics, who saw him as the "Honorable Arthur W. Mitchell," leader of the "colored race." One Afro-Cuban admirer informed Mitchell that he "read with extraordinary satisfaction about your liberal, valiant and realistic laws favorable to democracy, to workers, and to men of our race." Such efforts were "worthy of the most sincere praise and imitation."[47]

But when Congressman Mitchell and his wife, Annie Harris Mitchell, decided to visit Cuba in December 1937, they came not to develop political connections, but rather to take a holiday vacation. To organize their itinerary, they called upon José García Inerarity. While the precise origins of García's relationship with Mitchell are uncertain, it is likely that the Afro-Cuban entrepreneur sought out the politician because he was the only African American in the U.S. Congress. In his correspondence with Pickens and other African American associates, García frequently asked for information on prominent African American figures. In fact, in his first letter to Mitchell he asked for the congressman's photograph and biography.[48] It is possible that García's repeated entreaties to African Americans to come to the island prompted the congressman to stop in Cuba on his holiday sojourn.

Thanks to the efforts of García and other Afro-Cuban journalists, the Afro-

Cuban elite in Havana was prepared to greet Congressman Mitchell. When he stepped off the ss *Virginia* on 28 December 1937, he found an enthusiastic welcome from the who's who of the Afro-Cuban community in Havana. García introduced Mitchell to several leading black and mulatto intellectuals and politicians on the island, including Miguel Angel Céspedes, Manuel Capestany Abreu, and Martín Antonio Iglesias. Throughout his brief stay in Cuba, the press repeatedly saluted Mitchell for his status as the only black elected official serving in the U.S. Congress. His membership in Franklin Roosevelt's Democratic Party and his ardent support of the president's New Deal programs enhanced his prestige.[49]

Mitchell was literally besieged by Cubans from the moment he arrived on the island. It was a reception he was unprepared for: "For the love of Heaven," Mitchell cried to reporters before he stepped off the steamship that brought him to Havana, "is this what was waiting for me when I left to get some rest from the exigencies of the press? — and I have yet to step on Cuban soil!"[50] Despite his exasperated mood of the moment, Mitchell granted an interview to Gustavo Urrutia later that evening in the halls of the Club Atenas. The journalist's questions reflected the keen awareness that Afro-Cuban intellectuals possessed of U.S. racial politics. Urrutia asked Mitchell about the opportunities for blacks under Franklin Roosevelt's New Deal. Mitchell, the true party loyalist, insisted to Urrutia that "the Negro has awoken and is now filling the ranks of the Democrats because of the benefits accruing to him by Rooseveltian politics. . . . Roosevelt is advocating the improvement of the downtrodden classes and the Negro is found in one of the lowliest of these." He claimed that the "Rooseveltian policy is such that the intelligence of the Negro can serve as a lever with which to improve his status on a solid economic base offered to all the impoverished classes."[51] To Urrutia's remark to Mitchell that "a few Afro-Cubans believe that money from the North American Negro may come to help us in Cuba," the congressman replied that since "the Negro is poor in every corner of the earth," it was best for blacks in Cuba and the United States to "establish and maintain an intimate spiritual contact for the study and solution of our problems which are essentially identical."[52] Urrutia's question highlights the ways in which Afro-Cuban elites sought assistance from the population they perceived to be the vanguard of the "colored race."

The Mitchell tour continued for the next two days, as he was greeted by other Afro-Cuban public figures. Besides Céspedes, Capestany Abreu, and Iglesias, Mitchell met leaders of other Afro-Cuban societies, including Pastor de Albear Friol of the Unión Fraternal, who would become an important figure in Cuban racial politics in subsequent years, and representatives of La Unión, the Antilla Sport Club, and the Asociación Cultural Femenina. The Mitchells visited the Senate chambers, where Capestany Abreu saluted them with a champagne punch. After another luncheon with Miguel Angel Céspedes, then undersecretary of justice, the Mitchells boarded the ss *Virginia* to return to the United States.[53]

Despite the fanfare generated by Mitchell's visit, his trip did not conclude without incident. Following the reception at the Club Atenas, Mitchell and his party, which included his wife, Lieutenant Feliciano González, and José García Inerarity, ran into difficulties securing a table for dinner at the Hotel Saratoga. Though the details are somewhat sketchy, word quickly spread that the proprietor refused to serve them because they were persons of African descent.[54] The incident seems to have occurred quietly, so subtly that even members of Mitchell's party were not quite sure exactly what happened. After admitting that "some people have said that I did not act as I should, being a lieutenant, that I should have punished the man," Lieutenant González wrote to Mitchell weeks later claiming that he still did "not yet know what happened," wondering whether Mitchell himself knew precisely what had occurred at the hotel. "You imagined, as I did," wrote González, "that something happened," even though García "never told us."[55]

The ambiguity evident in González's letter and in other correspondence between Mitchell and his Afro-Cuban hosts makes it difficult to ascertain their motives for deciding on the Saratoga for their dinner plans that evening. It is unclear whether they arrived at the Saratoga fully expecting to be served without encountering difficulties or whether they went to the hotel intending to challenge the notoriously discriminatory practices of many Havana establishments connected to the tourist sector. As we have seen, García himself was well aware of the discriminatory practices of the tourist industry on the island. Therefore, it is highly unlikely that he was ignorant of the possibility that he and his guests would encounter difficulties dining at the Hotel Saratoga. Despite the absence of evidence of their motives, it seems reasonable to suspect that García and González believed that the presence of a well-known visitor, who also happened to be a congressman from the United States, would override any possibility of racial discrimination.

Although members of Mitchell's party were in the dark about what occurred at the hotel that evening, the Cuban public quickly received the unambiguous message that their distinguished visitor had been a victim of racial discrimination. In the days after the dinner at the Saratoga, a firestorm of protest was published in the Havana press. Antonio Villanueva, the owner of the hotel, quickly dismissed the charges of racial discrimination. In a letter written to the U.S. ambassador published in the *Diario de la Marina* Villanueva wanted to "definitively deny" the accusations of racial discrimination and insist that the delays in service were due to the overwhelming number of tourists at the hotel's restaurant that evening. Furthermore, Villanueva insisted that "the head waiter personally served the congressman and his associates" in an effort to make up for any inconveniences experienced by the Mitchell party.[56] Villanueva's account was reiterated by José I. Rivero, the director of the *Diario de la Marina*. An exchange appeared in Rivero's newspaper over the director's decision not to publish an article of protest penned by Urrutia. Rivero defended his decision, claiming that the accusations against Villanueva were unfounded. In his reply to Urrutia, the editor argued that he found it "hard to believe that a businessman would openly insult an official of our Army, and that official would accept the insult in as mild a manner as a Franciscan Friar." Any delays experienced by the "distinguished Negroes," according to Rivero, were due to the lack of available tables that evening. While maintaining that nothing discriminatory occurred at the hotel, the newspaper editor defended the right of businessmen to cater to the sensibilities of their more powerful and numerous white clientele. "If a businessman refuses to do business with a Negro," Rivero argued, "in truth it is not he who refuses, but rather his white customers, who are in the majority and possess greater buying power." Thus, Rivero argued against the adoption of an antidiscrimination law because it would punish the "innocent" merchant. "Any coercive legislative or governmental measures in this matter would only aggravate or create more conflicts," he concluded.[57]

Yet, the defenses put forth by Rivero and Villanueva did little to stem the growing tide of protest. Letters calling for the punishment of Villanueva came from various sectors of Cuban society. José García Inerarity was among the first Cubans to inform Mitchell of the storm unleashed by the incident at the hotel. "All colored people are getting there every night," García wrote. He followed with the startling claim that "some people came to see me to kill him [the hotel owner]."[58] Another letter from Clara Ruíz, whom Mitchell met during his visit, conveyed the anger generated by the episode. "The local press has commented bitterly and forcefully on the incident," Ruíz claimed, "and all organizations have denounced the deed, demanding of the authorities the immediate expulsion of the proprietor of the Hotel Saratoga."[59]

Ruíz and García were not exaggerating the uproar generated by the incident. News of the Saratoga episode rapidly spread throughout the island, and leaders of the colored societies sprang to action. Leading the mobilization of Afro-Cubans in Havana in particular was the Club Atenas. On 2 January 1938, the club held an assembly designed to draw up a legal campaign against the management of the Hotel Saratoga. The attendees of the meeting included many of the radical intellectuals who were part of the antidiscrimination movement in Cuba, such as Fernando Ortiz, Emilio Roig de Leuchshenring, José Luciano Franco, Juan Marinello, Salvador García Agüero, and Benjamin Muñoz Ginarte. They argued that the Mitchell episode illustrated the necessity of adding an antidiscrimination clause to the Cuban constitution. In previous years, Cuban politicians had routinely dismissed protests against racial discrimination by invoking article 11 of the constitution, which stipulated that "all Cubans are equal before the law." However, the delegates at the Club Atenas meeting argued that additional legislation that called for fines and imprisonment against those found guilty of racial discriminatory acts was needed to "prevent and suppress all acts of racial discrimination."[60] Moreover, the delegates formed a legal team to file a lawsuit against the management of the Hotel Saratoga. In this way, the Mitchell incident provided an important stimulus for the resurgent campaign for Afro-Cuban rights in the late 1930s and early 1940s.

As antidiscrimination activists worked to publicize the "Mitchell Case" in the Cuban public sphere, news of the upsurge of mobilization continued to flow to the congressman's Washington, D.C., office. A few weeks after his return to the United States, a letter arrived from Feliciano González, the military officer who was with the Mitchell party at the hotel. Writing from his military base in Cayo Mambí, Oriente, he informed Mitchell that "the people have raised hell" over the incident. Noting the widespread publicity, the lieutenant related to Mitchell that "your name and mine have practically been in the newspaper every day. Members of different societies have come together protesting the case." González claimed that the episode had caused concern even among the upper levels of the Cuban government, prompting Fulgencio Batista, then chief of the Cuban army and de facto president of the republic, to summon him to Havana from his post in Oriente in order to find out "what happened, how it happened, and what was my opinion about the matter." González stated that Batista wanted to know "what you said and if you left Cuba happy or not."[61]

Afro-Cuban activists in Havana were not the only ones who were mobilized by the treatment Mitchell received at the Hotel Saratoga. It is clear that the Cuban government's concern about *el caso Mitchell* stemmed from the shower of angry telegrams it received from numerous Afro-Cuban societies and other associations throughout the island. The scope of surviving letters and telegrams is truly astonishing and reflects the charged political atmosphere on the island at this time. Afro-Cubans were mobilized on an unparalleled scale. The outrage was clearly fueled by Mitchell's stature as a "distinguished leader of the colored race" from the United States. The embarrassing incident seemed to suggest that even an official representative of the U.S. government could not avoid racial discrimination in Cuba. The insult dealt to Mitchell signified to many across the island that more active measures were needed to protect the rights of people of African descent in Cuba.

No less than thirty-eight associations, mostly Afro-Cuban societies, sent telegrams and letters to President Federico Laredo Brú.[62] The Sociedad La Antorcha of Artemisa argued that the government needed to "take all measures in order to avoid the repetition of such deplorable acts in honor of the harmony and fraternity that ought to prevail among all Cubans."[63] "It is humiliating," wrote Francisco Pérez of the Club Artístico Cultural in another letter of protest, "that the democratic and liberal spirit of our Constitution has been trampled on and that even the duty of the most elementary courtesy has been ignored in our fatherland and under your government which owes its freedom to a Maceo, to a Moncada, and so many other Negroes who publicly confronted problems of a racial nature."[64] Meanwhile, in the town of Encrucijada in Las Villas province, the leaders of the Sociedad La Unión held a meeting with other organizations, including "labor groups," and subsequently wrote a letter to President Laredo Brú following a meeting. "It is necessary for such an order of things to disappear," they wrote, insisting that the "rulers of our country work to guarantee the true equality of rights for our race."[65] Finally, the Asociación Más Luz of Santiago de las Vegas echoed these sentiments in their protest to the president. They called upon the government to take "swift and energetic action," which was summed up in the concluding line of the letter: "For the expulsion of the owner of the Saratoga Hotel!"[66]

While many Afro-Cubans were outraged by the episode, few if any corresponding sentiments were emanating from Congressman Mitchell's office in Washington. Curiously, Mitchell himself hardly mentioned the episode in the letters he wrote to Cubans following his return to the United States. In a letter to García, for example, Mitchell thanked his Cuban friend for the "wonderful reception given us by the distinguished citizens of your great country." Moreover, he communicated to his host the "happiness that was ours during our short stay in Havana."[67] In one of his few references to the incident, Mitchell asked in a letter written to Clara Ruíz for "newspaper clippings expressing the attitude of the Cuban public toward the Saratoga Hotel affair."[68] Aside from such brief inquiries, Mitchell kept whatever feelings he had about the incident to himself.[69]

Despite the significant impact of the wave of protests in Cuba, the campaign against Villanueva did not produce any immediate results. Spurred by the angry telegrams from Afro-Cuban societies throughout the island, the lawyers hired by the Club Atenas, along with representatives from an organization called the Committee against Racial Discrimination, filed a lawsuit against the hotel owner before the Municipal Court of Havana. However, the legal proceedings against the alleged perpetrators of racial discrimination ended in frustration. A few months later, the Havana municipal court ruled that there was insufficient evidence to convict Villanueva of any wrongdoing.[70]

Although the judicial ruling was a bitter defeat for Cuban antidiscrimination activists, the Mitchell case helped recharge the movement. The case involving a black elected official from the United States legitimized claims about the necessity of more concrete measures to ensure the equality of all Cuban citizens. Throughout the 1930s, Cubans from a wide range of political persuasions had argued for the creation of a new constitution. After years of ongoing conflict between Fulgencio Batista, the de facto ruler of Cuba, and his numerous political opponents, by the end of the decade the path was clear for the creation of a new contract between the Cuban state and its citizenry. In 1940, the Cuban government adopted a new constitution. Although many measures proposed by antidiscrimination activists were omitted, the constitution of 1940 implemented clauses that gave the antidiscrimination movement new leverage against ongoing practices of racial exclusion.[71]

While the new Cuban constitution seemed to present possibilities for a new racial order in Cuba, Afro-Cubans and African American travelers continued to be subject to racism on the island. Indeed, the Mitchell episode was by no means the last instance of racial discrimination against black travelers in Cuba. Meanwhile, in the United States the battle against racial discrimination in transit was just getting under way. If elite African Americans wanted to travel to Cuba or anywhere else, they still needed to develop their own networks to navigate the racist structures of the transportation industry while the political battle unfolded over the next two decades. As the tourist industry rebounded in the 1940s and 1950s, Cuba continued to attract the attention of African American travelers. It was the task of transcultural Afro-diasporic subjects with roots in Cuba and the United States to forge these linkages.

Cultural Exchanges in the Era of Good Neighborism

In the early 1940s, a changing configuration of international politics created the circumstances for a resurgence of black tourism to Cuba. Much of it was due to the U.S. government's shift in foreign policy from military intervention and "dollar diplomacy" to an emphasis on cultural exchange and hemispheric collaboration. This shift was initiated by Franklin Roosevelt's "Good Neighbor" policy, which began soon after he took office in 1933 and reached its apogee during World War II, when the U.S. government sought to cultivate a hemispheric block of allies against the Axis powers. The main arm of this propaganda initiative was the Office of the Coordinator of Inter-American Affairs (OCIAA), the governmental agency headed by Nelson Rockefeller designed to promote cultural exchanges across the Americas. While good-neighborism had its roots in a project designed to bolster U.S. hegemony in the hemisphere, African Americans used the new policy as a way to create linkages among Afro-descended populations throughout the Americas. Black activists and intellectuals sought to intervene in inter-American exchanges by highlighting the particular struggles for "democracy" by the "colored" peoples of the region.[72] In fact, Washington's new policies created a political environment where all sorts of hemispheric connections could flourish. African American and Afro-Cuban organizations developed their own cross-border linkages independent of the objectives of the U.S. State Department. Once again, Cuba's geographic proximity to the United States gave it a special place of importance in these initiatives for hemispheric solidarity.

Good-neighborism not only created an environment conducive to the expansion of black tourism to Cuba but also facilitated the emergence of other types of cultural interactions. In this period, cultural tourism and intellectual exchanges were placed in the foreground by the tourist industry and the U.S. and Cuban governments. As Muna Lee of the U.S. State Department's Division of Cultural Relations stated to the National Council of Negro Women in a speech at Howard University, "The bonds of union must necessarily be cultured bonds and the interchanges cultural exchanges."[73] Aspirations for cultural interactions by African American and Afro-Cuban institutions were given a boost by the emergence of foundational and governmental grants that promoted international cultural exchange programs. Scholars at black educational institutions suddenly found themselves eligible for programs to fund student and faculty exchanges. By traveling to Cuba and other parts of the Americas and writing about their experiences in African American publications, these scholars became de facto promoters of black tourism. To be sure, African Americans' motivations to travel to Cuba varied. Undoubtedly, many went to the island for sun and the rumba. Nevertheless, in the Good Neighbor era many black travelers also sought to harmonize their desires for leisure with motives for cultural exchange and intellectual stimulation.

The arrival of Roosevelt's New Deal and Good Neighbor policy heightened the importance of Washington, D.C., and its African American community in the forging of transnational Afro-diasporic linkages. While Havana continued to be the hub of Afro-Cuban and African American interaction in Cuba, Washington joined New York and Tampa as important sites of cultural interaction between these communities. This was partially due to the fact that the federal government became a primary locus of activity for civil rights organizations such as the NAACP and other groups. It was in this period that the Roosevelt administration enacted Executive Order 8802, which banned racial discrimination in defense industries, prompted by A. Philip Randolph's "March on Washington Movement" in 1941. Such initiatives led many civil rights activists to pursue connections with an administration that seemed to be more responsive to the demands of African Americans in the United States and other parts of the Americas. Thus, Washington became an attractive place for a politicized intelligentsia looking to influence governmental policy with respect to Negroes at home and abroad.[74]

Another factor that pushed Washington to the forefront of Afro-Cuban and African American linkages was the ascendancy of Howard University. Under the leadership of President Mordecai Johnson, Howard became the center of black education in the 1930s and 1940s. It housed an impressive cadre of black scholars including Ralph Bunche, E. Franklin Frazier, Charles Wesley, Carter G. Woodson, and Howard Thurman among many others. Howard was also the home of the young Eric Williams, the Trinidadian-born historian, whose *Capitalism and Slavery* revolutionized the field of slavery studies. The university also played a key role in Good Neighbor academic initiatives. Howard's connections to Cuba were established by the historian Rayford Logan, whose scholarship and advisory work for the OCIAA made the "Negro in Latin America" a part of the university's intellectual community. So did the activities of the lesser-known literary scholar Ben Frederic Carruthers, whose research on Afro-Cuban literature made him a key player in Washington's African American community's developing relationship with Havana's Afro-Cuban intellectual community.[75]

Carruthers's career highlights the ways in which African American intellectuals could benefit from the changing international political climate of the period. While the relatively obscure Carruthers is best known for his collaborative translation of Nicolás Guillén's poems with Langston Hughes, he also played a key role in the forging of cultural exchanges between Afro-Cuban and African American institutions in the late 1930s and early 1940s.[76] Born in St. Louis and raised in Chicago, Carruthers was from a well-to-do, light-skinned "colored" family. He obtained his bachelor's and master's degrees in Romance languages at the University of Illinois. After teaching at Tillotson College in Austin, Texas, for four years he moved on to Howard University in 1938. A General Education Board fellowship allowed him to pursue a Ph.D. in Romance languages at Illinois. The fellowship also funded a residency in Havana, where he developed close ties to members of the Afro-Cuban intelligentsia, particularly Angel Suárez Rocabruna and Teodoro Ramos Blanco. Fittingly, his doctoral dissertation was a study of the life and work of Gabriel Concepción de Valdés ("Plácido"), the nineteenth-century Afro-Cuban poet who was executed by Spanish colonial authorities for his alleged connection to the La Escalera conspiracy in 1844.[77]

Carruthers's residency in Cuba and his position at Howard allowed him to eventually take positions at the Pan American Union, the OCIAA, and the U.S. State Department, where he worked for the International Broadcasting Division. Most of his energies were devoted to coordinating the joint State Department and CBS radio program *Cadena de las Américas* (Network of the Americas). Hence Carruthers's activities during this period illustrate the ways in which Afro-Cubans could take advantage of opportunities made possible by the U.S. government's Good Neighbor foreign policy.[78]

Rayford Logan was another African American scholar who attempted to use the project of good-neighborism for cultural exchanges between African descendants in Cuba and the United States. As we have seen, he promoted travel to Cuba in the *Afro-American* during the tumultuous period of Machado's overthrow. In the early 1940s, he sought to use his expertise to shape the Roosevelt administration's policies with respect to African descendants in the hemisphere. He accepted Rockefeller's invitation to be part of the advisory committee of the OCIAA. Among the projects he proposed was increasing "the number of black students, teachers, and artists involved in exchanges with Latin American countries," and, not surprisingly, "an investigation into discrimination by common carriers in inter-American travel." His own experiences of racial discrimination by steamship companies during a trip to Haiti in

Ben Frederic Carruthers (*left*) with Angel Suárez Rocabruna on the *Cadena de las Américas* radio program. Courtesy of Photographs and Prints Division, Schomburg Center for Research in Black Culture, The New York Public Library, Astor, Lenox and Tilden Foundations.

1934 made him particularly attuned to the issue of racial discrimination by the international transit industry.[79]

While Logan struggled against the racism of his colleagues on the advisory committee, who could not imagine taking the recommendations of a black scholar seriously, he still managed to secure support for a research trip in March 1942 on the "Negro Contribution to Hemispheric Solidarity with Special Reference to Cuba, the Dominican Republic, and Haiti." Logan spent part of his research trip in Cuba, where he interacted with Havana's Afro-Cuban cultural elite, including Urrutia, Ramos Blanco, and Suárez Rocabruna. He also visited with the leaders of the Afro-Cuban societies, including the Unión Fraternal and the Club Atenas. By the end of his stay on the island, Logan pondered the possibility of a "People's InterAmerican Rehabilitation Fund" that would be funded by the United States and other large Latin American nations "for low cost housing, schools, etc. *in other words a kind of Western Hemisphere New Deal largely financed by the people of the U.S.*"[80] Not surprisingly, the OCIAA did not adopt Logan's recommendations.

Although Logan's vision of a New Deal for the hemisphere was ignored by the white-dominated OCIAA, his idea of promoting international exchange programs between African American and Latin American students and teachers was taken up by black educational institutions. In the early 1940s, Howard provided a residency for Angel Suárez Rocabruna. It was also during this period that the university hosted an exhibition of Teodoro Ramos Blanco's sculptures, including a bust of Antonio Maceo that the artist gave to the school.[81] Mercer Cook, another African American scholar with a specialty in Romance languages, taught at the University of Havana around the same time. His numerous articles for the *Afro-American* newspaper in the early 1940s publicized other exchange programs organized by African American institutions and the University of Havana.[82]

Another set of intellectual linkages was generated by the visit of W. E. B. Du Bois and Irene Diggs to Cuba in June 1941. Upon their arrival, they received a warm welcome from their Cuban hosts, many of whom were the same figures who coordinated receptions for African American visitors in previous years, including Miguel Angel Céspedes, who along with Fernando Ortiz coordinated their itinerary. Soon after Du Bois and Diggs unpacked their bags in Havana, they made what was now a familiar stop at the Club Atenas, where they enjoyed a concert organized by the association's Sección Femenina (Women's Section) and directed by Zoila Gálvez, the soprano often compared to Marian Anderson, the African American opera singer. Like other African American elite travelers to Cuba, Du Bois left the island enamored with Atenas, telling Céspedes, who was then president of the club, that he had a "deep admiration for the splendid organization which you have."[83] Du Bois and Diggs then drove the length of the island in his Buick to Santiago, where they met with other Afro-Cuban intellectuals and public officials. The governor of Oriente province arranged for Du Bois to motor into the mountains of the Sierra Maestra, where he was mesmerized by the sight of "Santiago clasping the little bay in her arms with the jewel of Morro Castle" and "the hills of Haiti" from five thousand feet above sea level.[84] The seventy-three-year-old Du Bois was rejuvenated by the trip, writing to Ortiz following his return to the United States that he "had not only opportunity for thought and observation, but one of the best vacations and periods of rest that I have ever experienced. I come back with renewed vigor to attack the world problems of race and color."[85]

The 1941 trip was important for Diggs, who returned to Cuba to study with Fernando Ortiz at the University of Havana two years later. After serving for many years as Du Bois's assistant, she was eventually able to pursue her own anthropological research in Cuba. Like Carruthers, she obtained foundation money—a Roosevelt fellowship to study at the University of Havana. During her residency in Havana, she associated herself with the Afro-Cuban intellectual community, including Afro-Cuban feminists such as Ana Echegoyen de Cañizares. Like Du Bois, Diggs disseminated her knowledge of Afro-Cuban culture through her role as the Cuban correspondent for Claude Barnett's ANP. Her stay in Cuba turned out to be a seminal moment for the young anthropologist. After she earned her Ph.D. in 1946, she continued her work as a specialist on the experiences of people of African descent in the Spanish-speaking Americas. Diggs, like Zora Neale Hurston and Katherine Dunham, became part of a pathbreaking group of black women intellectuals who studied the cultural practices of people of African descent outside the United States. In so doing, she managed to carve out a space for herself as an important figure in an arena that was generally dominated by educated men of African descent. Moreover, her academic and journalistic writings on Afro-Cubans and other Afro–Latin Americans made her a key figure in the cultural and intellectual exchanges of the early 1940s.[86]

Even the ever-resourceful José García Inerarity figured out a way to enact his own form of intellectual exchanges. In the early 1940s, he used his connections to the Hampton Alumni Association and his position in the Department of Agriculture in the Fulgencio Batista administration to create student exchange programs. García remained true to the "Hampton-Tuskegee Idea" of technical education. He secured scholarships from the Cuban government to fund students to study agricultural engineering at Tuskegee and Hampton. Moreover, he continually kept Claude Barnett and his ANP abreast of his many business initiatives. Thus, García's activities in the 1940s illustrate the continuing importance of Hampton, Tuskegee, and other black educational institutions in the forging of Afro-diasporic linkages.[87]

In the Land of the Mother of Maceo

Irene Diggs's involvement in African American and Afro-Cuban intellectual exchanges in the early 1940s was preceded by another cultural exchange initiative by African American and Afro-Cuban women. In the summer of 1940, Mary McLeod Bethune's National Council of Negro Women (NCNW) organized a "seminar" in Cuba. Founded by the indefatigable and seemingly omnipresent Bethune in 1935, the NCNW represented a new type of black women's organization that went beyond racial uplift educational activities and adopted a more explicit orientation toward political advocacy. The NCNW's effectiveness was enhanced by Bethune's relationship to the White House, particularly to Eleanor Roosevelt. In 1943 the NCNW moved into a house at 1318 Vermont Avenue Northwest, where it would be strategically located between the White House, the Washington Mall, and the center of the city's black community in the Howard University area.[88]

While the NCNW's advocacy for black women in the United States is well known, their Pan-American-oriented activism has been less documented by historians. Beginning in 1940—before the creation of the OCIAA, the U.S. government's official "Good Neighbor" agency—the NCNW developed a Pan-Americanist vision that highlighted the interests of Afro-descended women across the hemisphere. The NCNW was particularly interested in connecting with Cuban and Haitian women. The seeds of this effort could have been planted during Bethune's 1930 trip to Cuba. However, it was Sue Bailey Thurman, the former YWCA secretary who was also detained by Cuban immigration authorities in 1930, who spearheaded this Pan-Afro-American initiative. Led by Thurman, who was the editor of the NCNW's *Aframerican Woman's Journal*, the council sought to make their presence known in the world of inter-American organizations. Thurman made these objectives clear in a letter she wrote to Bethune in March 1941. "If the white women's organizations will depend on ours to discover and bring to the public the contribution and need of the Negroid population of Latin countries," Bailey wrote, "we will be doing a great thing for all our people in this hemisphere."[89] Bailey's declaration highlights her desire to make the NCNW an authority on the "Negroid population" of the hemisphere vis-à-vis the predominantly white policy-making community in Washington. Taking advantage of its close relationship to the U.S. government, the NCNW reached out to the Commission of Inter-American Women, an organization dominated by elite white women across the hemisphere. In a manner similar to the ways Bethune developed ties to Eleanor Roosevelt, the council leader's organization established a relationship to Muna Lee, the head of the U.S. State Department's Division of Cultural Affairs. Lee agreed to serve as a guest editor of a special issue of *Aframerican Woman's Journal* dedicated to hemispheric solidarity among women. It was within this context that the NCNW decided to reach out to black women's groups in Cuba.

The co-organizer of the NCNW's trip to Cuba was the Asociación Cultural Femenina (Women's Cultural Association), the leading Afro-Cuban women's association of the period.[90] Like the NCNW, the ACF illustrated the changing character of Afro-descended women's associations. Founded in 1935, the organization represented the interests of elite and aspiring-class Afro-Cuban women, many of whom were related to members of leading Afro-Cuban societies in Havana, such as the Club Atenas and the Unión Fraternal. The association's constitution clearly shows that it was steeped in the elite project of racial uplift, evidenced by the repeated references to *mejoramiento* (improvement) in its constitution. The group sought to work toward the "civic and cultural improvement of women." However, it was a marked departure from earlier Afro-Cuban women's collectives, which tended to remain confined to the role of "women's sections" in the male-dominated Afro-Cuban societies. The key difference was the association's emphasis on Afro-Cubans' civic involvement, which undoubtedly was propelled by the need to mobilize new women voters, who gained suffrage rights in 1934. The founding of the ACF, even with its limited elite vision of female affirmation, highlights the growing influence of women's organizations in the 1930s.[91]

A major force behind the ACF was Ana Echegoyen de Cañizares. Echegoyen earned her status as one of the most prominent Afro-Cuban women in this period because she was the first woman of color to hold a teaching post at the University of Havana. This "prototypical" Cuban woman was celebrated in Afro-Cuban publications as embodying the qualities of "sacrifice," "love for family and her country," and a "thirst for knowledge." Aside from her work as an educator, where she extended her influence to "the humble homes of those who are in such a need for this apostolic dedication," Echegoyen was an active member of the feminist community. The emergence of Echegoyen and the ACF highlights the ways Afro-Cuban elite women were able to push against the male-dominated confines of their societies in this period.[92]

In the 1930s, Afro-Cuban feminists celebrated and publicized the work of Afro-Cuban female educators like Echegoyen. As we have seen, they had always placed a premium on education, which they viewed as the key to the "progress" and "improvement" of a population recently removed from slavery. This project of education was highly gendered and largely placed on the shoulders of women. As a historic tendency, it persisted into the 1930s and 1940s, since teaching remained one of the few fields open to women of color. Thus, Afro-Cuban women teachers were celebrated as "exemplary women," serving their role in the *reivindicación* (revindication) of the rights of the "colored race."[93]

But the work of organizing the "'first conferring together' of the two distinct Negro Women's Councils and participating groups, of the two Americas," as Thurman described the event, was accomplished by Sergio ("Henry"), Sylvia, and Evelio Grillo, three Afro-Cuban-American siblings who lived in Washington, D.C.[94] The Grillo story is known thanks to Evelio's fascinating memoir, which he titled, as he identified himself, *Black Cuban, Black American*, an exceedingly rare account of a man who struggled against discrimination while growing up in the segregated worlds of Tampa, Washington, and New Orleans. Evelio Grillo's elegant narrative shows how Jim Crow segregation separated him from his white Cuban-American counterparts and led him to embrace an African American identification.[95] In the 1930s, he found himself in the midst of the African American elite in Washington, D.C., after Nicholas Martin, a black acquaintance, took him north to continue his education. He wound up enrolling in the prestigious Dunbar High, formerly the M Street High School, which was the leading African American institution of secondary education in the country. Moreover, he was taken in by Sue Bailey and her husband Howard Thurman, the dean of Howard University's Rankin Chapel, which put him in contact with some of the leading members of the city's African American intelligentsia, including Rayford Logan, Ralph Bunche, and Alain Locke. It was this experience in Washington that led him to feel "free to be unambiguously black."[96]

While Evelio Grillo's story seems to easily lend itself to an assimilationist narrative, the experiences he and his family had actually highlight the process of transculturation, the making of a proto-Afro-Latino culture and identification. The Grillos' encounters with African Americans widen the notion of "blackness" so that it transcends the confines of an English-speaking "African American" construction. Because of their deep roots in Cuban and African American communities, the family served as cultural brokers between these two communities. Like the Afro-Cuban, West Indian, and African American Garveyites of the 1920s, the Grillos became transcultural subjects whose experiences elude the conceptual frame of race and nation. Their role as cultural emissaries in the NCNW's connections with Cuba highlights the ongoing dynamic of their multiple Afro-descended lineages.[97]

The Grillos' relationship with Bethune, Thurman, the NCNW, and Howard University illustrates their transcultural experience. Evelio's encounter with the Thurmans and the Howard University community was clearly made possible by his older brother Henry. While details of the elder Grillo's life are fragmented, even in Evelio's narrative, it is clear that he was an important factor in his younger brother's transition to Washington. Unlike Evelio, Henry appears to have maintained a stronger connection to Cuba, due to his stays on the island during his youth. Henry's eventual move to the nation's capital was an outgrowth of his relationship with Bethune, which began when he was a student at Bethune-Cookman in the early 1930s.[98] Henry Grillo's enrollment at the African American school is not surprising, given the ways racial segregation shaped the educational options for Afro-Cubans, especially those living in Jim Crow Florida. Evelio himself recalled in his memoir that he "did not know any black Cuban college graduate of my generation, and [of] all the generations preceding desegregation, who is not a graduate of a historically black college."[99]

Not unlike the Afro-Cuban alumni of Tuskegee and Hampton who maintained connections to their school, Henry Grillo seems to have felt a deep attachment to Bethune and her school. As Evelio recalled, Henry "thoroughly enjoyed being one of Mrs. Bethune's boys."[100] He followed Bethune to Washington when she took a position with the National Youth Administration. Not unlike José García Inerarity, Henry Grillo combined his loyalty to Bethune with his entrepreneurial interests. He was the "business manager" of the NCNW's 1940 trip to Cuba. Moreover, his siblings Evelio and Sylvia, a student at Miner's Teachers College in Washington, organized the NCNW's contacts with the ACF and other Afro-Cuban institutions. As Thurman wrote in her summation of the trip, Sylvia Grillo and her husband José Griñán, along with Echegoyen, had "prepared a comprehensive program of study consisting of nine conferences to be given during the Seminar period." In short, the Grillos as transcultural Afro-Cuban-American subjects provided the necessary links between the associations. As we shall see, Henry continued to act as a cultural emissary between African American and Afro-Cuban communities in subsequent years.

To the NCNW, the trip to Cuba was a "mission of contact and study," a characterization that underscores the cultural tourist thrust of Afro-diasporic travel in this period. To Pedro Portuondo Calá, one of the Afro-Cuban organizers of the tour, the seminar gave "the Cuban woman of the colored race" the opportunity to show her guests how she "concerns herself with and works for justice and social equality." Likewise, Thurman was confident that "in the land of the mother of a Maceo the record of the American Negro woman's achievements would join eminent company and be given a welcome place." By all accounts, these aspirations for cultural exchange were realized. The host institutions were the ACF, the Unión Fraternal, and of course, the Club Atenas. Thurman's summary of the trip reported that the delegates heard nine different lectures by members of the Afro-Cuban intelligentsia, including one by Echegoyen ("The Social Life of Cuba and the Negro Woman"), another by Francisco Goyri Reyes, the president of the Provincial Federation of Colored Societies of Havana, who lectured on "The Negro during the Period of Slavery in Cuba," and another by the "brilliant young lawyer, doctor in pedagogy, as well as a doctor in civil rights, Pedro Oliva Acosta," who spoke about "The History of Thirty Years of Revolutionary Action." The final two lectures were given by Juan Jiménez Pastrana, the "eminent historian" who spoke about "The Negro in the Republic," and Ramos Blanco, who informed readers about the status of "The Cuban Negro in the Arts." Along with the lectures, the NCNW delegation and their hosts witnessed two performances, one by Ada Fisher, a member of the delegation who interpreted "the worship moods of two early Negro Spirituals, a contribution warmly received," and a rendition of "Ave María" by the Afro-Cuban soprano Zoila Gálvez.[101]

Thurman's references to the performances by Fisher and Gálvez provide glimpses of the leisure activities that took place during the NCNW's "mission of contact and study." The NCNW's chronicle of their itinerary reveals how the group represented their trip under the cloak of respectable entertainment. Along with the seminars that were held at the headquarters of the ACF, the Unión Fraternal, and the Club Atenas, the delegation visited the homes of ACF members, attended a wedding, and sampled the "finest delicacies of the Cuban cuisine" at a banquet held at the Polar Gardens, an outdoor venue on the outskirts of Havana where many Afro-Cuban societies held dances. At the gardens, the NCNW visitors "were permitted a share in the Cuban's famed and enviable capacity for enjoyment." Although the precise aspects of this "capacity for enjoyment" are unclear, it is probable that the delegation listened and danced to a Cuban band that day. One can only wonder if other sorts of Afro-diasporic linkages were enacted on the dance floor at the Polar Gardens in addition to the exchanges foregrounded in Thurman's report. Such descriptions suggest the ways the black cultural exchange tours of the Good Neighbor era sought to merge leisure activities with the loftier goals of cultural elevation and coalition building.

The seminar turned out to be an invigorating experience that cemented the NCNW's ties to Afro-Cuban associations. Pedro Portuondo Calá, the best-known Afro-Cuban journalist in Havana after Gustavo Urrutia, hailed the trip a success. "One immediate lesson we can learn from this visit," he wrote in his column in *El País*, was "the conviction which the American Negro holds that one of the basic pillars of his general progress is to be found precisely in his own organization."[102] Here again, one notes Afro-Cuban elite desires to emulate the organizational traditions of African Americans. To the NCNW, the trip to Cuba strengthened its credibility within Washington's Good Neighbor policy circles. However, the ties that were forged "in the land of the mother of a Maceo" in the summer of 1940 continued after the era of good-neighborism. The relationships made by Grillo, the NCNW, and Afro-Cuban societies would persist as one war ended and a new one began.

Black Tourism in the Post–World War II Era

The postwar economic boom in the United States and Cuba led to a resurgence of tourism in Cuba. Indeed, the 1950s was the heyday of the Cuban tourist industry, driven by the expansion of air travel, of the American middle class, and of the influence of organized crime figures in the Cuban tourist sector. The growth of tourism was also shaped by the emerging consumer culture of the postwar era. These broader transformations gave the American middle class, including some African Americans, more income for travel and recreation.[103] Elite Afro-Cubans, like their white Cuban counterparts, also benefited from the postwar boom due to the island's deep integration into the U.S. economy. In the late 1940s, they began to take annual vacations to the United States. However, as the emerging civil rights movement waged an assault on Jim Crow, black travelers still had to contend with the racialization of travel and recreational options. It was in this period that the networks that had first emerged in the 1930s became more elaborate as Afro-descended entrepreneurs and organizations in Cuba and the United States sought to accommodate greater numbers of black travelers between the two countries.

Emerging black tourist linkages between Cuba and the United States were also shaped by the geopolitics of the Cold War. The U.S. government's shift from the Good Neighbor policy to the holy war against communism only enhanced the urgency to promote linkages with Latin American countries. In an attempt to counter the Cuban Communist Party's track record of support for Afro-Cuban rights, the U.S. government touted democracy by promoting the achievements of the "American Negro" to Cubans of African descent. Such efforts, which began during the Second World War, intensified during the Cold War.[104] In the 1950s, the U.S. embassy in Havana disseminated the writings of African American intellectuals in Cuba, especially the works of anticommunists such as George Schuyler. Moreover, they forged connections with Afro-Cuban associations, including the Instituto Interamericano de lucha contra la discriminación racial (Inter-American Institute for the Struggle against Racial Discrimination), an organization led by Serapio Páez Zamora. The U.S. embassy apparently convinced the Instituto Interamericano that the U.S. government was in fact responsible for the desegregation measures taking shape in the southern United States. In 1955, the institute organized a tribute to President Dwight Eisenhower for his administration's efforts "to eradicate racial segregation in education and other sectors of the country." Thus, U.S. imperial objectives continued to influence the contours of Afro-Cuban and African.American interaction during the early years of the Cold War.[105]

As in the past, Afro-Cuban and African American cultural institutions, rather than the U.S. State Department, were the primary initiators of the relationships between the two communities in the early postwar years. The emphasis on travel in the 1950s is not surprising, given the resurgence of civil rights activism by both populations. In the United States, the Montgomery Bus Boycott in 1955 was a tremendous boost for the movement against Jim Crow transit.[106] In Cuba, Afro-Cuban organizations continued their long-standing campaign against racism in leisure and hiring practices. They called on Cuban legislators to enact harsher penalties against employers who were found guilty of racial discrimination. However, such efforts were frustrated by the rampant political corruption on the island.[107] Still, some Afro-Cuban activists sought to act on Pedro Portuondo Calá's "lesson" on the importance of black autonomous mobilization that he proclaimed after the 1940 NCNW visit. Juan René Betancourt's Organización Nacional de Rehabilitación Económica (ONRE, National Organization of Economic Rehabilitation), an umbrella organization that sought to stimulate black economic development, was perhaps the boldest attempt at black autonomous organization. As Betancourt's writings illustrate, his orientation to the question of racial discrimination was clearly inspired by his understanding of African American freedom struggles. As he wrote in his *El negro: Ciudadano del futuro* (The Negro: Citizen of the Future), "Negro Americano . . . The Discriminated Men of the world entrust themselves to you."[108]

While Afro-Cuban organizations continued to press the Cuban state to eliminate racial discrimination in recreational practices, others expanded their options for recreation by traveling abroad. In the late 1940s and early 1950s, the Unión Fraternal and the Club Atenas organized annual trips to the United States for Afro-Cuban travelers. In August 1947, Ramón Cabrera Torres, the president of the Unión Fraternal, began the "social-cultural excursion" movement for prospective Afro-Cuban tourists. For $146.50, travelers could enjoy an eighteen-day trip to the United States. Their itinerary included a Pan-American flight from Havana to Miami, followed by a two-day Greyhound bus ride northward to Washington, D.C., before continuing on for an eleven-day stay in New York City. While the tour included visits to popular tourist sites in New York City, such as Coney Island, Radio City, the Metropolitan Museum of Art, and even the Bronx Zoo, Afro-Cuban travelers devoted most of their time to visiting African American cultural institutions. During their two days in Washington, the travelers visited Howard University and the headquarters of the NCNW. During their stay in New York, the group visited the NAACP and the newly formed Club Cubano Interamericano, a predominantly Afro-Cuban cultural institution founded in the Bronx in 1945. The emergence of the Club Cubano Interamericano highlights the growth of the Caribbean Latino community in New York in the 1940s and its ties to older Afro-Cuban associational traditions in Cuba and Tampa.[109]

Afro-Cuban tour organizers clearly saw this as an opportunity to model their trip after those of their "illustrious" African American visitors in previous years. "No one can deny the importance and transcendence of this trip that will allow us, not only to reciprocate the frequent visits of illustrious representatives of our race residing in the United States, but also to establish linkages and relations with sister organizations that effectively contribute to the elevation of our culture." The brochure's marketing of the trip's potential to "elevate" Afro-Cuban culture reveals the ways Afro-Cuban associations continued to project the notion that African Americans were the most modern sector of the African diaspora even in the 1950s. While Afro-Cubans had read about African American cultural institutions for decades, few had the opportunity to experience them in person. The excursions of this period promised what was an unprecedented form of cultural contact.

Cabrera's correspondence with the NCNW conveys the enthusiasm of the excursionists. A few weeks before the delegation's arrival, he informed the council that his group was excited about the "opportunity to express our great desire for fraternal, social, and spiritual exchange between Negroes of the United States and Cuba." He also informed NCNW leaders that "the women in the group are elated over the prospects of visiting you." The letter ended with Cabrera expressing the "great desire to know Howard University." Thus, the Afro-Cuban travelers were well aware of the school's reputation as the "capstone of Negro education."[110]

Documents from the NCNW papers show that the council presented prominent members of the black Washington community to its visitors from Cuba. On at least one occasion, the Reverend Robert Moten Williams of the Asbury Methodist Church, "the largest Negro Methodist Church in the world," extended an invitation to the "distinguished group." Moreover, the NCNW organized receptions for the Afro-Cuban delegation during their stopovers in 1947, 1948, 1949, and probably beyond. It had prominent African American figures—people such as Charles Hamilton Houston, the well-known civil rights lawyer who pioneered the legal campaign against Jim Crow; Emmer Lancaster, the "Special Advisor" on Negro Affairs for the Department of Commerce; and of course Bethune herself— "tell the delegation about the Negro in America." The NCNW asked attending organizations to bring greetings for the Afro-Cuban delegation "so they can be placed in a scrap book and presented to Mr. Cala for the delegation."[111] Guests were given flyers with information on the NCNW translated into Spanish. Their visitors reciprocated by presenting the council with a Cuban flag, which Bethune viewed as a "gesture of friendliness, love and understanding." The NCNW leader warmly conveyed to her visitors that it made her "heart glad to see us fellowship together even though we did not understand too well our different languages." Bethune's comments once again highlight the ways in which bodily gestures such as the donation of the Cuban flag could communicate "friendliness, love, and understanding" across linguistic and cultural differences.[112]

The delegation's itinerary also reveals the presence of a small Cuban community in the U.S. capital. The Comité Cubano de Washington (Cuban Committee of Washington), in which the Grillos were prominent members, organized a night of entertainment for their Afro-Cuban visitors. Guests were taken from the newly opened Dunbar Hotel to the Stardust Club, where they danced, drank Cuba Libres and other rum-based drinks, and ate Cuban-style sandwiches. The Cuban committee saw the event as a "humble offering of the small number of Cubans in this Capital."[113] The existence of the Cuban committee, however small, complicates prevailing understandings of African American history in Washington. In some ways, the committee's participation in the coordination of the visit is an example of African American and proto-Latino cultural interaction.

The advent of these Afro-Cuban excursions in the late 1940s and early 1950s reveals the existence of an intricate tourist network, organized by an assortment of organizations under the coordination of the Cuban-American Goodwill Association, an obscure organization headed by none other than Sergio "Henry" Grillo and Pedro Portuondo Calá that promoted cultural exchanges between Afro-Cubans and African Americans. While the founding of the association is uncertain, what is clear is that Grillo's experience as coordinator of the NCNW's 1940 seminar informed his participation in the development of the association. The Cuban-American Goodwill Association seems to have specialized in creating tourist opportunities specifically for Afro-Cuban travelers. The association worked with African American institutions, as well as white travel agencies and passenger carriers, including Pan-American Airways and Greyhound Bus Lines. Grillo's linguistic facility, evidenced by the fact that he frequently served as a translator for visiting delegations, and his connections to African American and Afro-Cuban communities enabled him to play a decisive role in the creation of the tourist network. Thus, the Cuban-American Goodwill Association was an attempt to profit from the emerging market in black tourism.

Getting to northern cities such as Washington, New York, and eventually Montreal required many Afro-Cuban travelers to navigate the bumpy roads of Jim Crow southern bus routes of the late 1940s and 1950s. While tour brochures played up the scenic stops in southern towns such as "Daytona and its beautiful beach," Saint Augustine, Savannah, and Richmond, finding places to eat and rest was no easy task. The correspondence between the Cuban-American Goodwill Association and African American institutions highlights the ways tour organizers tried to evade the ever-present possibility of humiliating experiences in the Jim Crow South. Before their 1952 excursion, Pedro Portuondo Calá solicited Claude Barnett's help in finding rest stops along their route through parts of the South. "In order to avoid possible racial discrimination," he wrote, "I wish to make a stop in any place, restaurant or hotel of Negro people." Portuondo Calá hoped that Barnett could recommend places where they could stop for "one or two hours at Charleston, S.C., Georgetown, S.C.; Wilmington, N.C.; Raleigh and Richmond, in order to rest a little and take a meal."[114]

The coordination of the Afro-Cuban delegation's itinerary highlights the ways the tours depended upon connections between transit companies and African American hotels that thrived on Jim Crow segregation in the early postwar era. Barnett, who himself traveled with a group of African American physicians to Cuba and other parts of the Caribbean that same year, had contacts with bus lines and hotels throughout the South. With Barnett's help, Portuondo Calá contacted T. B. O'Steen, a manager for Greyhound, who informed him that his company could "easily arrange to have the passengers taken care of at the Richmond Hotel in Jacksonville, and the Arcade Hotel in Raleigh." "You may rest assured," the Greyhound manager informed Portuondo Calá, "they will be well taken care of."[115] Barnett and the Greyhound manager's assistance allowed the Afro-Cuban travelers to find accommodations in the emerging black tourist sector of the Jim Crow South. They rested and dined at black establishments along the way, including the Arcade Hotel in Raleigh, North Carolina, and Slaughter's Hotel in Richmond, Virginia. By the end of the trip, Portuondo Calá was satisfied with the excursion. Writing from the historic Lord Calvert Hotel (later renamed the St. John), the establishment in Miami's black Overtown district where African American travelers and celebrities laid their heads at night, Portuondo Calá stretched his limited English to extend to Barnett his "personal regards and distinguish[ed] consideration to you for your aid in order to [ensure a] more happy trip for my Cuban group. We are very happy because we [had a] very good trip to New York, Montreal, Can., and Washington."[116]

But not all Afro-Cubans were enamored with the messages conveyed by black tourism. Serapio Páez Zamora, the president of the Instituto Interamericano, complained to Claude Barnett that the excursions perpetuated misconceptions about Afro-Cuban life. In a 1955 letter, he emphatically argued that the "touring negroes who annually visit the United States of North America, have never shown to YOU, our racial [brethren], the message of the true living ways and sufferings annihilating the negro population of the island." Páez Zamora warned Barnett that he should not be misled by the fact that Afro-Cuban visitors portrayed themselves as "rich tourists," arguing that they lacked real economic power like "all the rest of their brethrens of [their] race."[117] Páez Zamora's claims highlight the sharpening political and economic crisis in

Cuba during the 1950s, a turmoil that would give rise to a revolution that at once promoted racial equality in an unprecedented manner while destroying the structural foundations that had animated Afro-Cuban and African American cultural interaction during the previous five decades.

However, the ramifications of the Cuban Revolution were not at all apparent in 1952. The excursions of the early 1950s prompted some to enroll their sons and daughters in African American educational institutions. Like the Afro-Cuban parents who sent their children to Tuskegee in the opening decades of the century, they viewed black schools as opportunities for social mobility even though they were in the midst of the Jim Crow South. Portuondo Calá's visits to Bethune-Cookman College in Daytona Beach led him to send his son, Pedrito, to study at the school. While the details of his tenure at BCC are uncertain, it is clear that Pedrito's experience at the college made an impression on Henry Grillo, himself an alumnus of the school. Writing as representative of the Cuban-American Goodwill Association to school president Richard V. Moore, Grillo proposed his "pet idea of encouraging students from Cuba to come to BCC." Grillo informed Moore that his group was "very much encouraged with the wonderful results you have achieved with young Pedro Portuondo. I saw him in Washington this summer and his progress amazed me."[118] Thus the Afro-Cuban excursions of the early 1950s led to further cultural exchanges. Grillo and Portuondo Calá recruited a few more students to Bethune-Cookman during the early 1950s. As in the era of Good Neighborism, tourism and cultural exchange went hand-in-hand in the 1950s. The experience of one of Bethune-Cookman's Afro-Cuban alumni allows us to uncover remnants of the history of Afro-Cuban and African American diasporic linkages from the prerevolutionary period in the post-1959 era. It is to that story we now turn.

Epilogue

In November 1976, a delegation of African American artists and writers arrived at the José Martí International Airport in Havana on a flight from Mexico City. The trip, which was led by Robert Chrisman, editor of the journal *Black Scholar*, the leading publication of the radicalized black intelligentsia in the United States, occurred only a few weeks after the frightening bombing of a Cubana Airlines flight by anti-Castro terrorists. Chrisman hailed the group as the "first black American delegation of cultural workers to visit Cuba" since the triumph of the Cuban Revolution in 1959. The group of "cultural workers" he assembled included some of the foremost African American writers and artists of the day: Bernice Reagon, Phyl Garland, Samella Lewis, Alice Walker, William Marshall, Theresa George, Conyus Calhoun, and Lance Jeffers. The delegation sought to witness the "development of culture within a revolutionary context," and more specifically, "the interface between the African components of Cuba with the non-African, to gauge the extent to which Cuba was developing a revolutionary national culture." The Instituto Cubano de Amistad con los Pueblos (Cuban Institute of Friendship with the People), a branch of the Cuban revolutionary government, arranged the visitors' itinerary. During their two-week stay on the island, the group listened to lectures on Cuban history and culture, attended a dance performance at the Parque Lenin, and visited various museums, including the Museo Histórico de Guanabacoa, where they saw an exhibit on the Abakuá secret society and other Afro-descended cultures in Cuba. The 1976 tour, which was one of a number of trips to the island led by Chrisman during the 1970s and 1980s, impressed him enough to lead him to conclude that Cuba was pioneering a "renaissance in the Third World."[1]

The visit of the *Black Scholar* delegation in 1976 illustrates the continuities and ruptures in African American and Afro-Cuban linkages after the Cuban revolutionary government of Fidel Castro took power in 1959. Like earlier generations of African American travelers to Cuba, the delegation was particularly interested in the island's Afro-descended population. However, unlike their predecessors, these African American visitors did not go to Cuba merely to see "their own people" or to take in the Caribbean sun, although they surely enjoyed the island's pleasant climate during their stay. Instead, they wanted to witness firsthand the Cuban government's effort to make a revolutionary national culture from the nation's African and non-African cultural roots. Chrisman's comments illustrate the ways in which the revolutionary government further nationalized (and internationalized) blackness in its representation of Cuban national culture. The delegation's objectives also show how the revolution's brand of *mestizaje* ideology had altered the debate on blackness in Cuba from an emphasis on "race relations" to a focus on "culture." This subtle shift was a by-product of the Cuban government's claim that the revolution had virtually eliminated racism on the island, a position that was championed by its supporters, including some African Americans.[2] After all, Fidel Castro himself had made the unprecedented declaration that Cubans were a "Latin African people" in a speech justifying the sending of Cuban troops in support of the revolutionary struggle in Angola earlier that year. Thus, while the *Black Scholar* group was attentive to evidence of racism and sexism on the island, it was more concerned with ascertaining how the revolution was integrating Afro-Cuban culture into a new Cuban revolutionary "national culture."[3]

The Cuban Revolution's explicit solidarity with Afro-descended people throughout the diaspora, along with the emergence of nation-states in Africa and other parts of the "Third World," dramatically altered the making of Afro-diasporic linkages after 1959. In the era of decolonization and Third World revolution, the discourse of diaspora was largely submerged by a competing discourse of "nation." Diasporization, which had been carried out largely by nonstate actors since the era of the slave trade, was championed by "black" or explicitly antiracist states and by "national liberation" movements that sought to overthrow colonial rule. African Americans, who were still embroiled in their own struggles for equality during the civil rights era, sought out linkages with many of these nation-states, including Ghana, Algeria, and Cuba. The heightened importance of the concept of "nation" in Afro-diasporic formations is clear in the *Black Scholar* group's itinerary in Cuba. Like previous African American visitors to the island, the delegation received a warm welcome from their Cuban hosts. Unlike Langston Hughes, William Pickens, the NCNW delegation, and countless other African American visitors who came to the island during the pre-1959 era, the *Black Scholar* group was greeted not by an Afro-Cuban organization, but rather by an institution of the Cuban state. This was perhaps the most important difference in Afro-Cuban and African American linkages between the pre- and post-1959 periods. The forging of Cuba's alliance with the Soviet Union in 1960 and the consolidation of U.S. hostility against the revolution in the years that followed ensured that Afro-Cuban and African American interaction would be determined by the policies of the governments in both Havana and Washington, D.C. The ramifications of this transformation were far-reaching, constraining the Afro-diasporic linkages between Afro-Cubans and African Americans within the polarizing politics of the Cold War. To express support for the revolution and its policies on race was to align oneself with the "communist" world, while criticizing the Castro regime for ongoing racism in Cuba could earn one the tag of "counter-revolutionary." It was for these reasons that African American linkages with Cuba and its Afro-descended population tended to be promoted by black radical intellectuals and activists, in contrast to the wider range of black political actors in the prerevolutionary era.[4]

On a more fundamental level, the rupture in Cuban-U.S. relations destroyed the structural basis of Afro-Cuban and African American interaction. The severing of diplomatic relations between Cuba and the United States and the revolutionary government's incorporation into the Soviet bloc abruptly removed Cuba from the U.S.-Caribbean transborder zone that had been in place since 1898. Cuba was no longer the center of the U.S. empire in the Caribbean, a region that came under even greater U.S. influence after the retreat of British colonialism during the 1960s and 1970s. While the Cuban government welcomed U.S. visitors to the island, particularly after its revival of tourism in the 1990s, the U.S. travel ban and trade embargo dramatically curtailed the intimate ties that had linked the two countries for more than a century. Travelers from the United States who sought to circumvent the travel ban, like the *Black Scholar* delegation, often had to use indirect routes to Cuba via Mexico or Canada. Thus, the Cold War dismantled the engine that drove the creation of Afro-diasporic linkages: the constant flow of people and ideas between the two countries.[5]

If the conflict between the Cuban and U.S. governments damaged the structures of cross-border connections that made diaspora in action possible before the 1960s, the decline of segregated black institutions further disassembled the foundations of Afro-Cuban and African American linkages. As historians have shown, an unforeseen consequence of the gains of the civil rights movement was the decline of some African American institutions of the Jim Crow era, particularly black schools. Despite their status as separate and unequal institutions and their vulnerability to the Jim Crow political machinery, segregated black schools played decisive roles in the sustenance of African American communities and in the reproduction of the African American elite and middle class. As doors to predominantly white schools and professions opened, upwardly mobile African Americans no longer had to rely on black institutions to advance in U.S. society. Thus, as the boundaries of citizenship in the United States expanded in the 1960s and 1970s, African Americans had a greater incentive to invest their energies in national institutions. To be sure, black organizations and schools continued to play key roles in the lives of African Americans. However, as they became more integrated into formerly inaccessible routes of upward mobility, the power of relatively autonomous institutions and associations such as the NAACP, the black press, and black schools, now known as "historically black colleges and universities" (HBCUs), diminished. This transformation lessened the need for African Americans to pursue cross-national linkages as a strategy to combat racial discrimination. The post–civil rights era produced new conditions that required different strategies of negotiating racialized power in the United States.[6]

In Cuba, the decline of Afro-descended institutions occurred much more rapidly. In the early years of the revolution, the Afro-Cuban societies, like all Cuban associations that were racially segregated, were positioned as symbols of the country's odious history of racial segregation and class exclusivity. With widespread support, the revolutionary government undertook a campaign against racial discrimination by targeting all societies that were segregated along racial lines regardless of their racial makeup. The Club Atenas fell victim to this initiative. In 1961, the state seized Atenas's property and converted it into a *círculo infantil* (daycare center). All references to the building's history as the Club Atenas were quickly erased. This was the fate that met virtually all Afro-Cuban associations. The Cuban government's project of national integration entailed attacking not only the structures of racial discrimination, but all forms of racially defined social activity, including the relatively autonomous Afro-Cuban associations.[7]

Although the triumph of the Cuban Revolution undeniably inspired visions of genuine racial equality in Cuba, especially among those in solidarity with the revolution, it also has had the effect of silencing the history of Afro-Cuban associations and their connections to African American institutions before 1959. This silence continued beyond the Cold War era into the contem-

The former Club Atenas building, July 2006. Photograph by the author.

porary period. On a typically hot and humid July afternoon in Havana in 2005, I embarked on a search for the old headquarters of the Club Atenas. After a day of research, I departed from the Archivo Nacional de Cuba in La Habana Vieja (Old Havana) and headed north on Avenida Bélgica, passing the remnants of the Hotel Las Villas, where Langston Hughes stayed in 1930 and 1931, and El Baturro, the restaurant directly across the street where he dined with Cuban intellectuals. After turning left on Apodaca Street, I saw the building on the northwest corner of Zulueta and Apodaca, across from a police station and not too far away from the old clubhouse of the Unión Fraternal. Although the building was open during my previous trips to the island, this time it was clearly abandoned, fenced off from the public so that no one could enter its doors. As I peeked through the holes of the fence in an attempt to ascertain the current

Ramiro de la Cuesta,
July 2005. Courtesy of
Deborah Paredez.

status of the structure, a woman of African descent, who looked to be in her
forties, walked by and, gesturing toward the building, said to me: "Es un círculo infantil" (It is a daycare center). I nodded, fully aware of the building's
postrevolutionary history. I turned toward her and responded by saying: "Fue
una sociedad de color antes del triunfo de la revolución" (It was a colored society before the triumph of the revolution). The woman looked somewhat surprised, but ultimately unmoved. She shrugged her shoulders and walked away.

Although the pre-1959 exchanges between Afro-Cubans and African Americans have been largely silenced in the five decades since the triumph of the
revolution, the memory of those years lives on among some Afro-Cubans who
came of age in the prerevolutionary era. A few days after my search for the old
Atenas building, I made my way through the Centro Habana district accompanied by two friends of mine: historian Barbara Danzie León, a specialist on
nineteenth-century Afro-Cuban history, and her father, Nelio "Nilo" Danzie
Cooper, who encouraged me to visit the home of sixty-nine-year-old Ramiro

Nelio Danzie Cooper, July 2005. Courtesy of Deborah Paredez.

de la Cuesta. Ramiro, as I soon discovered, was the son of Ramiro Cuesta Rendón, a famous Afro-Cuban lawyer who was one of the founding members of the Club Atenas. We went to Ramiro de la Cuesta's home, a top-floor apartment in a three-story building in the Cayo Hueso neighborhood, and as soon as we sat down, the conversation took an unexpected turn. Ramiro began by recounting some of his family history and his father's role in the movement against racial discrimination in Cuba. Then, to my surprise, he informed me that he loved jazz music and proceeded to put on John Coltrane's classic album *Blue Train*. "Do you know what this is?" he asked me. As a fervent Coltrane admirer myself, I said, *"Blue Train"* without hesitation. As Coltrane's saxophone solo took off into full flight, Ramiro told me about some of his favorite artists and then showed me a copy of Miles Davis's autobiography that had been signed by Quincy Troupe. I soon discovered that Ramiro himself was a singer, musicologist, and historian of Cuban music with a specialty in the "feeling" movement of the 1940s and 1950s.[8]

Barbara Danzie León, July 2005. Courtesy of Deborah Paredez.

Ramiro's love for jazz was not a product of mere curiosity. As he pulled out documents from his own life, he told me that he attended Bethune-Cookman College in the 1950s. I subsequently realized that he was one of the Afro-Cuban students who attended BCC as a result of the tourist excursions organized by Henry Grillo and Pedro Portuondo Calá's Cuban-American Goodwill Association. Ramiro's documents included one of his yearbooks from his time at the school, which contained pictures of him playing football, a program from the 1953 commencement where Ralph Bunche was the keynote speaker, and of course, pictures of Mary McLeod Bethune. Along with Pedrito Portuondo Calá, he had been among the latter cohorts of Afro-Cubans who studied at one of the HBCUs in the United States before the revolution.

Jazz clearly had been a topic of conversation among some Afro-Cuban intellectuals in the months preceding my 2005 visit to the island. During that visit Ramiro, Barbara, and Nilo informed me of Gloria Rolando's *Nosotros y el Jazz* (Jazz and Us), a documentary about Afro-Cuban encounters with

American jazz during the 1940s and 1950s.[9] The documentary highlights the role of *Stormy Weather*, a 1943 Hollywood musical film that starred a slew of famous African American performers including Lena Horne and Bill "Bojangles" Robinson, in the popularization of jazz and African American dance styles in Cuba. As our conversation continued, Ramiro told us he had a VHS copy of *Stormy Weather* that he wanted us to watch with him. For the next hour and a half, we sat and watched the movie, surrounded by walls that contained emblems of Cuba's history of diaspora-making. On the wall to my left was an image of the Virgen de la Caridad del Cobre (Our Lady of Charity of El Cobre) alongside a number of jazz festival posters. In front of the wall to my right was an altar to Yemayá, the Yoruba-derived orisha. As I watched Lena Horne, Bill Robinson, Cab Calloway, and Katherine Dunham sing and dance on the TV screen, I felt the past and present of Afro-diasporic encounters come together. The irony of the moment was inescapable. This history was enacted in the home of an Afro-Cuban who had been schooled in the tenets of racial respectability and disidentification with Africa by the old Afro-Cuban elite and who now exemplified and embraced the histories of Afro-diasporic transculturation in Cuba.

This powerful encounter brought me back to visit with Ramiro one year later. This time I met him and four of his friends, Osvaldo, Angela, José, and Mari, at his apartment to watch Gloria Rolando's *Nosotros y el Jazz*.[10] Like Ramiro, his friends are Afro-Cubans in their sixties and seventies who are known as the "Santa Amalia dancers," an informal cluster of Afro-Cubans who have gathered together to dance to the sounds of Duke Ellington, Cab Calloway, Dizzy Gillespie, and other African American jazz performers since the 1980s.[11] As we sat around the television set, I quickly discovered that Rolando's documentary is a groundbreaking historical work. The film uses the gatherings of the Santa Amalia group to illustrate the ways Afro-Cubans in the 1940s and 1950s encountered African American popular culture. Among the many persons Rolando interviewed was Ramiro himself. As Ramiro sat on the *malecón* (bayfront), looking dapper in a Kangol beret, he recounted his encounters with jazz at a club called the "Chicken Shack" while he was a student at BCC. Rolando's footage of Afro-Cuban elders dancing to jazz and swing was particularly striking. Rather than engaging in Afro-Cuban folkloric dance, the dancers were moving to the music of another Afro-diasporic culture — African American jazz. In *Nosotros y el Jazz*, dancing is portrayed as a way to enact memories of a diasporic experience, as opposed to an expression of an exoticized innate Africanness.

After the documentary ended, a conversation spontaneously ensued between Ramiro and his friends about the film's significance for Afro-Cubans today. Osvaldo complained that "los negros no conocen su historia" (blacks do not know their history). That history, he insisted, was "more than the *comparsa*," the popular carnival traditions that have been practiced in Cuba for generations. He also pointed out the widespread rejection of the rumba "dentro los propios negros" (among blacks themselves). But Osvaldo wanted to make it clear that he was not one of these *negros*. In order to prove his point, he spontaneously decided to play a rumba track on Ramiro's laptop computer. Soon thereafter, he began to dance and urged Ramiro to join him. Ramiro initially refused. However, after repeated entreaties by his friends, he eventually got up and danced for several minutes, to the delight of us all.

The reaction of Ramiro and his friends to Rolando's documentary highlights the relevance of Afro-diasporic history to contemporary Cuba. In this context, Osvaldo's complaints about blacks not knowing their history is not merely a critique of a younger generation of Afro-Cubans, but an indictment of nationalist historical narratives that make it difficult to access that history. As a way to counter this historical silence, Osvaldo and Ramiro used kinesthetic forms of knowledge—the rumba—to enact that history. Here, the rumba was not prompted by some inherent African essence, but instead by a moment of connection to another diasporic cultural form—African American jazz. In short, what I witnessed that evening was the legacy of diaspora in action—an Afro-diasporic identification that was originally formed by a transregional history of slavery and subsequently nourished by the ongoing encounters of transcultural people of African descent who moved through the circuits of empire and segregation in the U.S.-Caribbean world. Although the transformations engendered by the Cold War, the Cuban Revolution, and the civil rights movement had obscured much of that history, it still lives on in the lives of Ramiro de la Cuesta and those who are featured in Rolando's documentary. The release of *Nostros y el Jazz*, along with the emergence of hip-hop and other diasporic musical forms in Cuba in recent years, might indicate that a new chapter in the history of Afro-diasporic linkages is at hand.

Notes

Abbreviations

AASP   Arthur A. Schomburg Papers, Schomburg Center for Research in Black Culture, New York Public Library, New York, N.Y.

AHPVC   Archivo Histórico Provincial de Villa Clara, Santa Clara, Cuba

AMP   Arthur Mitchell Papers, Chicago Historical Society, Chicago, Ill.

BTW   Booker T. Washington

BTWP   Booker T. Washington Papers, Library of Congress, Washington, D.C.

CBP   Claude Barnett Papers, Chicago Historical Society, Chicago, Ill.

GP   *The Marcus Garvey and Universal Negro Improvement Association Papers*, edited by Robert A. Hill, 7 vols. (Los Angeles: University of California Press, 1983–90)

LHP   Langston Hughes Papers, James Weldon Johnson Memorial Collection, Beinecke Rare Book and Manuscript Library, Yale University, New Haven, Conn.

NCNWP   Papers of the National Council of Negro Women, National Archives for Black Women's History, Mary McLeod Bethune Council House, Washington, D.C.

NW   *Negro World*

RA   Registro de Asociaciones, Archivo Nacional de Cuba, Havana

RG   Record Group

USNA   National Archives and Records Administration, Northeast Region, New York, N.Y.

WPPA   William Pickens Papers (Additions), Schomburg Center for Research in Black Culture, New York Public Library, New York, N.Y.

Introduction

1 Betancourt, "Castro and the Cuban Negro."

2 See Benedict Anderson, *Imagined Communities*, 113–40. Of course the author of *The Wretched of the Earth*, Frantz Fanon, had warned decolonizing populations about the "pitfall of national consciousness" in this exact period. See *Wretched of the Earth*, 148–205.

3 See Plummer, "Castro in Harlem"; Gosse, "African-American Press Greets the Cuban Revolution" and *Where the Boys Are*, 147–54; and Mealy, *Fidel and Malcolm X*.

4 American studies scholar Cynthia Young highlights the impact of the Cuban Revolution on the emergence of a U.S. "Third World Left" in which African American activists played a prominent role. See *Soul Power*, 18–53.

5 Clifford, *Routes*, 249–50. The notion of "routes" informed Paul Gilroy's notion of the Black Atlantic. See *Black Atlantic*.

6 For a useful intellectual history of the diaspora concept as it pertains to Afro-descended populations, see Edwards, "Uses of Diaspora."

7 See, for example, Robin Cohen, *Global Diasporas*; and Butler, "Defining Diaspora."

8 Along with the voluminous scholarship on slavery, the scholarship on Cuba's relationship to the African diaspora is dominated by studies of Afro-Cuban religions inspired by the anthropological and folkloric studies of Fernando Ortiz and Lydia Cabrera. See, for example, Ortiz, *Hampa afrocubana*; Cabrera, *La sociedad secreta Abakuá*; Brandon, *Santería from Africa to the New World*; and Fernández Robaina, *Hablen paleros y santeros*.

9 On the "live dialogue" between Africa and the Americas, see Matory, "Afro-Atlantic Culture" and "English Professors of Brazil"; and Gomez, *Reversing Sail*.

10 On racialization in twentieth-century Cuba, see Fernández Robaina, *El Negro en Cuba*; Helg, *Our Rightful Share* and "Black Men"; Ferrer, *Insurgent Cuba*; de la Fuente, *Nation for All*; and Bronfman, *Measures of Equality*.

11 Earl Lewis, "To Turn as on a Pivot."

12 Among the historians who have recently been reemphasizing the transnational dimensions of African American history, see Robin D. G. Kelley's many essays, especially "'But a Local Phase of a World Problem'"; Brock and Castañeda Fuertes, *Between Race and Empire*; Meriwether, *Proudly We Can Be Africans*; and Gaines, *American Africans in Ghana*.

13 On Afro-Cuban attention to African American struggles for citizenship rights, see Schwartz, "Cuba's Roaring Twenties"; Bronfman, *Measures of Equality*, 144–46; and Rebecca Scott, *Degrees of Freedom*. On the limits of the concept of identity, see Cooper and Brubaker, "Beyond Identity."

14 Edwards, *Practice of Diaspora*.

15 Verrill, *Cuba of Today*, 205–7; Inglish, "Transportation System of the United Fruit Company."

16 On U.S. military interventions in this period, see Schmidt, *United States Occupa-*

tion of Haiti; and Calder, *Impact of Intervention*. On the cultural ramifications of the U.S. presence in this period, see Pérez, *On Becoming Cuban*; Renda, *Taking Haiti*; and Gobat, *Confronting the American Dream*.

17 Here I am following historian Frederick Cooper's call for greater historical specificity in the writing of transregional histories. See "What Is the Concept of Globalization Good For?" This U.S.-Caribbean formulation is also inspired by scholarship on the Mediterranean and Indian Ocean worlds in the early modern and modern periods, as well as the histories of the "South Atlantic" or the "African-Portuguese" worlds. See, for example, Braudel, *Mediterranean and the Mediterranean World*; Chaudhuri, *Asia before Europe*; and Sweet, *Recreating Africa*. On "imperial formations" as an analytic framework for the study of empires, see Stoler, McGranahan, and Perdue, *Imperial Formations*. For a recent study of overlapping empires in the Caribbean, see Neptune, *Caliban and the Yankees*.

18 Joseph, LeGrand, and Salvatore, *Close Encounters of Empire*, 5.

19 Between 1904 and 1914, an estimated 150,000 to 200,000 West Indians migrated to work in Panama, transforming cities like Colón into black enclaves. Another 110,450 migrated to Cuba between 1912 and 1927, many of them coming from Panama and Costa Rica. On Afro-Caribbean "West Indian" migration throughout the region, see Conniff, *Black Labor on a White Canal*; Watkins-Owens, *Blood Relations*; James, *Holding Aloft the Banner of Ethiopia*; McLeod, "Garveyism in Cuba"; Giovannetti, "Black British Subjects in Cuba"; and Putnam, *Company They Kept*.

20 The "Great Migration" scholarship is voluminous. For a useful overview, see Trotter, *Great Migration in Historical Perspective*.

21 As is well known, the term "transculturation" was first coined by Fernando Ortiz, who employed it to describe the making of Cuban culture from its distinct European and African elements. See *Cuban Counterpoint*, 97–98. While most scholars employ the term to describe the creation of new Afro-American cultures from their European and African components (such as Cuban culture), I use it here to describe the creation of new Afro-diasporic cultures from two or more already existing Afro-American cultures.

22 Slave resistance movements inspired by the Haitian Revolution and the black emigrationist movement are just a few of many examples of nineteenth-century Afro-diasporic encounters. See Childs, *1812 Aponte Rebellion in Cuba*; and Miller, *Search for a Black Nationality*. For an innovative study of these encounters in the literary realm in the mid-nineteenth century, see Nwankwo, *Black Cosmopolitanism*.

23 Pérez, *On Becoming Cuban*, 324.

24 Enclosed manifesto dated 20 August 1928 found in folder 70, Fondo Jorge Juárez Cano, Archivo Histórico Provincial de Camagüey. For more on Klan activities in Cuba, see Guridy, "Racial Knowledge in Cuba." On the merits of a hemispheric approach to racialization, see Dzidzienyo and Oboler, *Neither Enemies nor Friends*. On the dangers of comparative race relations models and the benefits of a transnational approach to race, see Seigel, "Beyond Compare."

25 I borrow the phrase "segregation into congregation" from historian Earl Lewis, whose discussion of black institution building in Norfolk, Virginia, in the same period inspires my reading of the history of Afro-Cuban societies. See *In Their Own Interests*. On the Afro-Cuban societies, see, for example, Deschamps Chapeaux, *El Negro en el periodismo cubano*; Rebecca Scott, *Slave Emancipation in Cuba*, 268–78; Rushing, "*Cabildos de Nación* and *Sociedades de la Raza de Color*"; Hevia Lanier, *El directorio central de las Sociedades Negras de Cuba*; and Howard, *Changing History*.

26 On the significance of racial uplift to African American communities during the Jim Crow era, see Gaines, *Uplifting the Race*; Stein, *World of Marcus Garvey*; and Kelly, "Sentinels for a New South Industry," which emphasizes the ways racial uplift exemplified the divergent interests of black workers and the black leadership class. Other historians, particularly scholars studying women of the black elite and aspiring upper middle class, emphasize the subversive potential of the practice of racial uplift in the southern United States. See Gilmore, *Gender and Jim Crow*; and Shaw, *What a Woman Ought to Be and to Do*.

27 I draw upon historian Michele Mitchell's notion of "aspiring class," instead of the more commonly used term "middle class," to characterize Afro-Cubans who were not part of the rural laboring majority—such as artisans—and the tiny class of black professionals that emerged in the early twentieth century. "Aspiring class" is a more historically specific category of class formation that underscores Afro-Cuban *aspirations* for upward mobility while recognizing the tenuousness of their economic position in comparison to that of their white contemporaries. See Mitchell, *Righteous Propagation*, xx.

28 See, for example, José-Manuel Navarro's treatment of Booker T. Washington's relationship to the U.S. imperial project in Puerto Rico, in *Creating Tropical Yankees*, 115–30.

29 Brock and Castañeda Fuertes, *Between Race and Empire*. See also Reitan, *Rise and Fall of an Alliance*. One important location of Afro-Cuban and African American interaction in the United States during this period was Tampa and Ybor City, Florida. See Greenbaum, *More than Black*; Mirabal, "Telling Silences and Making Community"; as well as Grillo, *Black Cuban, Black American*. On the interactions between Afro-Cuban and African American baseball players and musicians, see Burgos, *Playing America's Game*; Jacques, "CuBop!"; and Austerlitz, *Jazz Consciousness*, 42–97.

30 McHenry, *Forgotten Readers*, 17.

31 Gunning, Hunter, and Mitchell, introduction; Stephens, *Black Empire*; and Neptune, *Caliban and the Yankees*, 158–90.

Chapter 1

1 Juan Gualberto Gómez to BTW, 12 November 1901, reel 185, BTWP.

2 On Washington and Tuskegee, see James Anderson, *Education of Blacks*; Spivey, *Schooling for the New Slavery*; Harlan, *Booker T. Washington: The Making of a*

Black Leader and *Booker T. Washington: The Wizard of Tuskegee*. A recent reconsideration of BTW and his legacy is Brundage, *Booker T. Washington and Black Progress*.

3 It is important to recall that Tuskegee was a normal school and not a university in this period. It was designed to educate students between the ages of fifteen and twenty years. The school did not offer advanced degrees until the 1920s. It became a university in 1985.

4 On African American historiography in this period, see Meier and Rudwick, *Black History and the Historical Profession*. Examples of this scholarship are Meier, *Negro Thought in America*; Harlan, *Booker T. Washington: The Making of a Black Leader*; and David Levering Lewis, *W. E. B. Du Bois: Biography*. African American gender historians have illustrated the inadequacy of the Du Bois–Washington narrative of the Jim Crow era. See Higginbotham, *Righteous Discontent*; and Gilmore, *Gender and Jim Crow*.

5 Historians are heavily indebted to Harlan's pioneering labor with Washington's Papers. See Harlan et al., *Booker T. Washington Papers*.

6 See Navarro, *Creating Tropical Yankees*. See also Harlan, *Booker T. Washington: The Making of a Black Leader*.

7 See Helg, *Our Rightful Share*; Ferrer, *Insurgent Cuba*; de la Fuente, *Nation for All*; and Bronfman, *Measures of Equality*. For a study of the convergence of Afro-Cuban and African American aspirations for freedom in the postemancipation period, see Rebecca Scott, *Degrees of Freedom*.

8 On the impact of the U.S. intervention on Afro-Cuban mobilization for equality, see Helg, *Our Rightful Share*, 91–116.

9 Louis Harlan has argued that Washington's "outlook throughout his life remained that of a provincial southern American, though he traveled widely and had a worldwide following." *Booker T. Washington: The Wizard of Tuskegee*, 266.

10 Ibid., 266–77; King, *Pan-Africanism and Education*; Zimmerman, "German Alabama in Africa."

11 Jesse Hoffnung-Garskoff's excellent essay on Arturo "Arthur" Schomburg and his Afro-diasporic contemporaries in New York argues for the centrality of Harlem in the African diaspora in the early twentieth century. I seek to complicate his mapping of the African diaspora of that period by arguing that Tuskegee occupied the center before Harlem's ascendancy in the 1920s. See Hoffnung-Garskof, "Migrations of Arturo Schomburg."

12 Mitchell, *Righteous Propagation*, 51–75. See also Gatewood, *Black Americans*, 22–40.

13 BTW to John Davis Long, 15 March 1898, in Harlan et al., *Booker T. Washington Papers*, 4:389.

14 Gatewood, *Black Americans* and *"Smoked Yankees."*

15 Osgood Welsh to BTW, 10 November 1899, reel 156, BTWP. A few weeks later, Welsh backed off from his idea, informing Washington that the "social and political condition of the island is, as I have discovered, so unsettled that I question the wisdom of bringing here just now even one negro from the United States. Many

people here believe that sooner or later the race question will assert itself and there is a fear that the U.S. may try to send large numbers of negroes to the island." Welsh to BTW, 29 November 1899, reel 156, BTWP.

16 Presley Holliday to BTW, 12 April 1901, reel 178, BTWP.

17 Gatewood, *Black Americans*, 166–79; Woods, *Black Odyssey*; Rampersad, *Life of Langston Hughes*, 10–11. Despite his failure in Cuba, Hughes continued undeterred to act on his belief that he could not realize his ambitions in the United States. He eventually settled in Mexico. While Hughes's vexed relationship with his father has been well documented, his father's travels to Latin America significantly influenced the poet's cosmopolitan understanding of people of African descent. See chapter 3 below.

18 R. M. R. Nelson to BTW, 18 June 1904, reel 247, BTWP.

19 Nelson to Charles Henry Douglass, 18 October 1924, Records of the Macon Douglass Theatre, Digital Library of Georgia, ⟨http://dlg.galileo.usg.edu/douglass/dbr080.php⟩ (emphasis in original). In this letter, Nelson tried to get Douglass to invest in "Beso Dulce," a soft drink that he claimed was created by an unnamed Afro-Cuban businessman. Nelson informed Douglass that he was offering him "THE SOLE RIGHT to Manufacture and Sell a Black Man's Discovery in the State of Georgia! A Beverage that WILL SELL BIGGER THAN Coca Cola." Four years earlier, Nelson was courting Garveyites and Afro-Cubans to participate in his business schemes. See chapter 2 below.

20 BTW to John Stephens Durham, 2 December 1907, container 48, BTWP.

21 Durham to BTW, 16 April 1905, ibid. In contrast to other male members of the "Talented Tenth," very little has been written about Durham. See Toll, "Free Men, Freedmen, and Race."

22 Rebecca Scott, *Degrees of Freedom*, 162, 173. Antonio Maceo was the Afro-Cuban general who was revered for his heroic deeds in the Cuban Wars of Independence.

23 William Henry Baldwin Jr. to BTW, 18 July 1898, in Harlan et al., *Booker T. Washington Papers*, 4:449.

24 "Industrial Education for Cuban Negroes," *Christian Register*, 18 August 1898, 455.

25 Emmett Scott to BTW, 25 August 1898, reel 71, BTWP.

26 Edwin Atkins to BTW, 2 January 1902, reel 170; BTW to Atkins, 13 February 1904, reel 560, both in BTWP.

27 On the Phelps-Stokes Fund, see King, *Pan-Africanism and Education*.

28 Henry B. Plant to BTW, 22 October 1898, reel 142, BTWP.

29 Headrick, *Tools of Empire*. On black sailors during the slave trade, see Bolster, *Black Jacks*.

30 BTW to Allen Alexander Wesley, 8 November 1898, in Harlan et al., *Booker T. Washington Papers*, 4:506.

31 BTW to Thomas Austin, 8 November 1898, container 141, BTWP.

32 On Afro-Cuban émigré activity in Florida and New York in this period, see Greenbaum, *More than Black*, 68–79; Poyo, *"With All, and for the Good of All,"*

81–84; and Mirabal, "'No Country But the One We Must Fight For.'" Afro-Cuban diasporic activity in these communities remains inadequately studied, mostly because it continues to be overshadowed by the nationalist narrative of Cuban history and its fixation on the activities of José Martí. For hints at this activity, see Montejo Arrechea, "*Minerva*"; and the fascinating documents compiled by historian Oilda Hevia Lanier from the Archivo Nacional de Cuba in Horrego Estuch's republished work, *Juan Gualberto Gómez*.

33 Thomas Austin to BTW, 1 November 1898, in Harlan et al., *Booker T. Washington Papers*, 4:501. One of the students who did arrive from Key West was Juan Eusebio Gómez, the son of Juan Gualberto Gómez. The young Gómez was living with his mother and siblings in exile in Key West during the final War of Independence on the island. While the exact details of Juan Eusebio's recruitment are unclear, it is certain that he arrived sometime in the late fall of 1898. He left the school for health reasons in 1899 before returning in 1901.

34 On Wesley and Barnett, see Goode, *"Eighth Illinois,"* 73–78. On African American veneration of Maceo, see Gatewood, *Black Americans*, 17; and Rebecca Scott, *Degrees of Freedom*, 4.

35 Allen Alexander Wesley to BTW, 14 October 1898, reel 144, BTWP.

36 Wesley to BTW, 21 December 1898, ibid.

37 BTW to Joseph Forney Johnson, 5 July 1899, in Harlan et al., *Booker T. Washington Papers*, 5:148. The students were Juan Gómez, Sixto Rodríguez, Alfredo Pérez Encinosa, Julian Valdés, Luís Delfín Valdés, Guillermo Fernández, Antonio Soto, and Celestina Ramírez. Another student from the Spanish-speaking Caribbean in this group was Pedro Salina, a Puerto Rican who arrived in the fall of 1898.

38 Robert Lyman to BTW, 21 November 1899, reel 151, and Lyman to BTW, 30 January 1900, reel 163, both in BTWP.

39 Assistant secretary of the War Department to BTW, 11 May 1899, reel 151, BTWP.

40 Lyman to Leonard Wood, 11 January 1900, reel 163, BTWP.

41 BTW to Wood, 16 January 1900; Wood to BTW, 15 February 1900, both in reel 90, BTWP.

42 James Lewis to BTW, 22 May 1900, reel 164, BTWP. One month later, Lewis asked Washington to "remember me kindly to the little Cuban boys. I have been too busy to reply to their letter." Lewis to BTW, 25 June 1900, ibid.

43 Grace W. Minns to BTW, 10 January 1903, in Harlan et al., *Booker T. Washington Papers*, 6:124–25.

44 Ibid.

45 Marcelino Callaba Pérez of Camp Columbia, Cuba, 21 October 1915, reel 687, BTWP.

46 Gavino Barnet to BTW, 17 November 1902, reel 191, BTWP.

47 BTW, *Up from Slavery*, 53.

48 Juana María Cárdenas and Carmen Navarro to BTW, n.d., reel 159, BTWP.

49 Rebecca Scott, *Slave Emancipation in Cuba*; Helg, *Our Rightful Share*, 35–38; Hevia Lanier, *El directorio central*, 8–9, 29; Howard, *Changing History*, 140–47.

50 Eleno Lino to BTW, 20 September 1902, reel 683, BTWP.

51 Bernardo Calderón to BTW, 14 January 1912, reel 684, BTWP. The original quote reads: "Pero no tendré comodidad ni podre crearme familia para tener una vejez tranquila como deseo."

52 Mitchell, *Righteous Propagation*, xix–xxi.

53 B. Cabrera to BTW, 19 January 1900, reel 158, BTWP.

54 Cabrera to BTW, May 1900, reel 159, BTWP. Sadly, Miguel Marin died while he was a student at the school in April 1902.

55 Gómez to BTW, 8 August 1903, reel 217, BTWP. Ibañez appears to have been the father of Juan Gualberto "Yonny" Ibañez, the famous Cuban painter. See the online literary magazine, ⟨http://www.habanaelegante.com/Winter2001/Cafe .html⟩.

56 Luis del Risco to BTW, 3 October 1901; Celestina Ramírez to BTW, 14 November 1901, both in reel 185, BTWP.

57 Alfredo Pérez to BTW, 6 April 1899, reel 152, BTWP.

58 Pérez to BTW, 14 April 1900, reel 166, BTWP.

59 Palmer to BTW, 27 May 1901, reel 184, BTWP.

60 Tuskegee Institute, *Twenty-first Annual Catalogue, 1901–1902*, 151; Martin Brumbaugh to BTW, 17 April 1901, reel 172, BTWP.

61 Austin to BTW, 21 July 1901, reel 156, BTWP.

62 Ramón Edreira to BTW, n.d. (1901), reel 187; Manuel Valdés to BTW, n.d. (June 1901), reel 186; Carlos Pierra Edwards to BTW, 18 January 1901, reel 176, all in BTWP.

63 Juana Cárdenas to BTW, 28 June 1901, BTWP.

64 Manuela Gómez to BTW, 6 December 1898, reel 139, BTWP. Manuela Gómez is not listed in any of the Tuskegee catalogs from the period.

65 Lyman to BTW, 19 February 1900, reel 163, BTWP; Greenbaum, *More than Black*, 178–223. Evelio Grillo's recollections of his feelings of ambivalence when he left Tampa to attend Dunbar High School in Washington, D.C., are also revealing in this regard. His sister Sylvia was expected to stay at home while her brothers were able to pursue educational and employment opportunities outside the house. See Grillo, *Black Cuban, Black American*, 52.

66 Gonzalo de Quesada to BTW, 25 August 1909, reel 396, BTWP. Washington replied to this letter by informing Quesada that the student was too young to attend Tuskegee, and he recommended other schools that might admit the young orphan.

67 F. P. Machado to BTW, 4 July 1910, reel 319, BTWP.

68 Tuskegee Institute, *Twenty-fifth Annual Catalogue, 1905–1906*.

69 The history of Sagua's particular connections to the United States remains to be written. For a useful study of Afro-Cuban culture in Sagua, see Testa, *Como una memoria que dura*.

70 For example, some of the Cuban students at Tuskegee during the 1923–24 academic year were Frank Clarke, James A. Mitchell, George E. Thompson, and William Dalton, among others with Anglophone surnames. See Tuskegee Institute,

Forty-third Annual Catalogue, 1923–24, published in the *Tuskegee Bulletin* 18, no. 1 (January–March 1923).

71 The Puerto Rican student population was much more balanced along gender lines. This was probably due in part to the fact that the insular government of Puerto Rico specifically stipulated that women were to comprise one half of the number of pupils who were sent to study at Tuskegee each year. Afro-Cuban young women did not have the benefit of the law, since the relationship between the school and Cuba was carried out by nonstate actors.

72 Margaret Murray Washington, "What Girls Are Taught and How," 73.

73 BTW, *Working with the Hands*, 80–81.

74 On Armstrong and Hampton, see Engs, *Educating the Disfranchised and Disinherited*. On Armstrong's influence on Washington and Tuskegee's educational philosophy, see Harlan, *Booker T. Washington: The Making of a Black Leader*, 52–77; and James Anderson, *Education of Blacks*, 33–109.

75 James Anderson, *Education of Blacks*, 73.

76 Robert R. Moton, "Hampton Institute's Relation to Tuskegee," in BTW, *Tuskegee and Its People*, 90.

77 BTW, *Working with the Hands*, 78. On the challenges facing the school's implementation of "dovetailing," see Harlan, *Booker T. Washington: The Wizard of Tuskegee*, 145–51.

78 BTW, *Up from Slavery*, 121.

79 Ibid., 122.

80 Shaw, *What a Woman Ought to Be and to Do*, 88–90.

81 Summers, *Manliness and Its Discontents*.

82 "An Interview by Frank George Carpenter in the Memphis Commercial Appeal," in Harlan et al., *Booker T. Washington Papers*, 5:275.

83 BTW to Samuel McCune Lindsay, 20 May 1902, ibid., 13:504–8 (emphasis in original).

84 The phrase comes from Harlan, *Booker T. Washington: The Making of a Black Leader*, 272.

85 The most prominent critiques of Tuskegee are James Anderson, *Education of Blacks*; and Spivey, *Schooling for the New Slavery*.

86 Gómez to BTW, 8 August 1903, reel 217, BTWP.

87 This is essentially Harlan's interpretation. See *Booker T. Washington: The Making of a Black Leader*, 283.

88 BTW to Lindsay, 20 May 1902, in Harlan et al., *Booker T. Washington Papers*, 13:508.

89 BTW to Logan, 27 September 1900, box 4, Booker T. Washington Papers, Tuskegee University Archives.

90 Logan to BTW, 21 January 1899, in Harlan et al., *Booker T. Washington Papers*, 5:17.

91 Cuban students to BTW, 8 September 1899, ibid., 5:199–202.

92 Celestina Ramírez to BTW, 14 November 1901, reel 185, BTWP.

93 Manuel Gutierrez to BTW, 7 November 1906, reel 684, BTWP.

94 Cuban students to BTW, 8 September 1899, in Harlan et al., *Booker T. Washington Papers*, 5:201.

95 I want to thank Mike Wellen for making this point.

96 School catalogs show that the international student population became more numerous and more varied from the latter part of the opening decade of the century onward, including more students from Central America, Africa, and the various English-speaking Caribbean islands.

97 A. Escabí to Executive Council, 15 March 1910, reel 684, BTWP.

98 Pérez to Scott, 9 June 1904, reel 237, BTWP; Serra, *Para blancos y negros*, 147–50.

99 BTW to Durham, 9 July 1904, container 48, BTWP.

100 See the program of the "Twenty Fourth Anniversary Exercises, Thursday, May 25, 1905," in reel 453, BTWP.

101 Pérez Encinosa to BTW, 30 April 1907, reel 278, BTWP. Sadly, Pérez's last letters to the school detailed his troubles with his studies in Europe. In a number of letters, he pleaded with the school for financial assistance after he discovered that his scholarship did not adequately cover his expenses.

102 Tuskegee Institute, *Thirty-third Annual Catalogue, 1913–1914*, 110. Despaigne's Francophone name and native city indicate that he was a product of earlier diasporic processes. As is well known, many masters and slaves arrived in eastern Cuba during the Haitian Revolution. It seems possible that Despaigne was a descendant of these Haitian immigrants.

103 Julio Despaigne to BTW, 22 September 1905, reel 449, BTWP.

104 Despaigne to BTW, 7 April 1906, reel 684, BTWP.

105 BTW letter of introduction, 25 February 1908, reel 403, BTWP.

106 Gómez's career after his departure from Tuskegee is difficult to ascertain. Louis Harlan's claim that he died in 1910 contradicts evidence from the Booker T. Washington Papers, which contains a letter from Gómez to Tuskegee in 1915. See Manuela Gómez to BTW, 6 December 1898, in Harlan et al., *Booker T. Washington Papers*, 4:527; and John E. Gómez to Warren Logan, 11 December 1915, reel 687, BTWP.

107 De la Fuente, *Nation for All*, 138–71.

108 Emilio Céspedes Casado to BTW, 15 November 1905, reel 254, BTWP.

109 In his letter of application to Tuskegee, Bernardo Calderón claimed that he was a student at the Instituto Booker T. Washington. See Bernardo Calderón to BTW, 14 January 1912, reel 684, BTWP. For brief discussions of the Instituto Booker T. Washington, see Helg, *Our Rightful Share*, 130; and de la Fuente, *Nation for All*, 166. The Céspedes brothers were not the only Afro-Cuban male leaders who venerated Washington as a race leader. Others, including Rafael Serra and Ricardo Batrell, publicly celebrated Washington's achievements and/or sought out his advice. See Serra, *Para blancos y negros*, 141–44; and Ricardo Batrell to BTW, 18 July 1907, reel 276, BTWP.

110 BTW, *Working with the Hands*, 78. On Tuskegee's pioneering architectural program, see Dozier, "Tuskegee"; and Weiss, "Tuskegee."

111 Luís Delfín Valdés to BTW, 6 October 1906, reel 683; Valdés to BTW, 11 May 1908, reel 684, both in BTWP. The preponderance of Afro-Cuban students in the program probably partially arose from their effort to avoid the more physically strenuous aspects of the school's course of study.

112 See Atenas's building plans in bundle 1112, file 23270, RA. For Atenas's original objectives, see Evelio S. Chen, "1917–21 de Septiembre–1951," *Atenas* 2 (September 1951): 7.

113 Hughes, *I Wonder as I Wander*, 8. On the politics surrounding the opening of the Club Atenas's headquarters, see Guridy, "Racial Knowledge in Cuba," chapter 2; and Bronfman, *Measures of Equality*, 135–36.

114 Despaigne to BTW, 7 April 1906, reel 684, BTWP.

Chapter 2

1 Carlos del Castillo to Coronel Emiliano Amiell, 15 August 1929, bundle 77, no. 563, AHPVC. Wignall's nationality is unclear. Various Rural Guard and police reports claim that he was also known as Jaime, or Julian Guillén. Thus, it is difficult to ascertain his background with any certainty. In mid-August, he was elected president of the Sagua Division.

2 Joaquín Caballero Milanés to Gobernador Provincial, 26 August 1929, bundle 77, no. 558, AHPVC.

3 Benito Riera to Capitán Ayudante del 3er. Distrito Militar, 29 July 1929; Milanés to Gobernador Provincial, 26 August 1929, both in bundle 77, no. 563, AHPVC.

4 See Ortiz, *Cuban Counterpoint*, 97–98.

5 The UNIA had over fifty divisions on the island by the mid-1920s. Historians Marc McLeod and Jorge Giovannetti are largely responsible for our knowledge of Garveyism in Cuba. See McLeod, "Sin dejar de ser cubanos" and "Garveyism in Cuba"; and Giovannetti, "Black British Subjects in Cuba," 113–23, 193–201, and "Elusive Organization of 'Identity.'" See also Guridy, "'Enemies of the White Race' UNIA."

6 The literature on gender in the UNIA has demonstrated the hierarchal vision of the Garveyite model of nationhood. See, for example, Bair, "True Women, Real Men"; Taylor, *Veiled Garvey*; Summers, *Manliness and Its Discontents*, 66–110; Mitchell, *Righteous Propagation*, 218–39; and Stephens, *Black Empire*. For an interpretation of Garveyism as a form of "black fascism," see Gilroy, *Between Camps*, 135–237.

7 Diamond, *Performance and Cultural Politics*, 1.

8 Here I am following Richard Schechner's notion that performance is "always subject to revision" because it is never performed by the same performer in the same way nor for the same audience in the same moment. As Schechner observes, performance is "never for the first time . . . [but instead] for the second to the nth time" and thereby always and already repetition with a (critical) difference. *Between Theatre and Anthropology*, 36. Similarly, Diana Taylor argues that performance is an "act of transfer" that transmits social knowledge, cultural memory, and identities in the Americas. *Archive and the Repertoire*, 2.

9　*GP*, 6:46. The speech was given on 16 November 1924 and was subsequently published in *NW*, 22 November 1924.

10　The notion of "outpost" Garveyism was first employed by Emory Tolbert in *U.N.I.A. and Black Los Angeles*. For another recent study of the UNIA in a local context, see Rowlinson, *Grassroots Garveyism*.

11　On the complexities of identity formation among West Indian migrants in Cuba, see Giovannetti, "Elusive Organization of 'Identity.'"

12　Stein, *World of Marcus Garvey*; Hill, "Boundaries of Belonging," 18–19. For general histories of the UNIA, see also Cronon, *Black Moses*; and Martin, *Race First*.

13　For an example of the comparative approach to the study of Anglophone vs. Hispanophone black activism, see James, *Holding Aloft the Banner of Ethiopia*. On the dangers of comparative race scholarship, see Seigel, "Beyond Compare."

14　On the peripatetic nature of Caribbean migration in this period, see Putnam, *Company They Kept*.

15　On U.S. interventionism in the Caribbean and Central America in this period, see Schmidt, *United States Occupation of Haiti*; Calder, *Impact of Intervention*; Pérez, *Cuba under the Platt Amendment*; and Gobat, *Confronting the American Dream*.

16　On Afro-Caribbean migration throughout the region, see Newton, *Silver Men*; Conniff, *Black Labor on a White Canal*; Watkins-Owens, *Blood Relations*; James, *Holding Aloft the Banner of Ethiopia*; Chomsky, *West Indian Workers*; McLeod, "Undesirable Aliens"; and Putnam, *Company They Kept*, 25–75.

17　The "Great Migration" scholarship is voluminous. For a useful overview, see Trotter, *Great Migration in Historical Perspective*.

18　On La Mothe and García, see *GP*, 2:69, 120.

19　Henrietta Vinton Davis to BTW, 25 June and 16 July 1900, both in reel 159, BTWP.

20　The only existing study of Davis's life and work is Seraile, "Henrietta Vinton Davis."

21　Eduardo Morales to Emmett J. Scott, 6 May 1910, reel 319, BTWP.

22　On Morales's and Stoute's activities in Panama, see Burnett, "'Are We Slaves or Free Men?'" 68, 88. Burnett provides the most detailed analysis of Morales's activism in Panama. For an example of the comparative race relations model in the context of Caribbean activism, see James, *Holding Aloft the Banner of Ethiopia*.

23　See Morales's testimony in *Garvey v. United States*, U.S. Court of Appeals, 2d Cir. (1925), Case 8317, Row 73, Compartment 8, vol. 3:1505–6, RG 276, USNA.

24　*GP*, 1:274–75. On the Garveyite version of racial uplift, see *GP*, 1:xxxv–xc. On the religious character of the UNIA, see Burkett, *Garveyism as Religious Movement*.

25　"Regalmento de la División #55, de la ciudad de Sagua la Grande; de la Asociación Universal para el Adelanto de la raza negra," bundle 77, no. 558, AHPVC.

26　*GP*, 1:257.

27　On Garveyite notions of the "self-made man" and its role in the regeneration of the race, see *GP*, 1:xxxix–lviii; and Summers, *Manliness and Its Discontents*, 66–109.

28 On "racial *regeneración*," see Morrison, "Civilization and Citizenship."

29 "Opiniones," undated clipping from *Alma Joven* in the author's possession.

30 De la Fuente, *Nation for All*, 138.

31 "Alma Joven," *Alma Joven* 3 (15 August 1923): 2.

32 Deschamps Chapeaux, *El Negro en el periodismo cubano*; Rebecca Scott, *Slave Emancipation in Cuba*, 268–78; Rushing, "*Cabildos de Nación*"; Hevia Lanier, *El directorio central*, 43–60; Howard, *Changing History*, 172–205; Ferrer, *Insurgent Cuba*, 128–38.

33 Many of the more important colored societies during the republican era were organized during the 1898–1902 period, including El Gran Maceo in Santa Clara, Luz de Oriente in Santiago de Cuba, and the Sociedad Antonio Maceo in Camagüey. The Club Oriente in Santiago de Cuba reconstituted itself as the Club Aponte in 1900, after the Afro-Cuban rebel José Antonio Aponte, whom the group described as "the first martyr of independence for the fatherland." See "Club Aponte, Sociedad de Instrucción y Recreo," *Oriente Contemporaneo* (n.d.), located in the Archivo Histórico Provincial de Santiago de Cuba. On the colored societies during the republican era, see de la Fuente, *Nation for All*, 161–71; and Bronfman, *Measures of Equality*, 88–93, 135–44.

34 Within an American context, historian Earl Lewis shows how African Americans transformed racial exclusionary practices into a source of empowerment by creating institutions that were spaces of "congregation." See Earl Lewis, *In Their Own Interests*.

35 "Domingo Bernardo González," *Alma Joven* 2 (16 and 31 May 1932): 9.

36 One of the organizers of the event was, revealingly enough, the Dominican-born Belisario Heureaux, the son of Ulises Heureaux, the former president of the Dominican Republic in the late nineteenth century. Heureaux was a founding member of the organization and went on to become one of the more visible members of the Club Atenas during the 1920s and early 1930s. The masculinist conception of uplift is evidenced by the fact that membership was exclusively reserved for men. Women could only participate in associational activities if they were family members or invited guests of members. Moreover, invited women had to be respectable. Working-class women, particularly domestic workers, were usually barred from participating in the social activities of these associations.

37 "Nuestros socios fundadores," *Atenas* 2 (September 1951): 8.

38 Other Atenas members who studied at Tuskegee were Nicolás Edreira, who was sent to the school by Juan Gualberto Gómez in 1901, and Fermín Domenech, who graduated in 1909.

39 Margaret Ross Martin, "The Negro in Cuba," *Crisis* 39 (January 1932): 455.

40 Evelio S. Chen, "1917–21 de Septiembre–1951," *Atenas* 2 (September 1951): 7.

41 Miguel Angel Céspedes, "Discurso de apertura de la serie annual de conferencias," *Atenas* 1 (March 1921): 7.

42 On the UNIA's vision of the black transnational nation, see Stephens, *Black Empire*, 75–101.

43 "Report of the Convention," in *GP*, 2:642.

44 *GP*, 2:315.

45 *Garvey v. United States* (1925), box 2817, 4:2209, RG 276, USNA.

46 *NW*, 16 July 1921.

47 *NW*, 14 August 1920.

48 Ibid.; Bundles, *On Her Own Ground*, 200, 263. On the central role of black beauticians in this period, see Gill, *Civic Beauty*.

49 After sugar prices peaked at an all-time high of 22.5 cents per pound in May 1920, they plummeted to 3.8 cents per pound by the end of the year. See Pérez, *Cuba under the Platt Amendment*, 186–87.

50 On the emergence of the Afro-Cuban elite in this period, see Schwartz, "Displaced and the Disappointed"; and de la Fuente, *Nation for All*, 149–71.

51 *GP*, 2:162. As early as January 1920, the Black Star Line was already receiving money from Cuba from those who wanted to purchase stock in the company. See Defendant's Exhibit M in *Garvey v. United States* (1925), box 2817, 4:2674, RG 276, USNA.

52 Mulzac, *Star to Steer By*, 79.

53 GP, 2:313; "Reglamento de la Sociedad 'Universal Improvement Association and Communities League,'" 17 February 1920, bundle 288, file 11640, RA. Jorge Giovannetti argues that the omission of "Negro" from the association's name in Cuba was likely an attempt to evade punishment under the Morúa law, the amendment that banned political parties organized along racial lines. See "Black British Subjects in Cuba," 195–96. Garveyites in Cuba must have been less fearful of the law in subsequent years since many divisions that emerged after 1920 did not omit "Negro" from their name.

54 The Oblate Sisters of Providence were themselves products of Afro-diasporic migration in the nineteenth century. Founded by Elizabeth Lange and Mary Balas, two women refugees from the Caribbean, the Oblate Sisters established missions throughout the United States in the nineteenth century and in Cuba in 1900. On the Oblate Sisters, see Morrow, *Persons of Color*; and Montgomery, "Mission to Cuba and Costa Rica."

55 *Panama Star and Herald*, 9 March 1920. For one of the few discussions of the Unión Fraternal, see Bronfman, *Measures of Equality*, 88–93.

56 De la Fuente, *Nation for All*, 54–95. On Ramírez Ros, see Rodríguez, "Marcus Garvey en Cuba," 288. Ramírez Ros was the father of María Teresa Ramírez, who eventually became a lawyer and leader of the Asociación Cultural Femenina, an Afro-Cuban women's organization, in the 1950s. María Teresa was profiled for African American readers of the *Crisis* in an article published by Margaret Ross Martin in 1932. See "Negro in Cuba," *Crisis* 39 (January 1932): 453–55. For more on Martin, see chapter 4 below.

57 Mulzac, *Star to Steer By*, 80.

58 Alfredo Zayas, president of Cuba from 1921 to 1925, was probably motivated by political concerns when he agreed to meet with Marcus Garvey one year later. R. M. R. Nelson claims to have put Garvey in touch with Zayas. See *NW*, 26 November 1921.

59 The *Yarmouth* had been taken out of service by 1921, replaced by the more recently purchased *Kanawha*. However, the *Kanawha*'s voyage to the Caribbean was even more disastrous than the *Yarmouth*'s, blowing out its engine and crashing into a pier in Norfolk, Virginia, before finally arriving in Cuba on 9 April 1921. The *Kanawha* would continue to be plagued by mismanagement and crew infighting before it was finally abandoned off the coast of Cuba in August 1921. See *GP*, 3:lv–lvii; and Stein, *World of Marcus Garvey*, 96–97.

60 *Heraldo de Cuba*, 4 March 1921. I want to thank Marc McLeod for sharing his copy of this important document with me.

61 This argument pervades the existing scholarship on Garveyism in Cuba. See Rupert Lewis, *Marcus Garvey*, 108–12; and Fernández Robaina, "Marcus Garvey in Cuba." Marc McLeod's research has highlighted Afro-Cuban participation in the UNIA, yet he too views the Garvey-Atenas encounter as the Afro-Cuban elite's rejection of the UNIA. See "Sin dejar de ser cubanos," 75–77.

62 While the author of the article is unknown, the piece shares an unease that many Cuban newspapers revealed when reporting on the activities of people of African descent on the island. Moreover, the newspaper, which was founded by Manuel Marquez Sterling, the noted Cuban journalist and diplomat, was a pro-government publication controlled by authoritarian president Gerardo Machado in the late 1920s.

63 On the racist repression of the Partido Independiente de Color in 1912 and the limits placed on Afro-Cuban autonomous organization, see Helg, *Our Rightful Share*. For another perspective on the PIC and the dominant Cuban discourse of racial equality, see de la Fuente, "Myths of Racial Democracy."

64 *Heraldo de Cuba*, 4 March 1921.

65 Bronfman, *Measures of Equality*, 99–104. On the massacre of Afro-Caribbean migrants in the eastern town of Jobabo a few years earlier, see Giovannetti, "Black British Subjects," 69–110.

66 Bernardo García Domínguez claims that Atenas leaders Pablo Herrera and Ramírez Ros were at the rally, offering words of welcome and a Cuban flag to be placed on the SS *Antonio Maceo*. However, García Domínguez did not provide a source for this information, although the performative aspect of this exchange between Garvey and Afro-Cuban leaders is significant. See "Garvey and Cuba," 300.

67 According to the *Heraldo* article, Ramírez Ros escorted Garvey to a meeting with President Menocal. See *Heraldo de Cuba*, 4 March 1921; Rodríguez, "Marcus Garvey en Cuba"; and Domínguez, "Garvey and Cuba," 289.

68 Which language Céspedes spoke during this encounter is not clear. The little that survives of his correspondence indicates that he did know English.

69 *Heraldo de Cuba*, 4 March 1921.

70 "Blancos" was capitalized in the original. Predictably, "Negroes" was not.

71 Louis Pérez has highlighted the prevalence of English in Cuban society, employed as a way to exemplify Cuban facility with American culture during these years. See *On Becoming Cuban*, 144–55.

72 On Garvey's legal troubles and the financial disaster that was the Black Star Line,

see Cronon, *Black Moses*; and Stein, *World of Marcus Garvey*. On Garveyism in Cuba during the 1920s, see McLeod, "Garveyism in Cuba."

73 McLeod, "Garveyism in Cuba." McLeod's research illustrates the continuing presence of Afro-Cubans in the association throughout the 1920s. Particularly revealing was the founding of the Cuban Chapter 71 of the UNIA in Santiago de Cuba in the mid-1920s. See McLeod, "Sin dejar de ser cubanos," 86.

74 *NW*, 20 August 1927.

75 The "African Police" was likely some version of the Universal African Legion (UAL). For more on the UAL, see below.

76 *NW*, 19 March 1921. On the importance of translation across linguistic differences in Afro-diasporic encounters, see Edwards, *Practice of Diaspora*.

77 Hill, "Making Noise"; Abrahams, *Man of Words in the West Indies*.

78 For more on Afro-Cuban literary practices, see chapter 3 below. Martin Summers has highlighted similar discourses of black manliness between the UNIA and Prince Hall Freemasons. See *Manliness and Its Discontents*, 77, 97.

79 *NW*, 16 April 1921.

80 On UNIA auxiliaries, see Summers, *Manliness and Its Discontents*, 93–101; and MacPherson, "Colonial Matriarchs."

81 Hill, "Making Noise," 199–200.

82 *GP*, 2:209–10.

83 *NW*, 19 March 1921. I want to thank Frances Sullivan for bringing this reference to my attention.

84 *NW*, 16 July 1921.

85 Mulzac, *Star to Steer By*, 79, 80.

86 On the UNIA's penchant for "state fetishism," see Stephens, *Black Empire*, 99–101. Smith-Green's appraisal of his trip to Cuba appears in *GP*, 2:311.

87 The limits placed on Afro-Cuban activism during this period are clear in the repression of the Partido Independiente de Color (Independent Party of Color) in the summer of 1912. The party was banned by a constitutional amendment in 1910 and annihilated by the Cuban government two years later. See Helg, *Our Rightful Share*, 165–226.

88 This practice also occurred in a number of Cuban cities, particularly in the island's interior. On racial segregation in the Cuban central plazas during this period, see Guridy, "Racial Knowledge in Cuba," chapter 3. Unlike in the southern United States, racial segregation was not backed by a legal structure. In fact, the 1901 Cuban Constitution stipulated: "All Cubans will be equal before the law." Yet, racial segregation was a routinely practiced "custom" throughout this period.

89 *NW*, 20 September 1924.

90 Diana Taylor, *Archive and the Repertoire*, 2. On the question of "translation" in Afro-diasporic encounters, Brent Edwards's insightful analysis of Afro-diasporic print culture during the 1920s and 1930s shows how translation shaped these textual encounters. However, a focus on the production and interpretation of embodied practices enables us to examine how connections happen in ways that they might not in literary practices. See Edwards, *Practice of Diaspora*.

91 *GP*, 2:277.

92 "Copia de unos programas publicados en inglés y español," bundle 77, no. 558, AHPVC. The importance of music to the UNIA can be seen in the budget figures of the BSL compiled by the U.S. government in its investigation of Garvey and the steamship company. Between 1919 and 1920, music was among the highest company expenses, constituting $10,518.20, a shade less than the costs of travel ($10,649.26). See *GP*, 2:689.

93 Rubiera Castillo, *Reyita, sencillamente*, 23.

94 Ibid., 24.

95 *NW*, 9 July 1921.

96 Bair, "'Ethiopia Shall Stretch Forth.'" Bair's essay highlights the violent opposition to Laura Kofey, a black woman charismatic leader who assumed the role of preacher as a UNIA organizer. She was assassinated for overstepping the boundaries of leadership for women in the association.

97 *NW*, 16 April 1921. The usage of exclamation points by the recorder of this event is designed to convey the emotional response of Daniels and presumably the audience.

98 Ayala, *American Sugar Kingdom*, 233–34.

99 On racial politics during the *machadato*, see Bronfman, *Measures of Equality*, 135–58; and de la Fuente, *Nation for All*, 91–95.

100 "Copia de unos programas publicados en inglés y español," bundle 77, no. 558, AHPVC.

101 Gobernador Provincial to Alcalde Municipal, and Gobernador Provincial to Jefe de la Policía Especial, 24 August 1929, ibid.

102 Benito Riera to Capitán Ayudante de este Distrito-Santa Clara, 14 August 1929, bundle 77, no. 563, AHPVC.

103 Joaquín Caballero Milanés to Gobernador Provincial, 26 August 1929, bundle 77, no. 558, AHPVC.

104 Antonio Sierra Acosta to Alcalde Municipal, 29 August 1929, ibid.

105 Vega to Sr. Presidente de la Asociación Universal para el Adelanto de la Raza Negra y A.C.L., 31 August 1929, ibid.

106 Vega to Gobernador Provincial, 24 August 1929, ibid.

107 Manuel J. Delgado to Gobernador Provincial de Santa Clara, 2 October 1929, bundle 77, no. 563, AHPVC.

108 Taylor to Gobernador Provincial, n.d., ibid. Although the letter is not dated, it was received by the governor on 29 October 1929.

109 Alcalde Municipal to Gobernador Provincial, 11 November 1929, ibid.

110 Meanwhile some Afro-Cubans who were associated with the UNIA were not so fortunate. One year later, Abelardo Pacheco, the Afro-Cuban activist, was murdered by *machadista* agents. See Abelardo Pacheco to Sr. Embajador de los Estados Unidos de Norte América, 30 December 1929; and Edward L. Reed to secretary of state, 15 August 1930, both in Decimal File 837.00/2825, RG 59, USNA.

111 *NW*, 21 June 1930

Chapter 3

1 Hughes, "Cuban Sculptor."

2 For David Levering Lewis's discussion of "The Six"—Jesse Fauset, James Weldon Johnson, Charles Spurgeon Johnson, Walter White, Alain Locke, and Casper Holstein—see *When Harlem Was in Vogue*, 119–55.

3 Ibid.; Locke, *New Negro*. On crazes for the primitive in other parts of the Atlantic world, see Savigliano, *Tango and the Political Economy of Passion*; Delpar, *Enormous Vogue of Things Mexican*; and Jackson, *Making Jazz French*.

4 On Guillén's role in the refashioning of Cuban national identity, see his *Obra poética*, 1:91–92; Kutzinski, *Sugar's Secrets*; and Moore, *Nationalizing Blackness*. Guillén's critique of the blackness vogue is clear in his poem "Pequeña oda a un negro boxeador cubano," in *Obra poética*, 1:97. Historian Alejandro de la Fuente has argued that despite the movement's co-optation of Afro-Cuban culture, it ultimately resulted in a more racially inclusive Cuban national identity. See *Nation for All*, 175–89.

5 See, for example, Ellis, "Nicolás Guillén and Langston Hughes"; Kutzinski, *Sugar's Secrets*, 134–62; Cobb, *Harlem, Haiti, and Havana*; Richard Jackson, *Black Writers in Latin America*; Mullen, *Afro-Cuban Literature*; and Monica Kaup, "'Our America That Is Not One.'"

6 On the limits of comparative analyses, see Seigel, "Beyond Compare."

7 Scholars have identified the participation of white musicians and poets in Afro-Cubanism as a feature that distinguished it from the Harlem Renaissance. As we shall see, these arguments have tended to underestimate the role of Afro-Cuban societies in the formation of the movement while overlooking the role of Afro-Cuban *son* musicians.

8 Hughes, *I Wonder as I Wander*, 7.

9 A similar dynamic can be seen in the relationship between the Harlem Renaissance and the Negritude movement during this period. See, for example, Cook, "Some Literary Contacts"; Vaillant, *Black, French, and African*; and Edwards, *Practice of Diaspora*.

10 Reid, *Negro Immigrant*, 204; Watkins-Owens, *Blood Relations*, 5.

11 On Victor, see the company's official history by Barnum, *"His Master's Voice" in America*.

12 Blanco Aguilar, *80 años del son y soneros en el Caribe*, 37. Blanco's claim is striking, because the performance took place before the period in which black performers were allowed on the Apollo stage. According to historians of the Apollo Theater, the heyday of black performances at the theater began in 1934. See Fox, *Showtime at the Apollo*. A photograph of Machín's name on the Apollo's marquee is on page 68. On Bauzá, see Glasser, *My Music Is My Flag*, 74–75. The Van der Zee photograph of the Sexteto Habanero appears in Willis-Braithwaite, *VanDerZee*, 109.

13 On Schomburg, see Sinnette, *Arthur Alfonso Schomburg*; James, *Holding Aloft the Banner of Ethiopia*; Hoffnung-Garskof, "Migrations of Arturo Schomburg"; and Arroyo, "Technologies."

14 Arthur Schomburg, "General Evaristo Estenoz," *Crisis* 4 (1912): 143–44.

15 Arthur Schomburg, "My Trip to Cuba in Quest of Negro Books," *Opportunity*, November 1933, 50.

16 Sinnette, *Arthur Alfonso Schomburg*, 179. Many of the materials that were generated by that trip exist in the library's collection to this day, including the publications of Club Atenas, one of the more important sources for this book.

17 Schomburg to Guillén, 1 November 1932, Nicolás Guillén Scrapbook, Schomburg Center for Research in Black Culture, New York Public Library, New York, N.Y.

18 Teodoro Ramos Blanco to Arthur A. Schomburg, 23 March 1933, reel 1, AASP. On the Harmon Foundation's attempts to profit from African American artists, see David Lewis, *When Harlem Was in Vogue*, 263.

19 Harmon Foundation, *Negro Artists*, 6.

20 Alain Locke, "The Negro Takes His Place in Art," ibid., 11–12.

21 Ramos Blanco to Schomburg, 16 January and 4 February 1933, both in reel 1, AASP.

22 See *Phylon* 4 (1943): 119, for an image of Ramos Blanco's bust of Antonio Maceo that was on display at Howard University. Details on Ramos Blanco's career can be gleaned from his slim artist file in the Art and Artifacts Division at the Schomburg Center for Research in Black Culture. I would like to thank fellow Schomburg Scholar-in-Residence Winston Kennedy for alerting me to the presence of Ramos Blanco's sculpture of Langston Hughes at the library.

23 Hughes, "My Early Days in Harlem," 64.

24 Schomburg, "My Trip to Cuba," 50.

25 Gustavo Urrutia to Langston Hughes, 20 April 1930, box 70, folder 2926, LHP.

26 For example, the Unión Fraternal in the Jesús María neighborhood ran the best-known night school in Havana.

27 Guillén, *Páginas vueltas*, 68. Along with his autobiography, the other key source on Guillén's early years is the indispensable biographical study by Augier, *Nicolás Guillén*.

28 "Las tardes literarias del Club Atenas," *Boletín Oficial del Club Atenas* 1 (20 August 1930): 11–12. On African American literary societies, see McHenry, *Forgotten Readers*.

29 Guillén, *Páginas vueltas*, 48.

30 Trelles, "Bibliografía de autores de la raza de color"; Cervantes, "Publicaciones de la raza de color."

31 Guillén, *Páginas vueltas*, 66.

32 Ibid., 67.

33 Afro-Cuban women's professional lives resembled those of African American professional women during the Jim Crow era. On African American social reformers, see Shaw, *What a Woman Ought to Be and to Do*; Gilmore, *Gender and Jim Crow*; Hayre and Moore, *Tell Them We Are Rising*; and Wadelington and Knapp, *Charlotte Hawkins Brown*.

34 Dámasa Jova, *Arpegios íntimos* and *Ufanías*.

35 The few bits of evidence on Dámasa Jova are culled from "Maria Dámasa Jova," *La Lucha Santa Clara, 1926* (directory of institutions in the province of Santa Clara; n.p.), 91; "Esa gran maestra que fue María Dámasa Jova," *Vanguardia*, 11 July 1985; and Ordetx, *Coterráneos*.

36 *Diario de la Marina*, 5 May 1938; Cook, "Urrutia." Cook's essay is one of the few published works on Urrutia in English. Tomás Fernández Robaina has pioneered the study of Urrutia's life and work. Among his many works, see *El Negro en Cuba*, 124–33.

37 Urrutia to Hughes, 1 May 1930, box 70, folder 2926, LHP.

38 Rosalie Schwartz and Alejandra Bronfman have also noted Urrutia's attention to African Americans in his column. See Schwartz, "Cuba's Roaring Twenties"; and Bronfman, *Measures of Equality*, 145.

39 *Diario de la Marina*, 21 April 1929.

40 Rampersad, *Life of Langston Hughes*, 1:176. Hughes's attempt to collaborate with Roldán was apparently a failure because the composer "said he wasn't a Negro." Hughes, *Big Sea*, 324.

41 Langston Hughes to Charlotte Van der Veer Quick Mason, box 111, folder 2092, LHP.

42 Langston Hughes, "Soledad," in *Collected Works*, 1:53.

43 The 1930 trip was Hughes's second visit to Cuba. In 1927, he briefly visited the island for the first time, spending much of his time on San Isidro Street in Old Havana, a neighborhood near the waterfront that was heavily populated by Chinese men and sex workers. See Rampersad, *Life of Langston Hughes*, 1:150.

44 Swan, "Nineteen Twenties"; Benjamin, "Machadato and Cuban Nationalism"; Pérez, *Cuba under the Platt Amendment*, 214–300; and Instituto de Historia de Cuba, *La Neocolonia*, 240–81.

45 On tourism in Cuba during this period, see Schwartz, *Pleasure Island*; and Pérez, *On Becoming Cuban*.

46 Langston Hughes, "Trip to Havana: 1930," box 492, folder 12436, LHP.

47 Moore, *Nationalizing Blackness*, 98. The *retreta* was the nighttime custom of promenading that took place in Cuban towns during the republican period. In a number of provincial towns, the custom was racially segregated. See Guridy, "Racial Knowledge in Cuba," 106–68.

48 *Diario de la Marina*, 21 April 1929.

49 Nicolas Guillén to Langston Hughes, 21 April 1930, box 70, folder 1366, LHP.

50 Hughes, *Big Sea*, 324; Hughes, *I Wonder as I Wander*, 7.

51 Bueno, *Orbita de José Antonio Fernández de Castro*.

52 For Fernández de Castro's interpretation of the "Negro theme" in Cuban literature, see *Tema negro en las letras de Cuba*.

53 The best source on Covarrubias's life and career remains Williams, *Covarrubias*. See also Heinzelman, *Covarrubias Circle*.

54 "De Covarrubias," *Social* 13, no. 2 (February 1928): 43. On Covarrubias's Harlem sketches, see Nadell, *Enter the New Negroes*, 102–12.

55 Guillén, *Páginas vueltas*, 105.

56 Rampersad, *Life of Langston Hughes*, 1:177–78. On Massaguer's *Social* magazine, see Lobo Montalvo, Lapique Becali, Menocal, and Shaw, "Years of *Social*."

57 On Covarrubias's travels to Cuba, see Williams, *Covarrubias*, 46.

58 Scholars of Afro-Cuban literature have highlighted the racialized heterosexism that pervaded Afro-Cubanist poetry of this period, a fact that was clearly an outgrowth of the male-dominated worlds of the artists and intellectuals who were a part of this movement. See Kutzinski, *Sugar's Secrets*, 163–98.

59 Hughes, *I Wonder as I Wander*, 8.

60 Of course, Hughes never informs his reader if he accepted his host's offer. He ends the passage in characteristically cryptic fashion: "So it goes at a rumba party in Havana to which one does not invite one's wife, one's mother, or one's sweetheart." *I Wonder as I Wander*, 10. Hughes's evasion of offers to partake in the pleasures of *mulata* Cuban women emerges again in his short story based on his experience in Cuba. See "Little Old Spy," in *Collected Works*, 1:254–61.

61 *Diario de la Marina*, 9 March 1930.

62 Interestingly, Guillén's clever citation of the phrase "black as the night" was a direct quote from Hughes's introductory poem to *The Weary Blues*.

63 Hughes, *I Wonder as I Wander*, 7.

64 Hughes, *Big Sea*, 325.

65 On the affective dimensions of Afro-diasporic encounters, see Guridy, "Feeling Diaspora in Harlem and Havana."

66 Hughes, *I Wonder as I Wander*, 8.

67 See Valdés's image in *Boletín Oficial del Club Atenas* 1 (20 September 1930): 22. Valdés also dined with Hughes during the Blues Poet's visit the following year. His signature appears on the back of a photo of Hughes dining with Cuban intellectuals at the El Baturro Restaurant in Havana. See box 460, folder 11137, LHP.

68 Langston Hughes, "Trip to Havana: 1930," box 492, folder 12436, LHP.

69 "Una noche en el Club Atenas," *Boletín Oficial del Club Atenas* 1 (20 March 1930): 7.

70 "Socios de Atenas," *Boletín Oficial del Club Atenas* 1 (20 September 1930): 30. In the same issue, the club even published "Piedra Pulida," which of course was not one of Guillén's *son*-poems. See page 44.

71 Hughes, *Big Sea*, 324.

72 *Diario de la Marina*, 8 April 1931.

73 Elmer Anderson Carter to Hughes, 2 July 1930, box 42, folder 727, LHP.

74 See "A Page of West Indian Poetry," *Crisis* 40 (1931): 424. See also Hughes's translation of Guillén's "Mujer Nueva," in *Opportunity* 8 (1930): 240, and "Madrigal," *Opportunity* 9 (1931), 78, which can be contrasted with the translations performed by Hughes and Ben Carruthers in *Cuba Libre* published almost two decades later. On the politics of "black to black" translation, see Nwankwo, "Langston Hughes"; and Kaup, "'Our America That Is Not One.'"

75 Guillén, *Páginas vueltas*, 77.

76 Guillén to Hughes, 21 April 1930, box 70, folder 1366, LHP.

77 Guillén, *Obra poética*, 89.

78 See Rampersad, *Life of Langston Hughes*, 1:179, 181, which claims Hughes suggested that Guillén consider the *son* as a source for his poetry, and Ellis, "Nicolás Guillén and Langston Hughes," 129–67, which disputes this claim.

79 Fernández de Castro to Hughes, n.d., and 2 February 1931 (emphasis in original), both in box 61, folder 1179, LHP. The first letter was clearly written in 1930 sometime after the publication of *Motivos de son*.

80 Gustavo Urrutia to Langston Hughes, 20 April 1930, box 70, folder 2926, LHP (emphasis in original).

81 Lalita Zamora to Hughes, 22 April 1930, box 224, folder 3712, LHP.

82 Zamora to Hughes, 26 September 1930, ibid.

83 Edelmira Linares to Langston Hughes, 1942, ibid.

84 *Diario de la Marina*, 9 March 1930.

85 Caruca Alvarez to Gustavo Urrutia, 3 May 1930, box 224, folder 3712, LHP.

86 Alvarez to Hughes, 22 May and 3 May 1930, both in ibid.

87 Fara Crespo to Hughes, 28 April 1930, box 48, folder 903, LHP.

88 Crespo to Hughes, 4 September and 19 July 1930, LHP.

89 Crespo to Hughes, 4 September 1930, LHP. Crespo's file in the Langston Hughes Papers includes another letter dated 1936 from "the Crespos" in Mexico. It is not clear whether she is the same Crespo who wrote Hughes from Havana six years earlier.

90 For samples of the debate on Hughes's sexuality, see Rampersad, *Life of Langston Hughes*, 2:431–35; and Schwarz, *Gay Voices of the Harlem Renaissance*. Much of this debate was generated by Isaac Julien's film, *Looking for Langston*.

91 Urrutia to Hughes, 1 May 1930, box 70, folder 2926, LHP.

92 Hughes to Van Vechten, 27 May 1931, in Bernard, *Remember Me to Harlem*, 88. For more on Hughes's 1931 trip to Cuba with Zell Ingram, see chapter 4 below.

93 On the crisis in Cuba, see Benjamin, "Machadato and Cuban Nationalism," 66–91; and Pérez, *Cuba under the Platt Amendment*, 214–300. On the 1931 uprising, see Instituto de Historia de Cuba, *La Neocolonia*, 292–93.

94 Guillén to Hughes, 7 August 1931, box 70, folder 1366, LHP.

95 Fernández de Castro to Hughes, 2 February 1931, box 61, folder 1179, LHP.

96 David Lewis, *When Harlem Was in Vogue*, 282–307.

97 On Scottsboro, see Carter, *Scottsboro*; Goodman, *Stories of Scottsboro*; Solomon, *Cry Was Unity*. For an excellent discussion of the case's international impact, see Miller, Pennybacker, and Rosenhaft, "Mother Ada Wright." On Scottsboro's impact on Hughes, see Rampersad, *Life of Langston Hughes*, 1:216–20.

98 "Junta Directiva: Acuerdos," *Atenas* 2 (August–September 1931): 35. On Scottsboro protests in Cuba, see Guridy, "Racial Knowledge in Cuba," 214–22.

99 Pedroso, *Antología poética*, 114–16. As is well known, Guillén's poetry also became more politicized after *Motivos de Son*, as is evident in "Caña," one of his *Sóngoro Cosongo* poems that critiqued U.S. exploitation of Cuba, as well as his next collection of poems compiled for *West Indies, Ltd.*

100 Langston Hughes, "The Official Daily Log Book: Jersey to the West Indies Lang & Zell via 'Nazimova' April 1-1931," box 492, folder 12437, LHP.

101 Hughes, "To the Little Fort."

102 Gillespie, *To Be, or Not . . . to Bop*, 319.

103 Jayne Cortez, "I See Chano Pozo," in *Coagulations*, 65–67.

Chapter 4

1 For a history of African American travel to Africa, see Campbell, *Middle Passages*. On African American travel and leisure practices in the Jim Crow era, see Foster, "In the Face of 'Jim Crow.'" On contemporary "heritage tourism" to Africa, see Ebron, "Tourists as Pilgrims"; Holsey, "Transatlantic Dreaming"; Richards, "What Is to Be Remembered?"; and Pierre, "Beyond Heritage Tourism."

2 On African American ballplayers in the Mexican and Caribbean leagues, see Burgos, *Playing America's Game*, 111, 164–66.

3 On tourism in prerevolutionary Cuba, see Schwartz, *Pleasure Island*; and Pérez, *On Becoming Cuban*, 166–98. The "So Near and Yet So Foreign" advertisement appears in *On Becoming Cuban*, 172.

4 Verrill, *Cuba of Today*, 205–7. On the growth of the transatlantic tourist industry, see Coons and Varias, *Tourist Third Cabin*.

5 On Pan-American Airways, see Bender and Altschul, *Chosen Instrument*.

6 *NW*, 5 January 1929.

7 *Hackley and Harrison's Hotel and Apartment Guide for Colored Travelers*, in box 380, folder 7, CBP.

8 See, for example, Geiss, *Pan-African Movement*; Kelley, "World the Diaspora Made"; Plummer, *Rising Wind*; and Von Eschen, *Race against Empire*.

9 William Pickens to Henry Stimson, 27 August 1930, reel 11, "General Subject File: Cuba," WPPA.

10 Historian Catherine Barnes argues that the NAACP did not have the resources to launch a sustained attack against racial discrimination in transit until the 1940s. See *Journey from Jim Crow*, 35–37. The NAACP's protest against the mistreatment of African American travelers to Cuba highlights the association's earlier efforts to combat racial discrimination in transit.

11 Rampersad, *Life of Langston Hughes*, 1:176; Langston Hughes, "Trip to Havana: 1930," box 492, folder 12436, LHP.

12 Miguel A. Campa to Walter White, 22 February 1930, reel 11, WPPA.

13 William C. Campbell to Langston Hughes, 14 March 1930, box 120, folder 2266, LHP.

14 On the backlash against Afro-Caribbean migrants, see McLeod, "Undesirable Aliens"; and Chomsky, "'Barbados or Canada?'"

15 Pickens to Stimson, 27 August 1930, reel 11, WPPA.

16 The *Crisis* published an open letter from Bethune to the Afro-Cuban journalist Gustavo Urrutia about the episode. See "Our Readers Say," *Crisis* 37 (December 1930): 412.

17 Pickens to Stimson, 27 August 1930, reel 11, WPPA. Belisario Heureaux was indeed the son of the late nineteenth-century Dominican president Ulises Heureaux.

18 Pickens to R. P. Sims, and to Sue Bailey, both 12 September 1930, ibid.

19 *Diario de la Marina*, 7 September 1930.

20 E. Francis White to Pickens, 16 September 1930, reel 11, WPPA.

21 *El Mundo*, 10 September 1930.

22 Details of Margaret Ross Martin's biography were taken from a letter of application to the International People's College in Denmark. See Martin to John B. Barton, 18 March 1931, reel 11, WPPA.

23 Photos of both James and Margaret appear in the September 1930 of the *Boletín Oficial del Club Atenas* 1 (September 1930): 19, 56.

24 Pickens corresponded with another African American woman named Albertha Cundy, who worked for the Martins. See Pickens to Cundy, 17 September 1930, reel 11, WPPA.

25 Margaret Ross Martin to William Pickens, 19 June 1930, ibid.

26 Martin to Pickens, 30 April 1930, ibid.

27 Martin to Pickens, 19 June 1930, ibid. Eventually, Pickens secured passage on the maiden voyage of the Ward Line's *Morro Castle* on 23 August 1930. The apparent ease with which Pickens purchased the ticket highlights the unpredictable nature of racism in the transit industry in this period. Black travelers (outside of the Jim Crow South) could never be sure of the moment when white companies would draw the color line.

28 Margaret Ross Martin, "The Negro in Cuba," *Crisis* 39 (January 1932): 453–55. Martin also wrote a profile of Juan Gualberto Gómez following the Afro-Cuban patriot's death in March 1933. See Martin, "The Last Word in Cuba," *Crisis* 40 (May 1933): 105.

29 William Pickens to Percival Prattis, 6 October 1930, box 376, folder 6, CBP.

30 Pickens to Urrutia, 17 September 1930, reel 11, WPPA.

31 Pickens to Luís Delfín Valdés, 18 September 1930, ibid.

32 This information on García's background was found in the alumni files on José García Inerarity, Hampton University Museum and Archives, Hampton, Virginia.

33 "Former Student, J. G. Inerarity, Wins International Recognition," *Hampton Alumni Record*, vol. 1, April 1959. One wonders if the resourceful García was able to maintain his relationship with the Cuban revolutionary government after Fidel Castro declared the revolution socialist in 1961. I would like to thank Miriam Jiménez Román for bringing this piece to my attention.

34 García to Pickens, 21 November 1930, reel 11, WPPA.

35 Pickens to García, 29 November 1930, ibid.

36 García to Barnett, 30 December 1930, box 203, CBP.

37 Claude Barnett to Luís Delfín Valdés, 5 December 1954, box 203, folder 3, CBP. For a brief discussion of Barnett's tenure at Tuskegee, see Hogan, *Black National News Service*, 40–41.

38 *Diario de la Marina*, 8 April 1931.

39 On African American perceptions of the possibilities of "automobility," see Seiler, "'So That We as a Race.'"

40 Langston Hughes, "The Official Daily Log Book," box 492, folder 12437, LHP. Hughes indicated that he wanted to publish an article for black travelers entitled "War Lands to the South." However, such an article was never written. See the photos of the Atenas building in box 458, folder 11092, LHP.

41 Conrado Thorndike to Arthur A. Schomburg, 5 November 1932, reel 6, AASP.

42 *Baltimore Afro-American*, 19 August 1933.

43 The lecture was subsequently published in 1942. See Blanco, *El prejuicio racial en Puerto Rico*.

44 Ibid., 121. On the Mitchell incident and its impact on the desegregation of southern railways, see Barnes, *Journey from Jim Crow*, 1–34.

45 On the politics of the 1930s and its ramifications on the campaign against racial discrimination in Cuba, see Bronfman, *Measures of Equality*, 171–81; Whitney, *State and Revolution in Cuba*; and de la Fuente, *Nation for All*, 175–209.

46 See Nordin, *New Deal's Black Congressman*.

47 Letter to Arthur Mitchell, 5 February 1938, box 36, folder 6, AMP. The signature on the letter is illegible, but it is clear that it was written by an Afro-Cuban politician.

48 García to Mitchell, 11 December 1934, box 3, folder 5, AMP.

49 The warm reception Mitchell received was even noticed by the U.S. embassy in Havana. The embassy sent Mitchell several news clippings detailing his visit that were published in the Cuban press. W. E. B. Du Bois to Mitchell, 30 December 1937, box 35, folder 1, AMP. See also *Baltimore Afro-American*, 22 January 1938.

50 *Diario de la Marina*, 30 December 1937.

51 Ibid.

52 Ibid.

53 Enclosed news clippings in box 35, folder 1, AMP.

54 It seems that the Mitchell party did eventually secure a table after the initial snub, perhaps after some negotiation with the hotel manager.

55 Feliciano González to Mitchell, 22 January 1938, box 36, folder 4, AMP. González's comments suggest that García was likely the person who negotiated some agreement with the hotel's management.

56 *Diario de la Marina*, 1 January 1938.

57 Ibid., 5 January 1938.

58 García to Mitchell, 2 January 1938, box 35, folder 7, AMP.

59 Clara Ruíz to Mitchell, 19 January 1938, box 36, folder 4, AMP.

60 *Diario de la Marina*, 3 January 1938.

61 González to Mitchell, 22 January 1938, box 36, folder 4, AMP.

62 These letters and cablegrams were found in box 39, no. 14, Fondo Secretaría de la Presidencia, Archivo Nacional de Cuba, Havana.

63 Angel Martínez to Presidente de la República, 2 December 1937, ibid. The date is incorrect. Since the incident at the Hotel Saratoga occurred on the night of 29 December, the letter was likely written on 29 or 30 December.

64 Francisco A. Pérez to Colonel Federico Laredo Brú, 31 December 1937, ibid.

65 Sociedad La Unión to Presidente de la República, 8 January 1938, ibid.

66 Asociación Más Luz to Presidente de la República, 4 January 1938, ibid.

67 Mitchell to García, 15 January 1938, box 36, folder 3, AMP. The incident, like Mitchell's trip to Cuba in general, received scant treatment in the African American press, possibly because it occurred during the holiday season, and possibly because Mitchell was not beloved by the editors of major black newspapers, including Robert Vann of the *Chicago Defender*, the preeminent black publication in Mitchell's home city.

68 Mitchell to Clara Ruíz, 2 February 1938, box 36, folder 6, AMP.

69 Mitchell's silence could have been due to the fact that aside from periodic transgressions of racial etiquette on the quotidian level, African Americans had not yet waged a sustained national legal campaign against racial segregation in public facilities and accommodations in the United States during this period. Thus, perhaps to Mitchell, whatever took place at the hotel that evening was simply yet another encounter with the color line. In the 1930s, civil rights groups such as the NAACP were focusing their efforts on beginning an attack on racial segregation in education. On the evolution of the legal campaign for desegregation in the United States, see Tushnet, *NAACP's Legal Strategy against Segregated Education*. Meanwhile, the legal campaign against segregation in transportation industries in the United States was rejuvenated by Mitchell's own lawsuit against the Chicago, Rock Island & Pacific Railway Company, which was filed in April 1938. See Barnes, *Journey from Jim Crow*, 20–37.

70 "La Ley Convertida en Letra Muerta," *Adelante* 3 (April 1938): 1.

71 On the debates on racial discrimination during the constitutional conventions of 1940, see de la Fuente, *Nation for All*, 212–22; and Bronfman, *Measures of Equality*, 171–81.

72 For a history of African American engagements with Haitians that was articulated through the discourse of Pan-Americanism, see Polyné, *Black Pan-Americanism*.

73 Muna Lee, "A New Point of View: America as a Continent," *Aframerican Woman's Journal* 3 (Summer and Fall 1942): 4. As historian Rosalie Schwartz has shown, the wider Cuban tourist industry took a "cultural turn" in this period. See *Pleasure Island*, 94–99.

74 On the New Deal and African Americans, see Sitkoff, *New Deal for Blacks*; and Sullivan, *Days of Hope*.

75 For a study of Howard's role in developing a cohort of black activist scholars during the 1930s, see Holloway, *Confronting the Veil*. On Logan, see Janken, *Rayford Logan*.

76 Guillén, *Cuba libre*.

77 Details of Carruthers's biography are taken from his resumes in box 1, Ben F. Carruthers Papers, Schomburg Center for Research in Black Culture, New York Public Library, New York, N.Y.

78 Documents in the Carruthers Papers files show that he eventually worked in the tourist industry for the Hilton hotel chain, highlighting his persistent interest in cultural tourism.

79 Janken, *Rayford Logan*, 97, 136–37.

80 See "Diary—1942," container 9, Rayford Logan Papers, Library of Congress (emphasis in original).

81 Carruthers to Claude Barnett, 30 April 1952, box 203, folder 3, CBP.

82 *Baltimore Afro-American*, 30 August 1941.

83 Du Bois to Miguel Angel Céspedes, 7 July 1941, reel 42, frame 771, W. E. B. Du Bois Papers, University of Massachusetts at Amherst Library, Amherst, Massachusetts.

84 *Amsterdam News*, 28 June 1941.

85 Du Bois to Ortiz, 7 July 1941, reel 53, frame 178, Du Bois Papers.

86 On Diggs's understudied life and work, see Bolles, "Ellen Irene Diggs." On her relationship with Du Bois, see David Lewis, *W. E. B. Du Bois: The Fight*, 485.

87 See news clippings in García's alumni file in the Hampton University Museum and Archives.

88 Hanson, *Mary McLeod Bethune*; White, *Too Heavy a Load*, 148–75.

89 Sue Bailey Thurman to Mary McLeod Bethune, 22 March 1941, Series 4, box 1, folder 17, NCNWP.

90 While the association did not have any explicit reference to race in its bylaws, the group's members and programming illustrate that it clearly was a group for the interests of Afro-Cuban women. Like many Afro-Cuban associations after the passage of the Morúa Law in 1912, the ACF seems to have downplayed its racial component in its correspondence with the Cuban state. See the association's constitution in bundle 1111, files 23246–48, RA.

91 For one of the few studies on the feminist movement in modern Cuba, see Stoner, *From the House to the Streets*.

92 Calixta Hernández de Cervantes, "Mujeres ejemplares: Ana Echegoyen," *Adelante* (February 1938): 13. Echegoyen's career also took a "Pan-American" turn in the 1940s. The ACF's participation in the seminar is not surprising. Ana Echegoyen also developed a hemispheric orientation to her work as an educator. In 1946, she coauthored a pamphlet on hemispheric education published in Spanish by the Pan-American Union. Echegoyen de Cañizares and Suárez, *El continente de enseñanza*.

93 Similar gender dynamics have been highlighted by historians of African American female teachers. See Shaw, *What a Woman Ought to Be and to Do*.

94 Sue Bailey Thurman, "The Seminar in Cuba," *Aframerican Woman's Journal* 1 (Summer and Fall 1940): 5.

95 On the Afro-Cuban experience in Tampa, see Greenbaum, *More than Black*. Greenbaum's work illustrates that Grillo's experience as a racialized subject in Tampa was not uncommon.

96 Grillo, *Black Cuban, Black American*, 61.

97 The experience of the Grillo family resonates with recent scholarly attempts to conceptualize racialization in a hemispheric perspective. See Dzidzienyo and Oboler, *Neither Enemies nor Friends*.

98 See Mary McLeod Bethune's diary, 1930, reel 4, part 1, Mary McLeod Bethune Papers, Bethune-Cookman College Collection, National Archives for Black Women's History, Washington, D.C., which lists Henry Grillo as a student in 1930.

99 Grillo, *Black Cuban, Black American*, 17–18.

100 Author's interview with Evelio Grillo, 13 October 2006, Oakland, California.

101 Thurman, "Seminar in Cuba," 4–5.

102 *El País*, 22 August 1940.

103 On the emergence of consumerism in the post–World War II United States, see Lisabeth Cohen, *Consumers' Republic*. On U.S. consumerism in Cuba, see Pérez, *On Becoming Cuban*.

104 On the U.S. embassy's attempts to court Afro-Cubans during World War II, see Guridy, "From Solidarity to Cross-Fertilization."

105 On the Instituto Interamericano's event, see the enclosed minutes in Serapio Páez Zamora and Cesar Guillén to Gobernador de la Habana, 1 August 1955, bundle 169, file 3220, RA.

106 Barnes, *Journey from Jim Crow*, 108–31.

107 On racial politics during the 1950s, see de la Fuente, *Nation for All*, 235–55.

108 Betancourt, *El negro*, 119.

109 On the Club Cubano Interamericano, see Mirabal, "Scripting Race, Finding Place."

110 Ramón Cabrera Torres to the Consejo de la Unión Nacional de Mujeres de Color, 17 July 1947, box 30, folder 5, NCNWP.

111 See enclosed flyers and invitations in box 30, folder 6, NCNWP. Houston apparently did not need the services of a translator, since it seems that he spoke to delegates in Spanish.

112 Bethune to Club Jóvenes del Vals, 18 August 1948, ibid.

113 See "El Comité Cubano" flyer in ibid.

114 Pedro Portuondo Calá to Claude Barnett, 23 June 1952, box 203, folder 3, CBP.

115 T. B. O'Steen to Pedro Portuondo Calá, 10 July 1952, ibid.

116 Portuondo Calá to Barnett, 25 August 1952, ibid. On the Lord Calvert Hotel and black tourism in the Overtown district, see Fields, "Tracing Overtown's Vernacular Architecture."

117 Páez Zamora and José Pacheco Vasconcelos to Barnett, 7 November 1955, box 203, folder 3, CBP.

118 Henry Grillo to Richard V. Moore, 10 October 1951, reel 8, Bethune Papers.

Epilogue

1 Chrisman, "National Culture."

2 See Cannon and Cole, *Free and Equal*.

3 On the Cuban government's support for African liberation struggles, see de la Fuente, *Nation for All*, 296–307, and Gleijeses, *Conflicting Missions*.

4 Of course, a number of these African American activists, such as Robert Williams, Stokely Carmichael, and Eldridge Cleaver, among others, eventually became dis-

affected by the Cuban Revolution. See Clytus, *Black Man in Red Cuba*; Cleaver, *Soul on Ice*. The most noteworthy Afro-Cuban critic of the revolution was Carlos Moore, who also framed his diatribe in black internationalist terms. See *Castro, the Blacks, and Africa*.

5 The history of Cuban-U.S. relations since 1959 complicates teleological narratives embedded in many globalization theories. Rather than demonstrating increasing global connectedness over time, Cuban-U.S. linkages during the past five decades illustrate the ebb and flow of cross-border interaction. For a useful critique of globalization theory, see Cooper, "What Is the Concept of Globalization Good For?"

6 For a recent appraisal of the consequences of the *Brown v. Board of Education* decision, see the essays in the *Journal of American History* 91 (June 2004).

7 Resolución de Sra. Edunia Ramírez, bundle 1112, file 23270, RA. On the closing of the Afro-Cuban societies, see de la Fuente, *Nation for All*, 280–85.

8 Ramiro sang with the Los Cavaliers group in the 1950s, which also included, among others, Tony Suárez Rocabruna, the son of Angel Suárez Rocabruna, who taught at Howard University in the 1940s. On the "feeling" movement in Cuba, see Acosta, *Cubano Be, Cubano Bop*, 60–61.

9 The film premiered in Havana in 2004 but has yet to be distributed in the United States. For more on the documentary, see ⟨http://afrocubaweb.com/gloriarolando/nosotrosjazz.htm⟩.

10 These names of Ramiro's friends are pseudonyms to protect their privacy.

11 For a brief profile of the group, see Gorry, "Timeless Cool."

Bibliography

Manuscript Sources

Cuba

Camagüey
   Archivo Histórico Provincial de Camagüey
      Fondo Jorge Juárez Cano
Havana
   Archivo Nacional de Cuba
      Fondo Secretaría de la Presidencia
      Registro de Asociaciones
Santa Clara
   Archivo Histórico Provincial de Villa Clara
      Fondo de Registro de Asociaciones

United States

Amherst, Massachusetts
   University of Massachusetts at Amherst Library
      W. E. B. Du Bois Papers
Chicago, Illinois
   Chicago Historical Society
      Claude Barnett Papers
      Arthur Mitchell Papers
Hampton, Virginia
   Hampton University Museum and Archives
New Haven, Connecticut
   Beinecke Rare Book and Manuscript Library, Yale University
      Langston Hughes Papers, James Weldon Johnson Memorial Collection
New York, New York
   National Archives and Records Administration, Northeast Region
      Records of the U.S. Department of State, RG 59
      Records of the U.S. Courts of Appeals, RG 276

Schomburg Center for Research in Black Culture, New York Public Library
  Ben F. Carruthers Papers
  William Pickens Papers (Additions)
  Arthur A. Schomburg Papers
  Universal Negro Improvement Association, Records of the Central Division
Tuskegee, Alabama
  Tuskegee University Archives
    Booker T. Washington Papers
Washington, D.C.
  Library of Congress
    Rayford Logan Papers
    Booker T. Washington Papers
  National Archives for Black Women's History, Mary McLeod Bethune
        Council House
    Mary McLeod Bethune Papers, Bethune-Cookman College Collection
    National Council of Negro Women Papers

Newspapers and Periodicals

Aframerican Woman's Journal (Washington, D.C.)
Alma Jóven (Trinidad)
Amsterdam News (New York)
Atenas (Havana)
Baltimore Afro-American
Boletín Oficial del Club Atenas (Havana)
Crisis (New York)
Diario de la Marina (Havana)
Hampton Alumni Record (Hampton, Va.)
Heraldo de Cuba (Havana)
La Lucha, 1926 (Santa Clara)
Negro World (New York)
Opportunity (New York)
Social (Havana)
Tuskegee Student (Tuskegee)

Published Primary Sources

Bernard, Emily, ed. *Remember Me to Harlem: The Letters of Langston Hughes and Carl Van Vechten, 1925–1964*. New York: Alfred Knopf, 2001.
Betancourt, Juan René. "Castro and the Cuban Negro." *Crisis* 67 (May 1961): 270–74.
———. *El negro: Ciudadano del futuro*. Havana: Cárdenas y Cía, 1959.
Blanco, Tomás. *El prejuicio racial en Puerto Rico*. San Juan, P.R.: Editorial Biblioteca de Autores Puertorriqueños, 1942.

Cannon, Terry, and Johnetta Cole. *Free and Equal: The End of Racial Discrimination in Cuba*. New York: Venceremos Brigade, 1978.

Cervantes, Carlos A. "Publicaciones de la raza de color." *Adelante* 3 (March 1938): 10–11.

Chrisman, Robert. "National Culture in Revolutionary Cuba." *Black Scholar* 8 (1977): 2–11.

Club Atenas. *Nuestros hombres faros en Cuba y Puerto Rico*. Havana: Club Atenas, 1921.

Cook, Mercer. "Urrutia." *Phylon* 4 (1943): 220–32.

Cortez, Jayne. *Coagulations: New and Selected Poems*. New York: Thunder's Mouth Press, 1984.

Dámasa Jova, Maria. *Arpegios intimos*. Santa Clara: Imprenta El Arte, 1925.

———. *Ufanías: Juicios y consideraciones acerca de "Arpegios intimos" y poesías*. Santa Clara, Cuba: Imp. De la A. Clapera, 1927.

Digital Library of Georgia. *The Blues, Black Vaudeville and the Silver Screen, 1912–1930s: Selections from the Records of Macon's Douglass Theatre*, ⟨dlg.galileo.usg.edu⟩.

Echegoyen de Cañizares, Ana, and Calixto Suárez. *El continente de enseñanza*. Washington, D.C.: Unión Panamericana, 1946.

Goode, W. T. *The "Eighth Illinois."* Chicago: Blakely, 1899.

Guillén, Nicolás. *Cuba libre: Poems*. Translated by Langston Hughes and Ben F. Carruthers. Los Angeles: Anderson & Ritchie, 1948.

———. *Obra poética*. Vol. 1. Havana: Letras Cubanas, 2004.

———. *Páginas vueltas: Memorias*. Havana: UNEAC, 1982.

Hackley and Harrison's Hotel and Apartment Guide for Colored Travelers. Philadelphia: Hackley & Harrison, 1930.

Harmon Foundation. *Negro Artists: Presented by the Harmon Foundation at the Art Center, 1933*. New York: Harmon Foundation, 1933.

Hill, Robert A. *The Marcus Garvey and Universal Negro Improvement Association Papers*. Vols. 1–7. Los Angeles: University of California Press, 1983–90.

Hughes, Langston. *The Big Sea*. 3rd ed. New York: Hill and Wang, 1993.

———. *The Collected Works of Langston Hughes: The Poems, 1921–1940*. Edited by Arnold Rampersad. Vol. 1. Columbia: University of Missouri Press, 2001.

———. "A Cuban Sculptor." *Opportunity* 8 (November 1930): 334.

———. *I Wonder as I Wander*. New York: Hill and Wang, 1956.

———. "My Early Days in Harlem." In *Harlem: A Community in Transition*, edited by John Henrik Clarke, 62–64. New York: Citadel, 1964.

———. "To the Little Fort of San Lazaro on the Ocean Front, Havana." *New Masses* 6 (May 1931): 11.

Pedroso, Regino. *Antología poética*. Havana: N.p., 1939.

Serra, Rafael. *Para blancos y negros: Ensayos políticos, sociales, y económicos*. Havana: Imprenta "El Score," 1907.

Trelles, Carlos M. "Bibliografía de autores de la raza de color." *Cuba Contemporánea* 43 (1927): 30–78.

Tuskegee Institute. *Annual Catalogue of the Tuskegee Normal and Industrial Institute.* Tuskegee, Ala.: Tuskegee Institute, 1898–1920.

Verrill, A. Hyatt. *Cuba of Today.* New York: Dodd, Mead, 1931.

Washington, Booker T. "Industrial Education for Cuban Negroes." *Christian Register*, 18 August 1898, 455.

———. *Up from Slavery.* Edited with a new introduction by W. Fitzhugh Brundage. Boston: Bedford/St. Martins, 2003.

———. *Working with the Hands.* New York: Doubleday, Page, 1904.

———, ed. *Tuskegee and Its People: Their Ideals and Achievements.* 1905. Reprint, New York: Negro Universities Press, 1969.

Washington, Margaret Murray. "What Girls Are Taught and How." In Booker T. Washington, *Tuskegee and Its People*, 68–88.

Secondary Sources

Abrahams, Roger D. *The Man of Words in the West Indies: Performance and the Emergence of Creole Culture.* Baltimore: Johns Hopkins University Press, 1983.

Acosta, Leonardo. *Cubano Be, Cubano Bop: One Hundred Years of Jazz in Cuba.* Translated by David S. Whitesell. Washington, D.C.: Smithsonian Books, 2003.

Anderson, Benedict. *Imagined Communities: Reflections on the Origins and Spread of Nationalism.* Rev. ed. London: Verso, 1991.

Anderson, James D. *The Education of Blacks in the South, 1860–1935.* Chapel Hill: University of North Carolina Press, 1988.

Arroyo, Jossianna. "Technologies: Transculturations of Race, Gender, and Ethnicity in Arturo A. Schomburg's Masonic Writings." *Centro Journal* 17 (Spring 2005): 4–29.

Augier, Angel. *Nicolás Guillén: Notas para un estudio biográfico-crítico.* 2nd ed. Santa Clara: Universidad Central de Las Villas, 1962.

Austerlitz, Paul. *Jazz Consciousness: Music, Race, and Humanity.* Middletown, Conn.: Wesleyan University Press, 2005.

Ayala, César J. *American Sugar Kingdom: The Plantation Economy of the Spanish Caribbean, 1898–1934.* Chapel Hill: University of North Carolina Press, 1999.

Bair, Barbara. "'Ethiopia Shall Stretch Forth Her Hands unto God': Laura Kofey and the Gendered Vision of Redemption in the Garvey Movement." In *A Mighty Baptism: Race, Gender, and the Creation of American Protestantism*, edited by Susan Juster and Lisa MacFarlane, 38–61. Ithaca, N.Y.: Cornell University Press, 1996.

———. "True Women, Real Men: Gender, Ideology, and Social Roles in the Garvey Movement." In *Gendered Domains: Rethinking Public and Private in Women's History*, edited by Dorothy O. Helly and Susan Reverby, 154–66. Ithaca, N.Y.: Cornell University Press, 1992.

Barnes, Catherine A. *Journey from Jim Crow: The Desegregation of Southern Transit.* New York: Columbia University Press, 1983.

Barnum, Fred. *"His Master's Voice" in America: Ninety Years of Communications*

Pioneering and Progress; Victor Talking Machine Company, Radio Corporation of America, General Electric Company. Camden, N.J.: General Electric, 1991.

Bender, Marilyn, and Selig Altschul. *The Chosen Instrument: Pan Am, Juan Trippe, the Rise and Fall of an American Entrepreneur.* New York: Simon and Schuster, 1982.

Benjamin, Jules. "The Machadato and Cuban Nationalism, 1928–1932." *Hispanic American Historical Review* 55 (1975): 66–91.

Blanco Aguilar, Jesús: *80 años del son y soneros en el Caribe.* Caracas: Fondo Editorial Tropykos, 1992.

Bolles, A. Lynn. "Ellen Irene Diggs: Coming of Age in Atlanta, Havana, and Baltimore." In *African-American Pioneers in Anthropology*, edited by Ira E. Harrison and Faye V. Harrison, 154–67. Urbana: University of Illinois Press, 1999.

Bolster, W. Jeffrey. *Black Jacks: African-American Seamen in the Age of Sail.* Cambridge, Mass.: Harvard University Press, 1997.

Brandon, George. *Santería from Africa to the New World: The Dead Cell Memories.* Bloomington: Indiana University Press, 1993.

Braudel, Fernand. *The Mediterranean and the Mediterranean World in the Age of Philip II.* Vol. 1. Berkeley: University of California Press, 1986.

Brock, Lisa, and Digna Castañeda Fuertes, eds. *Between Race and Empire: African-Americans and Cubans before the Cuban Revolution.* Philadelphia: Temple University Press, 1998.

Bronfman, Alejandra. *Measures of Equality: Social Science, Citizenship, and Race in Cuba, 1902–1940.* Chapel Hill: University of North Carolina Press, 2004.

Brundage, W. Fitzhugh, ed. *Booker T. Washington and Black Progress: Up from Slavery 100 Years Later.* Gainesville: University Press of Florida, 2003.

Bueno, Salvador, ed. *Orbita de José Antonio Fernández de Castro.* Havana: UNEAC, 1966.

Bundles, A'Lelia. *On Her Own Ground: The Life and Times of Madam C. J. Walker.* New York: Scribner, 2001.

Burgos, Adrian, Jr. *Playing America's Game: Baseball, Latinos, and the Color Line.* Berkeley: University of California Press, 2007.

Burkett, Randall K. *Garveyism as a Religious Movement: The Institutionalization of a Black Civil Religion.* Metuchen, N.J.: Scarecrow, 1978.

Burnett, Carla. "'Are We Slaves or Free Men?': Labor, Race, Garveyism and the 1920 Panama Canal Strike." Ph.D. diss., University of Illinois at Chicago, 2004.

Butler, Kim D. "Defining Diaspora, Refining a Discourse." *Diaspora* 10 (2001): 189–219.

Cabrera, Lydia. *La sociedad secreta Abakuá.* Miami: Ediciones C. R., 1970.

Calder, Bruce J. *The Impact of Intervention: The Dominican Republic during the U.S. Occupation of 1916–1924.* Austin: University of Texas Press, 1984.

Campbell, James T. *Middle Passages: African American Journeys to Africa, 1787–2005.* New York: Penguin, 2005.

Carter, Dan. *Scottsboro: A Tragedy of the American South.* Baton Rouge: Louisiana State University Press, 1969.

Chaudhuri, K. N. *Asia before Europe: Economy and Civilization in the Indian Ocean from the Rise of Islam to 1750.* Cambridge: Cambridge University Press, 1991.

Childs, Matt D. *The 1812 Aponte Rebellion in Cuba and the Struggle against Atlantic Slavery*. Chapel Hill: University of North Carolina Press, 2006.

Chomsky, Aviva. "'Barbados or Canada?' Race, Immigration, and Nation in Early-Twentieth-Century Cuba." *Hispanic American Historical Review* 80 (August 2000): 415–62.

———. *West Indian Workers and the United Fruit Company, 1870–1940*. Baton Rouge: Louisiana State University Press, 1996.

Clifford, James. *Routes: Travel and Translation in the Late Twentieth Century*. Cambridge, Mass.: Harvard University Press, 1997.

Cobb, Martha. *Harlem, Haiti, and Havana: A Comparative Critical Study of Langston Hughes, Jacques Roumain, Nicolás Guillén*. Washington, D.C.: Three Continents, 1979.

Cohen, Lisabeth. *A Consumers' Republic: The Politics of Mass Consumption in Postwar America*. New York: Knopf, 2003.

Cohen, Robin. *Global Diasporas: An Introduction*. London: Routledge, 2001.

Conniff, Michael. *Black Labor on a White Canal: Panama, 1904–1981*. Pittsburgh: University of Pittsburgh Press, 1985.

Cook, Mercer. "Some Literary Contacts: African, West Indian and Afro-American." In *The Black Writer*, edited by Lloyd W. Brown, 119–49. Los Angeles: Hennessey and Ingalls, 1973.

Coons, Lorraine, and Alexander Varias. *Tourist Third Cabin: Steamship Travel in the Interwar Years*. New York: Palgrave Macmillan, 2003.

Cooper, Frederick. "What Is the Concept of Globalization Good For? An African Historian's Perspective." *African Affairs* 100 (2001): 189–213.

Cooper, Frederick, and Rogers Brubaker. "Beyond Identity." *Theory and Society* 29 (2000): 1–47.

Cronon, Edmund. *Black Moses: The Story of Marcus Garvey and the Universal Negro Improvement Association*. Madison: University of Wisconsin Press, 1955.

de la Fuente, Alejandro. "Myths of Racial Democracy: Cuba, 1900–1912." *Latin American Research Review* 34 (1999): 39–73.

———. *A Nation for All: Race, Inequality, and Politics in Twentieth-Century Cuba*. Chapel Hill: University of North Carolina Press, 2001.

Delpar, Helen. *The Enormous Vogue of Things Mexican: Cultural Relations between the United States and Mexico, 1920–1935*. Tuscaloosa: University of Alabama Press, 1992.

Deschamps Chapeaux, Pedro. *El Negro en el periodismo cubano en el siglo XIX*. Havana: Ediciones R, 1963.

Diamond, Elin, ed. *Performance and Cultural Politics*. London and New York: Routledge, 1996.

Dominguez, Bernardo García. "Garvey and Cuba." In *Garvey: His Work and Impact*, edited by Rupert Lewis and Patrick Bryan, 299–305. Trenton, N.J.: Africa World, 1991.

Dozier, Richard K. "Tuskegee: Booker T. Washington's Contribution to the Training of Black Architects." Ph.D. diss., University of Michigan, 1990.

Dzidzienyo, Anani, and Suzanne Oboler, eds. *Neither Enemies nor Friends: Latinos, Blacks, Afro-Latinos*. New York: Palgrave Macmillan, 2005.

Ebron, Paulla A. "Tourists as Pilgrims: Commercial Fashioning of Transatlantic Politics." *American Ethnologist* 26 (1999): 910–32.

Edwards, Brent Hayes. *The Practice of Diaspora: Literature, Translation, and the Rise of Black Internationalism*. Cambridge, Mass.: Harvard University Press, 2003.

———. "The Uses of Diaspora." *Social Text* 19 (2001): 45–73.

Ellis, Keith. "Nicolás Guillén and Langston Hughes: Convergences and Divergences." In Brock and Castañeda Fuertes, *Between Race and Empire*, 129–67.

Engs, Robert Francis. *Educating the Disfranchised and Disinherited: Samuel Chapman Armstrong and Hampton Institute, 1839–1893*. Knoxville: University of Tennessee Press, 1999.

Fanon, Frantz. *The Wretched of the Earth*. New York: Grove, 1963.

Fernandes, Sujatha. *Cuba Represent! Cuban Arts, State Power, and the Making of New Revolutionary Cultures*. Durham, N.C.: Duke University Press, 2006.

Fernández de Castro, José Antonio. *Tema negro en las letras de Cuba*. Havana: Ediciones Mirador, 1943.

Fernández Robaina, Tomás. *Hablen paleros y santeros*. Havana: Editorial de Ciencias Sociales, 1997.

———. "Marcus Garvey in Cuba." In Brock and Castañeda Fuertes, *Between Race and Empire*, 120–28.

———. *El Negro en Cuba, 1902–1958: Apuntes para la historia de la lucha contra la discriminación racial*. Havana: Editorial de Ciencias Sociales, 1994.

Ferrer, Ada. *Insurgent Cuba: Race, Nation, and Revolution, 1868–1898*. Chapel Hill: University of North Carolina Press, 1999.

Fields, Dorothy Jenkins. "Tracing Overtown's Vernacular Architecture." *Journal of Decorative and Propaganda Arts* 23 (1998): 322–33.

Foster, Mark S. "In the Face of 'Jim Crow': Prosperous Blacks and Vacations, Travel and Outdoor Leisure, 1890–1945." *Journal of Negro History* 84 (Spring 1999): 130–49.

Fox, Ted. *Showtime at the Apollo*. New York: Holt, Rinehart, and Winston, 1983.

Gaines, Kevin K. *American Africans in Ghana: Black Expatriates and the Civil Rights Era*. Chapel Hill: University of North Carolina Press, 2006.

———. *Uplifting the Race: Black Leadership, Politics, and Culture in the Twentieth Century*. Chapel Hill: University of North Carolina Press, 1996.

Gatewood, Willard. *Black Americans and the White Man's Burden*. Urbana: University of Illinois Press, 1975.

———. *"Smoked Yankees" and the Struggle for Empire: Letters from Negro Soldiers, 1898–1902*. Urbana: University of Illinois Press, 1971.

Geiss, Immanuel. *The Pan-African Movement*. London: Methuen, 1974.

Gill, Tiffany M. *Civic Beauty: Beauticians, Beauty Salons, and the Politics of African American Female Entrepreneurship*. Urbana: University of Illinois Press, forthcoming.

Gillespie, Dizzy. *To Be, or Not . . . to Bop*. New York: Da Capo, 1979.

Gilmore, Glenda E. *Gender and Jim Crow: Women and the Politics of White Supremacy in North Carolina, 1896–1920*. Chapel Hill: University of North Carolina Press, 1996.

Gilroy, Paul. *Between Camps: Nations, Cultures, and the Allure of Race*. London: Routledge, 2004.

———. *The Black Atlantic: Modernity and Double Consciousness*. Cambridge, Mass.: Harvard University Press, 1993.

Giovannetti, Jorge L. "Black British Subjects in Cuba: Race, Ethnicity, Nation, Identity in the Migratory Experience, 1898–1938." Ph.D. diss., University of North London, 2001.

———. "The Elusive Organization of 'Identity': Race, Religion, and Empire among Caribbean Migrants in Cuba." *Small Axe* 10 (2006): 1–27.

Glasser, Ruth. *My Music Is My Flag: Puerto Rican Musicians and Their New York Communities, 1917–1940*. Berkeley: University of California Press, 1995.

Gleijeses, Piero. *Conflicting Missions: Havana, Washington, and Africa, 1959–1976*. Chapel Hill: University of North Carolina Press, 2002.

Gobat, Michel. *Confronting the American Dream: Nicaragua under U.S. Imperial Rule*. Durham, N.C.: Duke University Press, 2005.

Gomez, Michael. *Reversing Sail: A History of the African Diaspora*. Cambridge: Cambridge University Press, 2004.

Goodman, James E. *Stories of Scottsboro*. New York: Pantheon Books, 1994.

Gorry, Conner. "Timeless Cool." *Cuba Absolutely* 1 (2007), ⟨http://www.cubaabsolutely.com/music/Timeless_Cool.html.⟩, 1 December 2008.

Gosse, Van. "The African-American Press Greets the Cuban Revolution." In Brock and Castañeda Fuertes, *Between Race and Empire*, 266–80.

———. *Where the Boys Are: Cuba, Cold War America, and the Making of the New Left*. London: Verso, 1993.

Greenbaum, Susan. *More than Black: Afro-Cubans in Tampa*. Gainesville: University Press of Florida, 2002.

Grillo, Evelio. *Black Cuban, Black American: A Memoir*. Houston: Arte Público, 2000.

Gunning, Sandra, Tera W. Hunter, and Michele Mitchell. "Introduction: Gender, Sexuality, and African Diasporas." *Gender and History* 15 (2003): 397–408.

Guridy, Frank A. "'Enemies of the White Race': The Machadista State and the UNIA in Cuba." *Caribbean Studies* 31 (2003): 117–39.

———."Feeling Diaspora in Harlem and Havana." *Social Text* 27 (Spring 2009): 115–40.

———. "From Solidarity to Cross-Fertilization: Afro-Cuban/African American Interaction during the 1930s and 1940s." *Radical History Review* 87 (Fall 2003): 19–48.

———. "Racial Knowledge in Cuba: The Production of a Social Fact, 1912–1944." Ph.D. diss., University of Michigan, 2002.

Hanson, Joyce A. *Mary McLeod Bethune and Black Women's Political Activism*. Columbia: University of Missouri Press, 2003.

Harlan, Louis R. *Booker T. Washington: The Making of a Black Leader, 1856–1901*. New York: Oxford University Press, 1972.

——. *Booker T. Washington: The Wizard of Tuskegee, 1901–1915*. New York: Oxford University Press, 1983.

Harlan, Louis R., et al., eds. *The Booker T. Washington Papers*. 14 vols. Urbana: University of Illinois Press, 1972–89.

Hayre, Ruth Wright, and Alexis Moore. *Tell Them We Are Rising: A Memoir of Faith in Education*. Foreword by Ed Bradley. New York: John Wiley and Sons, 1997.

Headrick, Daniel. *Tools of Empire: Technology and European Expansion in the Nineteenth Century*. New York: Oxford University Press, 1981.

Heinzelman, Kurt, ed. *The Covarrubias Circle*. Austin: University of Texas Press, 2004.

Helg, Aline. "Black Men, Racial Stereotyping, and Violence in Cuba and the U.S. South at the Turn of the Century." *Comparative Studies in Society and History* 42 (2000): 576–604.

——. *Our Rightful Share: The Afro-Cuban Struggle for Equality, 1886–1912*. Chapel Hill: University of North Carolina Press, 1995.

Hevia Lanier, Oilda. *El directorio central de las Sociedades Negras de Cuba, 1886–1894*. Havana: Editorial de Ciencias Sociales, 1996.

Higginbotham, Evelyn Brooks. *Righteous Discontent: The Women's Movement in the Black Baptist Church, 1880–1920*. Cambridge, Mass.: Harvard University Press, 1993.

Hill, Robert A. "Boundaries of Belonging: Essay on Comparative Caribbean Garveyism." *Caribbean Studies* 31, no. 1 (2003): 11–22.

——. "Making Noise: Marcus Garvey's Dada, August 1922." In *Picturing Us: African American Identity in Photography*, edited by Deborah Willis, 181–205. New York: Free Press, 1994.

Hoffnung-Garskof, Jesse. "The Migrations of Arturo Schomburg: On Being *Antillano*, Negro, and Puerto Rican in New York, 1891–1938." *Journal of American Ethnic History* 21 (Fall 2002): 3–49.

Hogan, Lawrence D. *A Black National News Service: The Associated Negro Press and Claude Barnett, 1919–1945*. Rutherford, N.J.: Fairleigh Dickinson University Press, 1984.

Holloway, Jonathan Scott. *Confronting the Veil: Abram Harris Jr., E. Franklin Frazier, and Ralph Bunche, 1919–1941*. Chapel Hill: University of North Carolina Press, 2002.

Holsey, Bayo. "Transatlantic Dreaming: Slavery, Tourism, and Diasporic Encounters." In *Homecomings: Unsettling Paths of Return*, edited by F. A. S. Markowitz, 166–82. New York: Lexington Books, 2004.

Horrego Estuch, Leopoldo. *Juan Gualberto Gómez: Un gran inconforme*. Havana: Editorial de Ciencias Sociales, 2004.

Howard, Philip A. *Changing History: Afro-Cuban Cabildos and Societies of Color in the Nineteenth Century*. Baton Rouge: Louisiana State University Press, 1998.

Inglish, Leona Frances. "The Transportation System of the United Fruit Company." M.S. thesis, University of Chicago, 1932.

Instituto de Historia de Cuba. *La Neocolonia: Organización y crisis desde 1899 hasta 1940.* Havana: Editora Política, 1998.

Jackson, Jeffrey H. *Making Jazz French: Music and Modern Life in Interwar Paris.* Durham, N.C.: Duke University Press, 2003.

Jackson, Richard L. *Black Writers in Latin America.* Albuquerque: University of New Mexico Press, 1979.

Jacques, Geoffrey "CuBop! Afro-Cuban Music and Mid-Twentieth-Century American Culture." In Brock and Castañeda Fuertes, *Between Race and Empire,* 249–65.

James, Winston. *Holding Aloft the Banner of Ethiopia.* London: Verso, 1998.

Janken, Kenneth Robert. *Rayford Logan and the Dilemmas of the African-American Intellectual.* Amherst: University of Massachusetts Press, 1993.

Joseph, Gilbert M., Catherine C. LeGrand, and Ricardo D. Salvatore, eds. *Close Encounters of Empire: Writing the Cultural History of U.S.–Latin American Relations.* Durham, N.C.: Duke University Press, 1998.

Julien, Isaac. *Looking for Langston.* New York: Water Bearer Films, 1992.

Kaup, Monica. "'Our America That Is Not One': Transnational Black Atlantic Discourses in Nicolás Guillén and Langston Hughes." *Discourse* 22 (Fall 2000): 87–113.

Kelley, Robin D. G. "'But a Local Phase of a World Problem': Black History's Global Vision." *Journal of American History* 86 (1999): 1045–92.

———. *Freedom Dreams: The Black Radical Imagination.* New York: Beacon, 2002.

———. "The World the Diaspora Made: C. L. R. James and the Politics of History." In *Rethinking C. L. R. James,* edited by Grant Farred, 103–30. London: Blackwell, 1996.

Kelly, Brian. "Sentinels for a New South Industry: Booker T. Washington and Black Workers in the Jim Crow South." *Labor History* 44 (2003): 337–57.

King, Kenneth. *Pan-Africanism and Education: A Study of Race Philanthropy and Education in the Southern States of America and East Africa.* Oxford: Clarendon Press, 1971.

Kutzinski, Vera. *Sugar's Secrets: Race and the Erotics of Cuban Nationalism.* Charlottesville: University Press of Virginia, 1993.

———. "Yo También Soy America." *American Literary History* 18 (2006): 550–78.

Levine, Lawrence W. "Marcus Garvey and the Politics of Revitalization." In *Black Leaders of the Twentieth Century,* edited by John Hope Franklin and August Meier, 105–38. Urbana: University of Illinois Press, 1982.

Lewis, David Levering. *W. E. B. Du Bois: Biography of a Race, 1868–1919.* New York: Henry Holt, 1993.

———. *W. E. B. Du Bois: The Fight for Equality and the American Century, 1919–1963.* New York: Henry Holt, 2000.

———. *When Harlem Was in Vogue.* 2nd ed. New York: Penguin, 1997.

Lewis, Earl. *In Their Own Interests: Race, Class, and Power in Twentieth Century Norfolk.* Berkeley: University of California Press, 1991.

———. "To Turn as on a Pivot: Writing African Americans into a History of Overlapping Diasporas." *American Historical Review* 100 (June 1995): 765–87.

Lewis, Rupert. *Marcus Garvey: Anti-Colonial Champion*. Trenton, N.J.: Africa World Press, 1988.

Lobo Montalvo, María Luisa, Zoila Lapique Becali, Narciso G. Menocal, and Edward Shaw. "The Years of Social." *Journal of Decorative and Propaganda Arts* 22 (1996): 104–31.

Locke, Alain, ed. *The New Negro*. New York: Albert & Charles Boni, 1925.

MacPherson, Anne. "Colonial Matriarchs: Garveyism, Maternalism, and Belize's Black Cross Nurses." *Gender and History* 15 (2003): 507–27.

Marcus Garvey: Look for Me in the Whirlwind. Produced and directed by Stanley Nelson. Arlington, Va.: PBS Home Video, 2001.

Martin, Tony. *Race First: The Organizational and Ideological Struggles of Marcus Garvey and the Universal Negro Improvement Association*. Dover, Mass.: Majority Press, 1976.

Matory, J. Lorand. "Afro-Atlantic Culture: On the Live Dialogue between Africa and the Americas." In *Africana: The Encyclopedia of the African and African American Experience*, ed. Henry Louis Gates and K. Anthony Appiah, 36–44. New York: Basic Civitas Books, 1999.

———. "The English Professors of Brazil: On the Diasporic Roots of the Yoruba Nation." *Comparative Studies in Society and History* 41 (1999): 72–103.

McHenry, Elizabeth. *Forgotten Readers: Recovering the Lost History of African American Literary Societies*. Durham, N.C.: Duke University Press, 2002.

McLeod, Marc C. "Garveyism in Cuba, 1920–1940." *Journal of Caribbean History* 30 (1996): 132–68.

———. "Sin dejar de ser cubanos: Cuban Blacks and the Challenges of Garveyism in Cuba." *Caribbean Studies* 31 (2003): 75–104.

———. "Undesirable Aliens: Race, Ethnicity, and Nationalism in the Comparison of Haitian and British West Indian Immigrant Workers in Cuba, 1912–1939." *Journal of Social History* 31 (Spring 1998): 599–623.

Mealy, Rosemari. *Fidel and Malcolm X: Memories of a Meeting*. Melbourne: Ocean Press, 1990.

Meier, August. *Negro Thought in America: Racial Ideologies in the Age of Booker T. Washington*. Ann Arbor: University of Michigan Press, 1963.

Meier, August, and Elliot Rudwick. *Black History and the Historical Profession*. Urbana: University of Illinois Press, 1986.

Meriwether, James H. *Proudly We Can Be Africans: Black Americans and Africa, 1935–1961*. Chapel Hill: University of North Carolina Press, 2002.

Miller, Floyd J. *The Search for a Black Nationality: Black Emigrationism and Colonization, 1787–1863*. Urbana: University of Illinois Press, 1975.

Miller, James A., Susan D. Pennybacker, and Eve Rosenhaft. "Mother Ada Wright and the International Campaign to Free the Scottsboro Boys, 1931–1934." *American Historical Review* 106 (April 2001): 387–430.

Mirabal, Nancy Raquel. "'No Country but the One We Must Fight For': The Emergence of an Antillean Nation and Community in New York City, 1860–1901." In *Mambo Montage: The Latinization of New York*, edited by Agustín Laó-Montes and Arlene Dávila, 57–72. New York: Columbia University Press, 2001.

———. "Scripting Race, Finding Place: African Americans, Afro-Cubans, and the Diasporic Imaginary in the United States." In *Neither Enemies nor Friends: Latinos, Blacks, Afro-Latinos*, edited by Anani Dzidzienyo and Suzanne Oboler, 189–208. New York: Palgrave Macmillan, 2005.

———. "Telling Silences and Making Community: Afro-Cubans and African Americans in Ybor City and Tampa, 1899–1915." In Brock and Castañeda Fuertes, *Between Race and Empire*, 49–69.

Mitchell, Michele. *Righteous Propagation: African Americans and the Politics of Racial Destiny after Reconstruction*. Chapel Hill: University of North Carolina Press, 2004.

Montejo Arrechea, Carmen. "*Minerva*: A Magazine for Women (and Men) of Color." In Brock and Castañeda Fuertes, *Between Race and Empire*, 33–48.

Montgomery, William Leafonza. "Mission to Cuba and Costa Rica: The Oblate Sisters of Providence in Latin America, 1900–1970." Ph.D. diss., Catholic University of America, 1997.

Moore, Carlos. *Castro, the Blacks, and Africa*. Los Angeles: Center for African-American Studies, University of California Press, 1988.

Moore, Robin D. *Nationalizing Blackness: Afrocubanismo and Artistic Revolution in Havana, 1920–1940*. Pittsburgh: University of Pittsburgh Press, 1997.

Morrison, Karen Y. "Civilization and Citizenship through the Eyes of Afro-Cuban Intellectuals during the First Constitutional Era, 1902–1940." *Cuban Studies* 30 (2000): 76–99.

Morrow, Diane Batts. *Persons of Color and Religious at the Same Time: The Oblate Sisters of Providence, 1828–1860*. Chapel Hill: University of North Carolina Press, 2002.

Mullen, Edward J. *Afro-Cuban Literature: Critical Junctures*. Westport, Conn.: Greenwood Press, 1998.

Mulzac, Hugh. *A Star to Steer By*. New York: International Publishers, 1963.

Nadell, Martha Jane. *Enter the New Negroes: Images of Race in American Culture*. Cambridge, Mass.: Harvard University Press, 2004.

Navarro, José-Manuel. *Creating Tropical Yankees: Social Science Textbooks and U.S. Ideological Control in Puerto Rico, 1898–1908*. New York: Routledge, 2002.

Neptune, Harvey R. *Caliban and the Yankees: Trinidad and the United States Occupation*. Chapel Hill: University of North Carolina Press, 2007.

Newton, Velma. *The Silver Men: West Indian Labor Migration to Panama, 1850–1914*. Mona: University of the West Indies Press, 1984.

Nordin, Dennis S. *The New Deal's Black Congressman: A Life of Arthur Wergs Mitchell*. Columbia: University of Missouri Press, 1997.

Nwankwo, Ifeoma Kiddoe. *Black Cosmopolitanism: Racial Consciousness and Transnational Identity in the Nineteenth-Century Americas*. Philadelphia: University of Pennsylvania Press, 2005.

———. "Langston Hughes and the Translations of Nicolás Guillén's Afro-Cuban Culture and Language." *Langston Hughes Review* 16, nos. 1 and 2 (1999–2001): 55–72.

Ordetx, Luis Machado. *Coterráneos: Testimonio*. Santa Clara, Cuba: Ediciones Capiro, 1997.

Ortiz, Fernando. *Cuban Counterpoint: Tobacco and Sugar*. Durham, N.C.: Duke University Press, 1995.

———. *Hampa afrocubana: Los negros brujos*. Madrid: Librería de F. Fé, 1906.

Pérez, Louis A. *Cuba under the Platt Amendment, 1902–1934*. Pittsburgh: University of Pittsburgh Press, 1986.

———. *On Becoming Cuban: Identity, Nationality, and Culture*. Chapel Hill: University of North Carolina Press, 1999.

Pierre, Jemima. "Beyond Heritage Tourism: Race and the Politics of African-Diasporic Interactions." *Social Text* 27 (2009): 59–81.

Plummer, Brenda Gayle. "Castro in Harlem: A Cold War Watershed." In *Rethinking the Cold War*, edited by Allen Hunter, 133–53. Philadelphia: Temple University Press, 1998.

———. *Rising Wind: Black Americans and U.S. Foreign Affairs, 1935–1960*. Chapel Hill: University of North Carolina Press, 1996.

Polyné, Millery. *Black Pan-Americanism: U.S. African-Americans and Haitian Affairs*. Gainesville: University Press of Florida, forthcoming.

Poyo, Gerald. *"With All, and for the Good of All": The Emergence of Popular Nationalism in the Cuban Communities of the United States, 1848–1898*. Durham, N.C.: Duke University Press, 1989.

Putnam, Lara. *The Company They Kept: Migrants and the Politics of Gender in Caribbean Costa Rica, 1870–1960*. Chapel Hill: University of North Carolina Press, 2002.

Rampersad, Arnold. *The Life of Langston Hughes*. Vol. 1, *1902–1941: I, Too, Sing America*. New York: Oxford University Press, 1986.

———. *The Life of Langston Hughes*. Vol. 2, *1941–1967: I Dream a World*. New York: Oxford University Press, 1988.

Reid, Ira de Augustine. *The Negro Immigrant: His Background, Characteristics, and Social Adjustment, 1899–1937*. New York: Columbia University Press, 1939.

Reitan, Ruth. *The Rise and Fall of an Alliance: Cuba and African-American Leaders in the 1960s*. East Lansing: Michigan State University Press, 1999.

Renda, Mary A. *Taking Haiti: Military Occupation and the Culture of U.S. Imperialism*. Chapel Hill: University of North Carolina Press, 2001.

Richards, Sandra L. "What Is to Be Remembered? Tourism to Ghana's Slave Castle-Dungeons." *Theatre Journal* 57 (2005): 617–37.

Rodríguez, Pedro Pablo. "Marcus Garvey en Cuba." *Anales del Caribe* (1987–88): 279–301.

Rowlinson, Mary G. *Grassroots Garveyism: The Universal Negro Improvement Association in the Rural South, 1920–1927*. Chapel Hill: University of North Carolina Press, 2007.

Rubiera Castillo, Daisy. *Reyita, sencillamente.* Havana: Instituto del Libro Cubano, 1997.

Rushing, Fannie T. "*Cabildos de Nación* and *Sociedades de la Raza de Color*: Afro-Cuban Participation in Slave Emancipation and Cuban Independence, 1865–1895." Ph.D. diss., University of Chicago, 1992.

Savigliano, Mara. *Tango and the Political Economy of Passion: From Exoticism to Decolonization.* Boulder, Colo.: Westview, 1995.

Schechner, Richard. *Between Theatre and Anthropology.* Philadelphia: University of Pennsylvania Press, 1985.

Schmidt, Hans. *The United States Occupation of Haiti, 1915–1934.* New Brunswick, N.J.: Rutgers University Press, 1971.

Schwartz, Rosalie. "Cuba's Roaring Twenties: Race Consciousness and the Column 'Ideales de una Raza.'" In Brock and Castañeda Fuertes, *Between Race and Empire,* 104–19.

———. "The Displaced and the Disappointed: Cultural Nationalists and Black Activists in Cuba in the 1920s." Ph.D. diss., University of California at San Diego, 1977.

———. *Pleasure Island: Tourism and Temptation in Cuba.* Lincoln: University of Nebraska Press, 1999.

Schwarz, A. B. Christa. *Gay Voices of the Harlem Renaissance.* Bloomington: Indiana University Press, 2003.

Scott, Rebecca J. *Degrees of Freedom: Louisiana and Cuba after Slavery.* Cambridge, Mass.: Harvard University Press, 2005.

———. *Slave Emancipation in Cuba: The Transition to Free Labor, 1860–1899.* Princeton, N.J.: Princeton University Press, 1985.

Scott, William. "*Motivos* of Translation." *CR: The New Centennial Review* 5 (2005): 35–71.

Seigel, Micol. "Beyond Compare: The Comparative Method and the Transnational Turn." *Radical History Review* 91 (2005): 62–90.

Seiler, Cotton. "'So That We as a Race Might Have Something Authentic to Travel By': African American Automobility and Cold-War Liberalism." *American Quarterly* 58 (December 2006): 1091–1118.

Seraile, William. "Henrietta Vinton Davis and the Garvey Movement." *Afro-Americans in New York Life and History* 7 (1983): 7–24.

Shaw, Stephanie. *What a Woman Ought to Be and to Do: Black Professional Women Workers during the Jim Crow Era.* Chicago: University of Chicago Press, 1996.

Sinnette, Elinor Des Verney. *Arthur Alfonso Schomburg: Black Bibliophile and Collector.* New York: New York Public Library; Detroit: Wayne State University Press, 1989.

Sitkoff, Harvard. *A New Deal for Blacks: The Emergence of Civil Rights as a National Issue.* New York: Oxford University Press, 1978.

Solomon, Mark. *The Cry Was Unity: Communists and African Americans, 1917–1936.* Jackson: University Press of Mississippi, 1998.

Spivey, Donald. *Schooling for the New Slavery: Black Industrial Education, 1868–1915.* Westport, Conn.: Greenwood, 1978.

Stein, Judith. *The World of Marcus Garvey: Race and Class in Modern Society.* Baton Rouge: Louisiana State University Press, 1986.

Stephens, Michele. *Black Empire: The Masculine Global Imaginary of Caribbean Intellectuals in the United States, 1914–1962.* Durham, N.C.: Duke University Press, 2005.

Stoler, Ann Laura, Carole McGranahan, and Peter C. Perdue. *Imperial Formations.* Oxford: James Currey, 2007.

Stoner, K. Lynn. *From the House to the Streets: The Cuban Woman's Movement for Legal Reform, 1898–1940.* Durham, N.C.: Duke University Press, 1991.

Sullivan, Patricia. *Days of Hope: Race and Democracy in the New Deal Era.* Chapel Hill: University of North Carolina Press, 1996.

Summers, Martin. *Manliness and Its Discontents: The Black Middle Class and the Transformation of Masculinity, 1900–1930.* Chapel Hill: University of North Carolina Press, 2004.

Swan, Harry. "The Nineteen Twenties: A Decade of Intellectual Change in Cuba." *Revista/Review Interamericana* 8 (1978): 275–88.

Sweet, James. *Recreating Africa: Culture, Kinship, and Religion in the African-Portuguese World, 1441–1770.* Chapel Hill: University of North Carolina Press, 2003.

Taylor, Diana. *The Archive and the Repertoire: Performing Cultural Memory in the Americas.* Durham, N.C.: Duke University Press, 2003.

Taylor, Ula Y. *The Veiled Garvey: The Life and Times of Amy Jacques Garvey.* Chapel Hill: University of North Carolina Press, 2002.

Testa, Silvina. *Como una memoria que dura: Cabildos, sociedades y religiones afrocubanas de Sagua la Grande.* Havana: Ediciones La Memoria, Centro Cultural Pablo de la Torriente Brau, 2004.

Tolbert, Emory. *The U.N.I.A. and Black Los Angeles: Ideology and Community in the American Garvey Movement.* Los Angeles: University of California Press, 1980.

Toll, William. "Free Men, Freedmen, and Race: Black Social Theory in a Gilded Age." *Journal of Southern History* 44 (November 1978): 571–96.

Trotter, Joe William, ed. *The Great Migration in Historical Perspective: New Perspectives on Race, Class, and Gender.* Bloomington: Indiana University Press, 1991.

Tushnet, Mark V. *The NAACP's Legal Strategy against Segregated Education, 1925–1950.* Chapel Hill: University of North Carolina Press, 1987.

Vaillant, Janet. *Black, French, and African: A Life of Léopold Sédar Senghor.* Cambridge, Mass.: Harvard University Press, 1990.

Von Eschen, Penny. *Race against Empire: Black Americans and Anticolonialism, 1937–1957.* Ithaca, N.Y.: Cornell University Press, 1997.

Wadelington, Charles W., and Richard F. Knapp. *Charlotte Hawkins Brown and Palmer Memorial Institute: What One Young African American Woman Could Do.* Chapel Hill: University of North Carolina Press, 1999.

Watkins-Owens, Irma. *Blood Relations: Caribbean Immigrants and the Harlem Community, 1900–1930*. Bloomington: Indiana University Press, 1996.

Weiss, Ellen. "Tuskegee: Landscape in Black and White." *Winterthur Portfolio* 36 (2001): 19–37.

White, Deborah Gray. *Too Heavy a Load: Black Women in Defense of Themselves*. New York: Norton, 1999.

Whitney, Robert. *State and Revolution in Cuba: Mass Mobilization and Political Change, 1920–1940*. Chapel Hill: University of North Carolina Press, 2001.

Williams, Adriana. *Covarrubias*. Austin: University of Texas Press, 1994.

Willis-Braithwaite, Deborah. *VanDerZee: Photographer, 1886–1983*. New York: H. N. Adams, 1993.

Woods, Randall B. *A Black Odyssey: John Lewis Waller and the Promise of American Life, 1878–1900*. Lawrence: Kansas University Press, 1981.

Young, Cynthia A. *Soul Power: Culture, Radicalism, and the Making of a U.S. Third World Left*. Durham, N.C.: Duke University Press, 2006.

Zimmerman, Andrew. "A German Alabama in Africa: The Tuskegee Expedition to German Togo and the Transnational Origins of West African Cotton Growers." *American Historical Review* 110 (December 2005): 1362–98.

Index

Abraham Lincoln Club, 84–85
Abrahams, Roger, 90
Abreu, Ramótn, 17
Academias de baile. See Dance halls of
  Havana
Accommodationism: of Booker T. Wash-
  ington, 18, 20–21
ACF. *See* Asociación Cultural Femenina
ACL. *See* African Communities League
Activism: antidiscrimination activism in
  Cuba, 167–75, 188–89; civil rights activ-
  ism in U.S., 188; and tourism, 150, 155.
  See also specific groups
Aframerican Woman's Journal, 182, 183
Africa: in Afro-Cuban culture, 111, 133;
  Afro-Cubans' relationship to, 12, 60;
  in Cuban culture, 109; educational
  opportunities in, 22, 29; in Garveyism,
  63–64, 86–87; liberation struggles in, 2,
  196; racial uplift in, 12, 55, 86–87; valori-
  zation of culture of, 149
African American entrepreneurs. *See*
  Entrepreneurs, African American
African Americans: anticommunist, 188;
  Castro regime and, 3, 196–98; citizenship rights for, 12, 21, 23; diaspora in history of, 5–6; Great Depression's impact
  on, 145; as leaders of "colored race,"
  12; military service by, 23–24, 27, 31;
  opportunities in imperialism for, 21–27;
  radicalization of, 145, 147–48; in UNIA,
  69; views on Afro-Cuban culture, 111,
  137, 149; views on Afro-Cubans, 12

African Americans in Cuba: Club Atenas
  visited by, 58–59; migration of, 24–27,
  160; in "Spanish-American War," 21,
  23–24; in U.S. occupation, 24, 31.
  See also Tourism
African American women. *See* Women,
  African American
African Communities League (ACL), 99
African Cross, 93
African diaspora. *See* Diaspora, African
African Motor Corps, 91, 97, 99
African Police, 89, 220 (n. 75)
Africans: as Tuskegee students, 60
Afro-American Council, 33
Afro-Caribbeans: migration of, 67–68,
  158; performance traditions of, 90–91.
  See also specific groups
Afro-Cuban culture. *See* Artists, Afro-
  Cuban; Culture, Afro-Cuban; Music,
  Afro-Cuban; Writers, Afro-Cuban
Afro-Cuban elites. *See* Elites, Afro-Cuban
Afro-Cuban entrepreneurs. *See* Entrepre-
  neurs, Afro-Cuban
Afro-Cubanism (*afrocubanismo*): Afro-
  Cuban societies in, 117–18; as cross-racial
  movement, 109, 222 (n. 7); emergence of,
  109; establishment of Harlem Renais-
  sance links with, 15, 108. *See also* Harlem-
  Havana cultural nexus
Afro-Cubans: citizenship rights for, 58, 168;
  diaspora in history of, 5–6; government
  limits on activities of, 96–97, 103, 220
  (n. 87); Harlem influenced by, 112–17;

Batista, Fulgencio, 1, 154, 164, 173, 175

Batrell, Ricardo, 214 (n. 109)

Bauzá, Mario, 113, 149

BCC. *See* Bethune-Cookman College

Beach access, 153, 154, 160

Betancourt, Juan René: on African American leadership, 12; on Castro's revolution, 1; on racial discrimination, 1–2, 3, 188–89

Bethune, Mary McLeod: Afro-Cuban students and, 202; Afro-Cuban tourists and, 190; Grillos's relationship with, 185; Margaret Ross Martin and, 162; in NCNW, 182; visits to Cuba, 59, 116, 158–59

Bethune-Cookman College (BCC), 156, 158, 185, 193, 202

Big Sea, The (Hughes), 136

Black Cross Nurses, 84, 89, 97, 99

Blackman, W. W., 28

Black nationalism, 64, 122

Blackness: in Castro regime, 196; in Havana dance halls, 111; Hughes on, 133–34, 141, 146; vogue of, 109, 222 (n. 4)

Black Scholar (journal), 195–97

Black Star Line (BSL): Cuban reception of, 79–82, 94; establishment of, 79; failure of, 68, 77, 88; investment in, 79, 84, 218 (n. 51); La Mothe working for, 69; Menocal on, 81, 94–96; music in, 221 (n. 92); names of ships, 76, 79; in performance culture, 93–96; problems with ships, 79, 82, 219 (n. 59); purpose of, 77; routes of, 68

Blanco, Tomás, 167–68

Blanco Aguilar, Jesús, 112, 222 (n. 12)

Blues: in Hughes's poetry, 124, 135, 139; *son* compared to, 109–10, 149

Booker T. Washington Papers, 21

Brindis de Salas, Claudio, 114

Brooke, John, 39

Brooks, D., 61

BSL. *See* Black Star Line

Bunche, Ralph, 177, 184, 202

Bustamante, A. N., 98

Bus travel: in Cuba, 154; in U.S., 191, 192

Caballero Milanés, Joaquín, 102

Cabildos de nación, 11

Cabrera, Brijida, 37–38

Cabrera Torres, Ramón, 189, 190

Cadena de las Américas (radio program), 178, 179

Calá, Epifanio, 73

Calderón, Bernardo, 37, 214 (n. 109)

Calhoun, Conyus, 195

Callaba Pérez, Marcelino, 34–35

Calloway, Cab, 203

Camagüey: literary gatherings in, 118–19; UNIA in, 96–98

"Camino de Harlem, El" (Guillén), 123, 127

Campa, Miguel, 157

Campbell, William C., 157–58

Capestany Abreu, Manuel, 116, 170, 171

Capitalism: UNIA support for, 77–78

Capitalism and Slavery (Williams), 177

Carbó, Segundo, 32, 33

Cárdenas, Juana María, 36, 40–41

Cárdenas, Romualdo, 17

Carmichael, Stokely, 232–33 (n. 4)

Caroling Dusk (Cullen), 128

Carpentier, Alejo, 129

Carruthers, Ben Frederic, 116, 177–78, 179

Cars: travel by, 156, 166

Cartaya, Pedro, 159

Carter, Elmer Anderson, 137

Casanova, María, 41

Casanova, Patrocino, 41

Castalia (publication), 110, 120

Castillo Bueno, María "Reyita" de los Reyes, 98–99

Castillo Duany, Joaquín, 32, 41–42

Castro, Fidel: 1960 visit to Harlem, 3; rise to power, 1

Castro regime: African Americans' relationship with, 3, 196–98; Afro-Cuban entrepreneurship in, 164; Afro-Cubans' status under, 1, 196; blackness in, 196; on civil rights in U.S., 3; establishment of, 1, 196; racial discrimination in, 1, 3, 196, 198

Central America: Afro-Caribbean migration to, 67

Central Chaparra, 81

Central Francisco, 26

Céspedes, Miguel Angel: and Du Bois's 1941 visit to Cuba, 180, 181; elite status of, 85; and Garvey's 1921 visit to Cuba,

of, 219 (n. 62); of Mitchell's 1937 visit to
Cuba, 170, 172, 173, 175, 229 (n. 49), 230
(n. 67); of UNIA performance culture,
89–100. *See also specific publications*
Mella, Julio Antonio, 125
Memphis Commercial Appeal, 47
Men: as focus of scholarship, 14; self-made,
72, 74. *See also* Manhood/manliness
Menocal, Mario García: on Black Star Line,
81, 94–96; and Garvey's 1921 visit to
Cuba, 219 (n. 67); UNIA and, 81
Middle class: vs. aspiring class, 208 (n. 27);
travel by, 152–53, 187
Migration: of African Americans to Cuba,
24–27, 160; of Afro-Caribbeans, 67–68,
158; of black labor force, 9–10, 67–68,
158, 207 (n. 19); and Garveyism, 9, 65,
67–68; Great Migration, 9–10, 67–68
Militarism, UNIA, 64, 93
Military, U.S.: African Americans in,
23–24, 27, 31; interventions by, 8; uni-
forms of, 91
Mills, Jacob Samuel, 91–92
Mimicry: in UNIA uniforms, 91
Minns, Grace, 33–34
Minoristas, 125
Mitchell, Annie Harris, 169, 171
Mitchell, Arthur W.: career of, 168–69;
1937 visit to Cuba, 168–75
Mitchell, James A., 212 (n. 70)
Mitchell, Michele, 23, 37, 208 (n. 27)
Moncrief, R. P., 61
Montgomery Bus Boycott (1955), 188
Moore, Carlos, 233 (n. 4)
Moore, Richard V., 193
Morales, Eduardo: transcultural life of,
69–71; on UNIA uniforms, 93; on
United Fruit model, 77
Moreno, Arturo, 61–62
Morro Castle (steamship), 156, 161, 228
(n. 27)
Morúa Delgado, Martín, 38, 74
Morúa Law, 104, 218 (n. 53)
Moses, G. O., 61
Motivos de son (Guillén), 118, 122, 138, 139
Moton, Robert Russa, 45, 83
Movement culture. *See* Performance culture
of UNIA

Mule Bone (Hurston and Hughes), 144
Mulzac, Hugh, 79–80, 81, 94, 96
Muñoz, Andrés, 85
Muñoz Ginarte, Benjamin, 173
Museo Histórico de Guanabacoa, 195
Music: blues, 109–10, 124, 135, 139, 149;
commercialization of, 110; jazz, 201–4;
and UNIA, 61, 87, 89–90, 97–99
Music, Afro-Cuban: Africanness of, 133; in
Harlem, 112–13, 125; Hughes on, 125, 126–
27, 133–34; merged with African Ameri-
can music, 149; in NCNW visit to Cuba,
187; rumba, 134, 204. *See also Son*
"My Early Days in Harlem" (Hughes), 117

NAACP (National Association for the
Advancement of Colored People): Afro-
Cuban societies working with, 160, 163–
64; Afro-Cuban tourists visiting, 189;
campaign against travel discrimination,
156–57, 159, 227 (n. 10), 230 (n. 69);
Cuban branches of, 162, 164; decline in
power of, 198; racial uplift model of, 83;
in tourist networks, 156, 162–64, 189;
on travel as civil rights issue, 153. *See also
Crisis*
Nápoles, Félix, 120
National anthems: Cuban, 61, 97–98;
Ethiopian, 61, 62, 97, 98
National Association for the Advancement
of Colored People. *See* NAACP
National Confederation of Cuban Workers, 125
National Council for Negro Women
(NCNW): Afro-Cuban tourists visit-
ing, 189–91; linkages formed by, 156;
visit to Cuba by, 182–87
National Federation of Negro Societies, 1
National holidays, 52
Nationalism: black, 64, 122; and decoloni-
zation, 2, 196; diaspora's compatibility
with, 4, 6
Nationalism, Cuban: and Afro-Cubans,
86–88; anti-imperialism in, 125; after
Cuban Revolution, 196; of Juan
Gualberto Gómez, 17, 18; and identity,
6, 59–60; mixed-race, 109; and UNIA,
63, 76, 102

62, 64, 91, 106; elocution and oratory in, 89–91; forms of, 64; functions of, 64, 99; Garvey in, 84; media coverage of, 89–100; preexisting traditions in, 90–91; uniforms in, 64, 89, 91–93; women in, 99–100

Periodicals: Afro-Cuban, 110, 120, 122, 125; U.S., 136–37. *See also specific publications*

Phelps-Stokes, Caroline, 29

Phelps-Stokes, Olivia, 28, 29

PIC. *See* Partido Independiente de Color

Pickens, William: in development of tourist networks, 162–64; on discrimination against black travelers, 156–57, 159–62; Margaret Ross Martin and, 160–62; 1930 visit to Cuba, 156–57, 160, 228 (n. 27)

Pierra Edwards, Carlos, 40

Piñeiro, Ignacio, 112

Piracy: in Hughes's poetry, 147–48

Plant, Henry B., 29

Plant System, 29, 30

Platt Amendment, 17

Polar Gardens, 186–87

Political corruption in Cuba, 188

Political parties: Cuban, 104, 218 (n. 53); U.S., 169, 170

Politicization: of African Americans, 145, 147–48; of Afro-Cubans, 145–47, 226 (n. 99)

Portuondo Calá, Pedrito, 193, 202

Portuondo Calá, Pedro: and Afro-Cuban visits to U.S., 191–92, 193, 202; and NCNW's visit to Cuba, 186, 187, 188

Posey, Bethel Aldrick, 19

P. O. Steamship Company, 8, 155

Pozo, Chano, 113, 149–50

Prattis, Percival, 162

Presidents, Cuban: UNIA relations with, 81, 94–96, 218 (n. 58). *See also specific presidents*

Press coverage. *See* Media coverage

Primitivism: Covarrubias influenced by, 129, 131; Fernández de Castro influenced by, 129, 131; Hughes influenced by, 124, 131, 133–34; white fascination with, 109

Progressivism: of Du Bois, 20–21

Prohibition, 79

Prostitution: at dance halls, 126

"Protest of the Thirteen," 128

Provost, Ernest, 97

Puerto Ricans: at Tuskegee Institute, 18, 21, 39–40, 43, 49, 51–52, 213 (n. 71)

Puerto Rico: racial discrimination in, 167–68

Quesada, Gonzalo de, 42, 212 (n. 66)

"Race first" ideology, 63–64, 70, 76

Racial backwardness, 73

Racial discrimination in Cuba: activism against, 167–75, 188–89; Afro-Cuban writers on, 121–23, 146–47; Betancourt on, 1–2, 3, 188–89; in Castro regime, 1, 3, 196, 198; in employment, 61–62, 102, 104, 105, 188; against migrants, 83, 158; in Mitchell case, 168–75; UNIA activism against, 97, 102–3; U.S. influence on, 10, 21. *See also* Tourism in Cuba

Racial discrimination in Puerto Rico, 167–68

Racial discrimination in U.S.: Afro-Cuban writers on, 123, 146–47, 189; defense industry ban on, 177; against Mitchell, 168; in Scottsboro Case, 145–46; in transit, 152, 153, 157

Racial equality: Cuban activism for, 168; in Cuban Constitution, 104, 173, 220 (n. 88); in New Negro movement, 109; as transnational issue, 5

Racial hierarchy. *See* Hierarchy

Racial ideas: cross-fertilization of Cuban and U.S., 10–11

Racial segregation in Cuba: Afro-Cuban societies after end of, 198; as custom vs. law, 97, 220 (n. 88); in dance halls, 126–27, 128; in formation of societies, 11, 73; of leisure activities, 11, 65, 74, 126–27; and tourist networks, 152; UNIA activities and, 96–98

Racial segregation in U.S.: African American institutions after end of, 198; Afro-Cuban writers on, 123; in Cold War, 188; in New Orleans, 33; and tourist networks, 152; Booker T. Washington on, 22

Racial uplift: in Africa, 12, 55, 86–87; Afro-Cubans' understanding of, 71–78; in Asociación Cultural Femenina, 183; in Club Atenas, 75, 86–87; definition of, 71; education in, 36–37, 72, 73, 118; elocution in, 90–91; in Garveyism, 68, 71–78, 86–87; gender in, 41, 73–74, 217 (n. 36); Harlem-Havana cultural nexus in decline of, 111; imperialism and, 11–12; at Instituto Booker T. Washington, 57; social class and, 208 (n. 26); three theories of, 83; at Tuskegee Institute, 20, 45–47; Booker T. Washington's model of, 20, 35, 45–47, 59, 72, 83. *See also* Upward mobility

Racial violence: against West Indians in Cuba, 83

Racism. *See* Racial discrimination

Radicals: on Cuban Revolution, 197, 232–33 (n. 4); Garveyites as, 66; Hughes as radical, 145, 147–48

Radio programs, 178, 179

Railroads: and black tourism, 155, 166; discrimination in hiring for, 61–62; discrimination in travel on, 168; expansion of, 155

Ramírez, Celestina, 39, 41, 49–50, 211 (n. 37)

Ramírez, María Teresa, 161, 218 (n. 56)

Ramírez, Sixta, 39, 41

Ramírez Ros, Primitivo: death of, 161; as editor of *Atenas*, 80–81, 87; family of, 161, 218 (n. 56); and Garvey's 1921 visit to Cuba, 82, 219 (nn. 66–67); and Hughes's 1930 visit to Cuba, 135

Ramos Blanco, Teodoro: in Afro-Cubanism, 109; Harlem exhibition by, 114–16; Hughes's profile of, 107–8, 136; Hughes's relationship with, 130; NCNW lecture by, 186; U.S. intellectuals and, 178, 180

Ramsey, James, 50

Randolph, A. Philip, 177

Raymond, Luisa, 100

Raza de color, la. See "Colored race"

Reagon, Bernice, 195

Recording industry, 110, 112

Recreation. *See* Leisure activities in Cuba

Reid, Ira, 112

Repression in Cuba, 101, 144, 147

Republican Party, U.S., 169

Respectability: of rumba, 134; in UNIA, 72

Retreta, 127, 224 (n. 47)

Rey, Lorenzo del, Jr., 17

Risco, Armando del, 38–39

Risco, Luis del, 38–39

Rivera, A., 98

Rivero, José I. "Pepín," 121, 172

Robinson, Bill "Bojangles," 203

Rockefeller, Nelson, 176, 178

Rodríguez, Agapito, 121

Rodríguez, Sixto, 211 (n. 37)

Roig de Leuchshenring, Emilio, 173

Rojas, Alberto, 32, 33

Rolando, Gloria, 202–4

Roldán, Amadeo, 124, 136, 224 (n. 40)

Roosevelt, Eleanor, 182

Roosevelt, Franklin D., 170, 176, 177

Roosevelt, Theodore, 24

Roots: vs. routes, 4, 206 (n. 5)

Roumain, Jacques, 137, 146

Routes: vs. roots, 4, 206 (n. 5)

Rubiera Castillo, Daisy, 98

Ruíz, Clara, 172, 175

Rumba, 134, 204

Sagua la Grande: Black Star Line in, 79; Tuskegee students from, 43, 101; UNIA in, 61–62, 72, 101–5

Salina, Pedro, 211 (n. 37)

Samad, Mariamne, 92

Santa Amalia group, 203

Schechner, Richard, 215 (n. 8)

Schomburg, Arturo "Arthur": on Afro-Cuban writers, 113–14, 118; on Afro-diasporic history, 113–14; book collection of, 113, 114, 223 (n. 16); as promoter of Harlem-Havana cultural nexus, 108, 113–15; on tourism in Cuba, 166

Schomburg Center for Research in Black Culture, 113, 114

Schools: decline of African American, 198; tourism in Cuba promoted by, 176–82. *See also* Education; *specific schools*

Schuyler, George, 188

Schwartz, Rosalie, 230 (n. 73)

World War II: good-neighborism in, 176; tourism after, 187–93

Writers, African American: Afro-Cuban societies' study of, 119; anticommunist, 188; 1976 visit to Cuba by, 195–96. *See also specific writers*

Writers, Afro-Cuban: Afro-Cuban societies' promotion of, 118–20, 135; Hughes's promotion of, 107–8, 136–37; publication of, 110, 120; on racial discrimination, 121–23, 146–47, 189; Schomburg's promotion of, 113–14, 118; Urrutia's promotion of, 121–23; women, 120–21. *See also specific writers*

Yarmouth (ship), 79–82, 93–94, 219 (n. 59)

Young, Cynthia, 206 (n. 4)

YWCA, 158

Zamora, Lalita, 132, 139–40

Zayas, Alfredo, 128, 218 (n. 58)

Zionism, 64

Zuñiga, Fermín, 38

ENVISIONING CUBA

Frank Andre Guridy, *Forging Diaspora: Afro-Cubans and African Americans in a World of Empire and Jim Crow* (2010).

Ann Marie Stock, *On Location in Cuba: Street Filmmaking during Times of Transition* (2009).

Alejandro de la Fuente, *Havana and the Atlantic in the Sixteenth Century* (2008).

Reinaldo Funes Monzote, *From Rainforest to Cane Field in Cuba: An Environmental History since 1492* (2008).

Matt D. Childs, *The 1812 Aponte Rebellion in Cuba and the Struggle against Atlantic Slavery* (2006).

Eduardo González, *Cuba and the Tempest: Literature and Cinema in the Time of Diaspora* (2006).

John Lawrence Tone, *War and Genocide in Cuba, 1895–1898* (2006).

Samuel Farber, *The Origins of the Cuban Revolution Reconsidered* (2006).

Lillian Guerra, *The Myth of José Martí: Conflicting Nationalisms in Early Twentieth-Century Cuba* (2005).

Rodrigo Lazo, *Writing to Cuba: Filibustering and Cuban Exiles in the United States* (2005).

Alejandra Bronfman, *Measures of Equality: Social Science, Citizenship, and Race in Cuba, 1902–1940* (2004).

Edna M. Rodríguez-Mangual, *Lydia Cabrera and the Construction of an Afro-Cuban Cultural Identity* (2004).

Gabino La Rosa Corzo, *Runaway Slave Settlements in Cuba: Resistance and Repression* (2003).

Piero Gleijeses, *Conflicting Missions: Havana, Washington, and Africa, 1959–1976* (2002).

Robert Whitney, *State and Revolution in Cuba: Mass Mobilization and Political Change, 1920–1940* (2001).

Alejandro de la Fuente, *A Nation for All: Race, Inequality, and Politics in Twentieth-Century Cuba* (2001).